T3-BOG-497

The Economics of Business Investment Abroad

THE ECONOMICS OF BUSINESS INVESTMENT ABROAD

H. PETER GRAY

Crane, Russak & Company, Inc.
New York

Published in the United States by

Crane, Russak & Company, Inc.

52 Vanderbilt Avenue

New York, N.Y. 10017

Library of Congress Catalog Card No. 72–83311

ISBN 0–8448–0064–3

Printed in Great Britain

To

Robert and Ruelle Mathieson

CONTENTS

LIST OF TABLES, FIGURES
AND CHART

List of Tables

List of Figures

Chart

PREFACE

My interest in the subject of business investment abroad dates back to the early fifties. At that time I was one of a group engaged in obtaining permission from the (British) Board of Trade for the export of capital to Canada. In the course of time I was associated with the actual creation and operation of that subsidiary. The rapid post-World War II growth of direct investment coupled with the failure of balance-of-payments theory to allow explicitly for direct investments, has sustained my interest.

One of the points made in the text is that business investment abroad is still in evolution. As a consequence, anything written on the subject is likely to have only fleeting validity. What is offered here is a conceptual approach to the multi-faceted problem of the social and economic implications of direct international investment. Definitive judgements are not given. It is hoped that the approach will help scholars, politicians, civil servants and businessmen to have a better understanding of some of the indirect relationships of the process of business investment abroad.

Two economists, Professors Carlisle and Maldonado, have written short pieces on topics in which they have specialist knowledge and insights. They should not be held responsible for any views other than those expressed in their own contributions. Similarly, the Rutgers University Research Council and the Brookings Institution are exonerated from any blame attaching to the contents despite the assistance that they provided me while I was writing. The manuscript itself benefited from being read in its entirety by Professors Jean M. Gray and Gail E. Makinen. The treatment of the Canadian and Ivorian experiences owes a great deal to the most courteous and thorough assistance given me by Mrs Mary Freeman of the Canadian Embassy and Mr Jean Batigne of the Ivorian Embassy in Washington. Professors E. Ray Canterbery and Ingo Walter read parts of the manuscript and my understanding of the whole topic gained from many conversations with

Dr Lawrence B. Krause. Mrs Doris K. Cunningham performed in her usual admirable way *qua* amanuensis. To all of the above, I am very grateful for their assistance.

H. PETER GRAY

New Brunswick, N.J., U.S.A.

CHAPTER I

BUSINESS INVESTMENT ABROAD: THE INFRASTRUCTURE FOR ANALYSIS

Jean-Jacques Servan-Schreiber wrote a book entitled, *Le Défi Américain* (*The American Challenge*)[1] that sold more than half a million copies to Frenchmen warning them of the dangers of too great a role for American subsidiary corporations in the French economy (as well as about a million copies in other languages). He told France to 'wake up' and, since that time, has become the leader of an important political party. His book was castigated by no less a critic than Nobel laureate Paul A. Samuelson who 'tore into' the logical and factual basis of Servan-Schreiber's thesis.[2] The incompatibility of the thinking of these two eminent men can be traced to the fundamental problem involved in any analysis or understanding of international business. Is a wholly-owned American subsidiary located in France, employing French labour (except perhaps for the top executives) and paying French taxes, a French or an American concern? Does geography or equity ownership determine nationality? If the subsidiary of an American parent *is* *American* even though located on French soil, then Samuelson's critique misses the point.

In Canada, J.-J. S.-S.'s counterpart accuses an eminent economist of being internationalist to the detriment of the welfare of the land of his birth.[3]

One of the root problems may be that the economists are locked too firmly into their own professional analytic frame of reference and refuse to countenance the legitimacy of a different

---

[1] (New York: Avon Books, 1969.)

[2] Paul A. Samuelson, 'The French Galbraith', *Newsweek*, 22 July 1968, p. 73.

[3] See Kari Levitt, *Silent Surrender* (Toronto: Macmillan of Canada, 1970) pp. 35-6 – the economist is Harry G. Johnson.

set of basic assumptions and values. Communication with people who wish to argue on different premises is then difficult. Economists have traditionally sought for their subject the status of a science where value judgements cannot affect a conclusion. For such a status to be achieved it is necessary for economic udgements about the relative desirability of two alternative patterns of production to be able to be indifferent to the distribution of the two outputs among men or groups of men. Economists have assumed that the efficiency of output is separable from questions of distribution and have allowed for distributional aspects to be taken care of, usually implicitly, by the hypothetical payment of transfers by gainers to losers. In the international sphere this is an important limitation of technique since there is even less justification in arguing the plausibility of compensating any losers. Thus, the welfare of a group of men (that group that constitutes a nation) cannot, in the traditional approach, be singled out for attention and have their interests considered apart from the interests of some global mass of humanity. Thus, nationalism in the sense that Servan-Schreiber, Levitt and others conceive of it – whereby the economic welfare of the citizens of the country in which the foreign investment is to be located is the primary (if not the only) concern and in which gross domestic product (or even gross 'global product') is not the unique determinant of economic welfare – this kind of nationalism is repugnant to orthodox economics.

The second half of the twentieth century has already witnessed a startling growth in the number and importance of business subsidiary operations located abroad and, with it, a nascent opposition to foreign subsidiaries. Perhaps of even greater importance in the long run is the emergence of multinational business on a large scale. Such is the importance – actual and potential – of this internationalisation of business that no businessman can afford to be ignorant of these developments or of their implications for his own corporation. Equally, no economist can afford to neglect the repercussions of these developments for the world economy, its interrelationships, its balance of payments strains and their effects upon individual national economies.

For the businessmen and economists who wish to keep

abreast of the developments and social implications of international business, this book attempts to provide a tool kit that will enable them to 'keep up-to-date'. An unguided case-by-case approach is likely to prove expensive in time and could possibly mislead. A more effective method of approaching the subject is to evolve a frame of reference that is broad and abstract, to attach new data to it as they become available and to see individual events not in isolation or in reference merely to one or two similar examples, but to incorporate new events into the totality of the analytic frame of reference. The tool kit that this book aims to provide will enable each individual to build his own framework within which problems can be solved and projects weighed. In the process of generating such a tool kit, it is important to ensure that each aspect of the problem can be included in the ultimate frame of reference. The going is not always easy, for the subject is intricate. However, the degree of reliance on technical-mathematical economics is small and the emphasis is placed on straight, logical thinking. In the generation of the frame of reference, orthodox international economics will be used but will also be transformed.

The balance of this introductory chapter is concerned with three distinct aspects of the foreign investment process. Acknowledging the limitations of the coverage of both political phenomena and the inter-relationship between the question of foreign investment and other dimensions of international political relations will comprise the first section. The second section examines the mechanism of international accounting – balance of payments accounting – particularly in so far as it pertains to the foreign investment process. This section will introduce the concept of international saving (by a nation) which is fundamental to the economic analysis to be constructed. Nothing can make the mechanics of international accounting interesting, so some attempt has been made to make the section very simple and quite short. Finally, a brief summary of the history of international investment through time is made. The emphasis of modern international investment must be largely based on the United States experience, but other nations do invest abroad currently and hold large stocks of overseas assets as a result of their investment in the past – even though they may be net recipients of direct investment in the sixties and seventies.

THE POLITICAL ENVIRONMENT

The overwhelming part of direct foreign investment involves the establishment by business of foreign subsidiary corporations or branch enterprises. These subsidiary firms constitute business investment abroad. The crucial aspect of a foreign corporate subsidiary is the *control* of a part of the productive resources of one nation by citizens and/or residents of a foreign nation. A nation's economic success depends directly upon the efficiency with which its productive resources are used for its own benefit. The existence in a nation (the *host* nation) of a foreign subsidiary controlled from the *investing* nation presents a possible clash of interests between the controllers or the executives of the parent corporation and the economic well-being of some or all of the people in the host nation. Such a clash would be similar to the familiar clash of interest between the executives of a domestic corporation and their employees, between stockholders and customers, and quite feasibly, between executives and stockholders. When the business is multinational in scope, the potential clash of interest can assume international aspects. It can involve governments, and the conflict of interest becomes a part of the infinitely complex world of international politics. The problems of international investment must therefore transcend purely economic considerations. Nor is it reasonable to ignore the casual chain whereby the economic welfare of the voter affects the security in office of the political leader and his ability to effect change. Because voters are interested in their own 'economic package', the nation will remain a separate unit in the international world seeking its own (collective) interest. This is not to say that nations are incapable of unselfish actions or of bilateral reductions of protective devices, but merely that the political process makes the leaders of a nation state sensitive to the feelings of its voters. There is a useful analogy here with a labour union whose leaders cannot with impunity sacrifice the economic welfare of its membership for a wider cause. While the purpose of this book is to emphasise the economic interrelationships and to attempt to provide a review of alternative costs and benefits that are likely to follow from the establishment or from the continuance of a foreign subsidiary, politics on a national level cannot be disregarded. In this modern world in which the process of foreign investment is seen by some as a part of a deliberately thought-out strategy of neo-colonialism by western nations seeking a substitute for their lost, former colonies, the potential for an ideological clash is apparent.[1] Equally, in a world in which mistrust of foreigners has been traditional (and frequently justified) and in which nationalism is an ever-present if not a growing phenomenon, the purely economic aspects of material costs and benefits may be temporarily overwhelmed by political disturbances.

The economic aspects of multinational business are important not only in the way in which they affect the economic variables of life – income, growth rates, income distribution and the terms of trade – but also in the way in which they can initiate or aggravate political disputes. They can also affect the internal politics of a nation in that a foreign response of a given type can strengthen the hand of a faction within a nation – one example of this in 1971 has been the intransigence of the attitude of the United States Government to Chile's nationalisation of copper mines strengthening the hand of the more extreme political factions in Chile.

The economic aspects of multinational business can be the source of an international dispute between the investing and host nations because one nation or the other believes that it can increase through political action, the net benefits which it derives from its foreign investment position. Given that a foreign subsidiary is always to some degree at the mercy of the host government which has the power to legislate against the subsidiary's interests, to favour its competitors, to tax it more heavily or, in the last resort, to confiscate it, a subsidiary is always *en prise*. As a consequence, the foreign affairs department of the investing country is often concerned with safeguarding the interest of the subsidiaries of its corporations and is likely to be more sensitive and even more aggressive in its relations with the host government, because of the subsidiaries' existence. Similarly, the host government is always tempted to use the captive subsidiary as a pawn in a complex, many-faceted

[1] A somewhat prolix, Marxist tract which makes some damaging points in its indictment of western nations' and western corporations' practices is Jack Woddis, *Introduction to Neo-Colonialism* (New York: International Publishers, 1967).

political disagreement which has as its origin something completely unconnected with multinational business or even with economic considerations. There will always be some people in the two countries who will feel themselves less well off (or who will be less well off) because of the existence of a foreign subsidiary. These people will be tempted to use any excuse for stirring up antipathy toward the subsidiary and will aggravate any disagreement by involving the issue of multinational business. Finally, the presence of a foreign subsidiary in a nation, particularly in a developing nation, will often prove a vehicle on which a group will hope to ride to political power (or to maintain power) and the subsidiary may become a political football to be kicked by opposing groups of politicians.

These aspects must always be in the back of the reader's mind. The province of economics, and even of political economy, is the production and distribution of goods and services. Therefore, the core of this book will be a dispassionate study of the influence of multinational business and direct investment on global production and consumption. Like most things, multinational business can arouse passions. Some people will see it as almost exclusively beneficial to the world, others – like Woddis – see multinational business as a new device designed for the exploitation of the masses. Like most extreme views, there are occasional examples that can be used to justify the contention – but these are isolated instances. Most investments are likely to prove less than wholly beneficial and less than wholly evil. The decision to invest in a foreign country is made by businessmen and, to a less degree, by bureaucrats. Such people are a mixture of saints and sinners just like any other group and their achievements will reflect their individual values.

When the yardstick of social desirability by which a transaction is judged includes the values and interests of a group larger than those directly concerned in the transaction, outside influences (externalities) can be both political and economic in their origin.[1] In any study of international economics, the nation state is the obvious unit to use as a basis for analysis.

---

[1] An externality can be defined as a service (disservice) rendered free (without compensation) by one economic entity to another and done so unintentionally. Another way of defining an externality is as an effect which escapes the market system.

Externalities make it possible for a transaction to be mutually advantageous to those directly concerned in it but not be beneficial for the nation taken as a whole. The problem with externalities is made quite apparent by reference to 'the national interest'. The national interest is a composite of the values and interests of the population. These values and interests have to be accorded relative importances before they can be welded into a whole and it is the assignment of these relatives that involves guesswork or arbitrary (and often not impartial) decisions. For problems such as international investment which will affect the interests of persons not even born at the time the decision is made, the externalities become an imponderable. This complication can be seen in the 1971 rift between Chile and the United States in which the bone of contention was American ownership of natural resource deposits. Natural resource deposits are depletable and therefore the decision to exploit these resources affects the inherited stock of wealth of future generations. Further, the decision to sell the natural resources to American corporations was probably made in the days before an awareness of externalities and interdependences was allowed to influence the actions of private citizens. Thus, nationalisation could be rationalised on the grounds that the philosophy underlying economic decision-making in Chile has changed since the time of the original sale – the argument would not, however, rationalise confiscation, i.e. nationalisation without compensation.

The inevitable lack of precision that must follow from the existence of externalities does not excuse ignoring these forces. But the lack of precision and the political aspects of international investment both mean that no reference to externalities can be accepted without question. Neither the author nor the reader can be completely objective. The whole question of foreign investment strikes at the heart of a person's economic philosophy and a sceptical attitude toward unsupported or oversimplified statements is a useful adjunct in attempting to assess the true benefits and costs of foreign investment in general and in particular instances.

When a corporation makes an investment, it does so in what it expects to be its own self-interest as seen through the (subjective) eyes of its executives. If any thought is given to the welfare of others affected by the investment decision on a philosophical or moral plane, the executive will tend to rely upon the benign working of the 'invisible hand' to outweigh any externalities involved – unless these are forcibly brought to his attention in which case they cease, probably, to be external considerations. There are many potential sources of self-interest that will encourage a corporation to create a foreign subsidiary. At this juncture they can be categorised quite aggregatively as subjective, aggressive or defensive. Subjective reasons involve the ego or the self-interest of the decision-maker, the fashionability of 'going abroad' and the desire to bask in the enhanced image of the expanded corporation. Aggressive reasons are the recognition of a profitable investment opportunity located abroad. Defensive reasons can involve the protection of an existing foreign market against inroads from local manufacture by a competitor or the securing of an assured source of supply of some raw material vital to the domestic operations of the parent company.

Direct investment abroad can be defined as the process of creation or expansion of some business in a foreign country, over which operational control is exerted by the parent corporation. The foreign enterprise may be extractive, manufacturing, sales or any other form of activity that contributes to the gross domestic product of the host country,[1] and will involve something more than the acquisition of a tangible asset for speculative purposes.

An act of investment results in the acquisition of an asset. If the investment is made possible by saving and is not merely a switching of existing assets or does not involve a simultaneous and equal increase in liabilities, the net worth of the investor increases. Investment or asset acquisition can be performed by any economic unit – individuals, corporations or governments. When international investment is the focus, flows of investment and stocks of international net worth (assets held abroad minus domestic assets held by foreigners) are usually computed on an aggregate national basis. Thus, the very real possibility exists that there will be offsetting balances within the investing

[1] Gross domestic product refers to the output of goods and services located in a country irrespective of the nationality of ownership of the factors of production.

country so that government dissaves on international account in order that the private sector may increase its asset holdings. Consequently, analysis of the process of international investment requires a familiarity with national balance of payments accounts. But the international economic relationship goes deeper than international accounting essentially because of the international political implications of the phenomenon.

Balance of payments accounting is concerned with debits and credits recorded in (domestic) money terms. The system of accounts is designed to measure whether or not monetary inflows exceed monetary outflows and the emphasis is on the monetary aspects of international transactions – if international liquid reserves are running down that is a sign of a deficit and of possible difficulty in defending the existing exchange rate of the national currency. On the other hand, international investment is concerned with changes in the stock of real tangible assets and with changes in holdings of long-term financial instruments owned abroad. These changes are necessarily interrelated with changes in liquid reserve positions. Secondly, investment analysis is concerned with the stock or net worth dimension of international transactions as well as with the flow aspects of economic transactions – if only because it is the proportionate foreign ownership of capital that is the principal measure of the impairment of a host nation's economic sovereignty. A final and more subtle distinction is that balance of payments analysis is based on the source and destination of the expenditure and therefore with the residence of the spender. Investment analysis is concerned with economic sovereignty and with a flow of investment income from abroad and therefore with the nationality or citizenship of the controlling party. This distinction will be seen to be an important one on which a crucial aspect of the argument of nationalists hinges.[1]

INTERNATIONAL ACCOUNTS

International accounts are quite straightforward. They are usually computed on an annual basis and comprise four separate sub-accounts. Where confusion exists about balance of payments analysis, the cause of the difficulty is either the

[1] See below pp. 9–10, pp. 148–9 and references cited there.

quite intricate economic analysis of the real or monetary forces which underlie any imbalance, or the complex inter-relationships which are involved in any adjustment by one economy to an imbalance in its international payments,[1] or the large number of different definitions of deficit and surplus. What follows is a minimal introduction to a system of international accounts cast in terms most suitable for the analysis of international investment.

The most important single category of transaction is the sale of commodities and services by residents of one country to residents of another country. These transactions involve the exchange of domestic money for a good or service and form the basis of both the mutual benefit derived from international trade and of the received body of international economic analysis. Each export uses factors of production as inputs and therefore detracts from the maximum amount of goods and services available for domestic use. Each import increases the amount of goods and services available for domestic absorption by adding to the available bundle of goods without directly using up factors of production.[2]

Goods and Services Account
(in millions of dollars)

	Receipts	Payments
Exports of commodities	135	
Imports of commodities		113
Exports of current services	38	
Imports of current services		49
Balance on goods and services	+11	

(A plus sign denotes a surplus or an excess of receipts over disbursements)

Provided that all goods are used in the period under review and no net investment or disinvestment in inventories of imported goods takes place, the balance on goods and services

[1] This is particularly true for students of international investment since the main body of adjustment theory ignores the process of international lending. The adjustment problem is analysed in Chapter VI below.

[2] Absorption is a technical term covering all categories of expenditure within a nation, i.e. $A = C + I + G$ including imports.

(BGS) shows the difference between the absorption by the focus country of foreign-made items and sales of domestic items to foreigners for their own absorption. If the focus country has a positive balance on goods and service account, it indicates that the focus country has produced more than it has consumed and therefore has saved. The balance on goods and services is therefore a first measure of *international saving* which can be defined as the increase in the international net worth of the focus country.[1]

A second category of transaction is that which covers all unilateral transfers. Transfers are current items in balance of payments accounts that either comprise gifts or payments made for services rendered that do *not* involve the using up of factors of production in the recipient country in the period under review. Thus a credit attributable to a transfer is distinguished from a credit attributable to a commodity export mainly by the difference in the current factor input required. Transfers cover a wide range of transactions and include foreign aid, private gifts, charitable donations made to residents of foreign nations or received from foreign economic units, reparations, pensions paid to persons living abroad and, very important, dividend and interest receipts and payments made by foreign debtors to residents of the focus country or by residents to creditors who live abroad. Foreign investment generates dividend income and therefore generates transfer receipts for the investing nation.

Together with transactions in goods and services, transfers make up the current account of a nation.

Current Account
(in millions of dollars)

	Receipts	Payments
BGS	+11	
Dividends and interest	83	49
Other transfers	17	42
Balance on current account	+20	

[1] This concept is developed throughout the book, but it should be clearly understood that a failure to save internationally does *not* imply living beyond one's total means since it is possible to have net capital formation as a result of domestic investment exceeding international dissaving.

Since both categories of transfers itemised are quite aggregative there is no reason why simultaneous debits and credits should not be recorded. The balance on current account (BCS) is a full measure of the excess of 'income' over expenditure and donations for the focus nation with the rest of the world. It is therefore a full measure of the amount of international saving of the nation in that it represents quite clearly the amount by which the nation can increase its net claims on foreigners as a result of the year's transactions – 20 millions of dollars. This increase in international net worth may be held in gold, in claims on foreign banks, or may be used up in the reduction of liabilities to foreigners. It can also be used to allow citizens to acquire real assets abroad through direct investments.

In addition to the unreliability of the component data in the real world, there is a fundamental problem which underlies the computation of the flow of international saving. A foreign corporate subsidiary seldom sends back to its parent all of its profits after taxes. The usual ratio is between one half and two thirds – the remainder being retained in the country of operation for the expansion of the business. For simplicity, consider a wholly-owned subsidiary. If the subsidiary earns a profit of ten units after payment of taxes, the net worth of the group of companies has increased by 10 units. If all of the profits are repatriated to the parent, the net worth of the investing country will be recorded as increasing by 10 units. If, however, the retained earnings are not included in dividend receipts by the investing country, the total international saving of the investing country will be understated by the amount of the retained profits. Similarly, the amount of domestic saving of the host country will, under the same accounting rules, tend to be overstated by the same amount. This is not an important problem in traditional balance of payments analysis which emphasises monetary flows and not net worth, but it can be very important in the analysis of international investment.[1] In balance of payments accounting, retained profits are sometimes ignored (as in the United States accounts) and sometimes entered in dividends or investment income and offset by a debit in the capital account as a matching outflow of investment (as in the recommended procedures of the International Monetary Fund). The IMF

[1] See footnote on p. 9 in this chapter and the apposite text.

practice is the more accurate for international investment analysis even though the actual repatriation and reinvestment are imagined transactions. There is a second problem with the computation of international saving and that is the valuation of existing foreign assets. It is not practicable for a nation to record or to estimate the change in value of outstanding assets and liabilities even though these changes will affect international net worth and therefore the flow of international saving in any one year. Thus, by concentrating on annual flows and not allowing for changes in capital values or for expropriations, data on international saving can be misleading and, over time, the sum of annual flows may not equal the change in the net worth figure. In this book, no further attention will be paid to this possibility.

The third kind of sub-account is the capital account.

Capital Account
(in millions of dollars)

	Receipts	Payments
Government investment (net)		9
Portfolio investment	7	11
Direct investment	3	22
	—	—
Balance on long-term capital		-32
	—	—

Capital account records transaction in which residents of one country acquire long-term, illiquid assets that are either tangible or represent liabilities of foreigners. Short-term capital is so liquid that it is most usefully integrated with money and ignored for purposes of analysis of direct investment. There are three types of assets that can be acquired: direct investment assets; portfolio assets and government assets – the latter being defined with reference to the creditor not the debtor. 'Government assets' are the result of government-to-government long-term loans. Portfolio assets are stocks or bonds purchased by the private sector of the investing country. The debtor can be a government, a foreign corporation or even a foreign financial corporation. Portfolio investment includes purchases of equity of foreign corporations provided that the acquisition of the equity does not involve a significant measure of managerial control. Portfolio investment is therefore motivated by normal economic considerations by which an asset-holder expects to achieve a better portfolio for his own purposes – usually involving some improvement in the trade-off between return and risk exposure.

The final category results from direct investment and represents the acquisition by a resident of the investing nation of a tangible real asset in a foreign country. This type of investment can vary from a Canadian purchasing a winter home in Florida to the acquisition of a French computer manufacturing corporation by an American conglomerate. The acquisition, creation or expansion of a corporate subsidiary is the predominant type of direct investment. Purchases of real estate by individuals or speculating corporations, while they can be important for Caribbean and other tourism-exporting nations, will not be further considered.

The essence of direct investment is not its tangibility so much as the fact that control of the tangible asset is vested in residents-citizens of the investing nation. The statistical criteria for distinguishing between portfolio and direct investments in the U.S. international accounts are that a holding is a direct investment if 25 per cent or more of the voting stock of the corporation is owned by a U.S. resident or an affiliated group of residents, or if 50 per cent or more of the stock is owned by U.S. residents regardless of affiliation. These criteria represent an attempt to gauge the location of managerial control. In fact, the arbitrary dividing lines are not important for U.S. subsidiaries since 97 per cent of subsidiaries involved more than 50 per cent ownership by U.S. residents and 75 per cent involved U.S. equity ownership of better than 95 per cent.[1]

Government investment is usually recorded as the difference between the reduction of outstanding government loans and the extension of new loans – loans both made and owed. The net figure of a payment of 9 million dollars shows that capital has been exported by the government of the investing country.

---

[1] Based on 1957 census data. See *The Balance of Payments Statistics of the United States – A Review and Appraisal*, Report of the Review Committee for Balance of Payments Statistics to the Bureau of the Budget (Washington, D.C., 1965) pp. 62–3.

Portfolio investment shows purchase of domestic bonds and stocks by foreigners in the amount of $7 million and purchases of foreign assets in the amount of $11 million. The international assets of the nation have increased as a result of transaction in long-term instruments by the private sector. Finally, direct investment shows a substantial net export of capital.[1] Overall transactions on long-term capital account resulted in net payments of $32 million – testimony to the fact that residents' desire to acquire foreign assets exceeded the desires of foreigners to acquire domestic assets.

The *basic balance* of payments is the sum of international saving (the change in international net worth) and international investment (the change in the net position in long-term assets). There is no reason why the basic balance for any single year should be zero. The forces that influence international saving and net long-term international investment are quite different. There must, therefore, be a fourth sub-account to serve as a balancing item if, as accountants insist, total payments are to equal total receipts. The items in the three sub-accounts covered so far all cover transactions that are made for their own sake. Transactions recorded in the 'liquid assets' account can be made either for their own sake or for the sake of balancing the overall demand for and supply of foreign exchange at the existing rate of exchange. The basic balance is:

Basic Balance
(in millions of dollars)

	Receipts	*Payments*
Balance on current account (international saving)	20	
Balance on long-term capital (international investment)		32
	—	—
Basic balance		– 12
	—	—

[1] A conceptual difficulty sometimes occurs when the act of foreign investment is thought of as an export of capital. The exports of goods and exports of capital have different 'signs'. This difficulty can be resolved by thinking of international investment as the importing of an IOU so that all payments involve imports and all receipts exports.

The fourth liquid assets account includes shipments of gold, reductions and increases in official stocks of convertible currencies,[1] and changes in private and public net positions in short-term assets *vis-à-vis* foreigners.

The total set of international accounts is:

		Net Receipts		*Net Payments*
Balance on goods and services	(a)	11		
Balance on transfers	(b)	9		
		—		
Balance on current account	(a + b)	20		
Balance on long-term capital	(c)			32
		—		—
Basic balance	(a + b + c)			12
Balance on liquid assets	(d)	12		
Accountants' balance or		—		—
identity	(a + b + c + d ≡ o)	32	=	32
		—		—

One point that is brought out by the balance of payments accounts is the fact that the acquisition of a foreign bond or a foreign piece of land constitutes an act of investment for the focus nation. This concept directly contradicts the usual definition of investment in the macroeconomic theory of a closed economy and merits a brief explanation.[2] The acquisition of an existing bond in a closed economy by a member of the population does not increase the total net worth of the nation since the transaction inevitably entails the sale of the bond by another member of the population. In an international framework, using international saving to acquire a bond from a foreign resident does increase the nation's international net worth in the same way as an addition to the stock of physical capital increases net worth in a closed economy. Both the bond acquired from the foreigner and the addition to the capital stock will generate a flow of income and increase potential national income.

[1] Domestic currencies of key currency nations do not count as international reserves – thus the U.S. dollar resources of the Federal Reserve System or the U.S. Treasury are not international reserves.

[2] Of course, if a resident purchases a foreign bond from another resident, the argument does not hold.

Implicit in the argument of the preceding paragraph was the assumption that the transaction in question was the only transaction on long-term capital account and that the basic balance was zero, or that the transaction was the marginal transaction which took place and prevented the investing nation from acquiring an equivalent amount of gold. It is, of course, possible for foreign portfolio assets to be acquired without any increase in the nation's international net worth and therefore without any increase in potential national income. Assume that the nation has a zero basic balance but that it has a net deficit on portfolio investment (capital export). This increase in assets could be offset by an equal sale of direct investment assets:

	Receipts	Payments
Government investment (net)		2
Portfolio investment	3	11
Direct investment	10	

With the flows postulated, the nation has experienced no net investment and no change, therefore, in its international net worth. Yet, by exchanging portfolio capital for direct investment it has weakened its own control over its industrial sector and, possibly, acquired the introduction of new technology into its economy via the establishment of foreign direct investments. It is possible that the return to government investment and to portfolio investment are less than the rate of return earned by direct investment (over and above any return to technology) and that the nation's net receipts of dividends and interest will have deteriorated.

Offsetting direct and portfolio investments are examples of the final noteworthy anomaly between the concepts used in balance of payments accounting and the concepts that are most useful in the analysis of business investment abroad. The problem of profits retained by a subsidiary and not recorded in the international accounts has already been referred to – if retained profits are not entered into the balance of payments accounts of a nation, the total value of its foreign business investments will exceed the cumulative sum of direct investments. However, asset size not net worth may be the more important indicator of the importance of foreign business to the host country and asset size can differ from net worth on a national basis because of international financing and because of internal financing.[1] The first possibility whereby asset size exceeds net worth exists when an investing nation does not achieve international saving equal to its net outflow of direct investment. In such instances, the direct investments of the business corporations based in the investing country are being financed either by the reduction of the liquid asset position of the investing country or by a portfolio inflow from the host country. The second possibility involves local financing in the host country of the direct investment. Such a loan will be a domestic transaction and will not be entered in the international accounts. Such loans do not increase the net worth of either the investing corporation or the investing nation but they do increase the asset size relative to the volume of real saving accomplished by the investing nation. In both examples, the host country has contributed to the capital formation under the control of foreign business – once through the investing nation's monetary authorities and once through its own banking system. In both cases, of course, the absolute profits accruing to the investing country will be smaller than they would have been had the requisite volume of international saving been transferred.[2]

To those concerned with the impairment of economic sovereignty by the volume of foreign business located in the host nation, a reasonable minimum requirement for the approval of the inflow of more direct investment is that the increase in the volume of assets under foreign control should be matched by international saving – the transfer of real resources. The essence of capital formation is abstinence from current consumption – or, in an international setting, current absorption. Real transfers are made by conveying to the host nation, the products of factors of production of the investing nation. This can only be accomplished when a nation uses less than it produces and has a positive balance on its current transactions with foreigners.

---

[1] Changes in the value of foreign enterprises can also cause discrepancies – such changes can come about through shifts in the terms of trade, appreciation of assets, improvement in market share, the acquisition of 'goodwill', etc.

[2] See C. P. Kindleberger, *American Business Abroad* (New Haven: Yale University Press, 1969) pp. 2–3.

The ability to effect a real transfer to another nation is measured by the flow of international saving achieved. International saving, defined for the balance of payments accounts as the balance on current account, is an important concept in the analysis of international direct investment. The concept is made more easily comprehensible by the examination of some familiar, *ex post facto* national income relationships.[1] The following notation is used:

Y =national income or product
I_D =domestic investment (capital formation at home)
C =domestic consumption
X =exports
M =imports
S =total saving (domestic plus international)
S_I =international saving
S_D =domestic saving
T_R =transfer receipts – international
T_P =transfer payments – international
I_I =international investment

Government expenditures are subsumed under C and I_D.

$$Y = C + I_D + I_I \tag{1}$$
$$Y = C + S_D + S_I \tag{2}$$
$$S_I = X - M + T_R - T_P \tag{3}$$
$$S = I_D + I_I \tag{4}$$
$$S_I = I_I \tag{5}$$

Equations (1), (2) and (3) are definitions. Equation (4) shows the condition for domestic equilibrium – that non-consumption equal total capital formation. Equation (5) shows the condition for (basic) international equilibrium – that international saving equal international investment. No causality is expressed in this 'model' and it differs from the orthodox model in one important respect. Orthodox thinking includes $(X - M)$ in equation (1)[2] in place of I_I. However, the investment equation, equation (1), is better used to show the intent of the nation and

---

[1] International saving is the equivalent of the more familiar concept of 'net foreign investment' in the national income accounts. The renaming is discussed below. The accepted nomenclature derives from J. M. Keynes, *A Treatise on Money*, I (London: The Macmillan Company, 1930) pp. 131–2.
[2] In the text $(X - M)$ is used as a 'shorthand' for $(X - M + T_R - T_P)$.

the way in which it plans to dispose of the fruits of its abstinence. Thus, equation (1) shows two possible avenues for the increase of national net worth and shows, explicitly, the substitutability between them. By putting $(X - M)$ or S_I in equation (2), a surplus on current account emphasises the abstinence that has been accomplished internationally and views it as an enabling process for capital formation either at home or abroad. Equally, the substitutability between S_D and S_I is explicit. A deficit on international account has a finite term though and ultimately S_I and I_I must be equated.

The framework presented above allows an important problem in the analysis of international investment to be clearly seen. There is no reason to expect that the volume of *planned* international investment should equal the volume of actual international saving that evolves – in the absence of some automatic international adjusting mechanism. The flow of international saving is determined by the competitiveness of prices, levels of income and net transfer receipts. The flow of planned international investment is determined by corporate expectations and decisions. There is a mechanism within a nation that will 'enforce' equation (4) but unless I_I is reduced by a portfolio inflow, there is no mechanism that guarantees that the nation will perform the volume of international saving that its corporations require. This is the crux of the problem of the adjustment of the investing economy to the international investment plans of its corporations.[1] In a regime of fixed rates of exchange, there is no mechanism that will equilibrate S_I and I_I for a nation by making sure that the investing nation actually foregoes the resources necessary for its corporations to acquire the real foreign assets that they seek.

INTERNATIONAL INVESTMENT: A HISTORICAL OVERVIEW

Historically, the evolution of foreign investment has three distinct stages. Prior to 1914, international investment was predominantly portfolio investment and the main – dominating – capital market was located in London.[2] The joint dominance

[1] This problem is discussed in detail in Chapter VI below.

[2] Douglass C. North, 'International Capital Movements in Historical Perspective', in Raymond F. Mikesell (ed.), *U.S. Private and Government*

of Great Britain both as a supplier of goods and as a supplier of capital meant that the adjustment mechanism worked well on an international basis – though there may well have been severe hardship incurred in the peripheral areas both within Britain and outside when the flows of capital needed adjusting. The joint dominance in goods and loans worked because, under a gold standard, the world was one country in effect and because the demands for loans from London virtually automatically increased the demand for goods from London. Under this set of conditions, the interest rate (Bank-rate) was able to act effectively as an allocative device for rationing capital demand among domestic and foreign users and it also managed to attract money capital (gold) from abroad quite efficiently. What direct investment took place in this period was largely from the colonial powers to their own colonial possessions and, given the close trading ties that existed, most of the direct investment funds could be expected to return to their source in the form of an increased demand for goods. Thus, for both direct and portfolio investment, there existed a mechanism that would bring international investment and international saving into something approaching equality *and* there existed a financing mechanism that would cope smoothly with small inequalities. Between the wars the breakdown of the international economy was a severe deterrent to any natural evolution of international investment. Certainly there was little incentive for direct investments to take place and, flight capital excepted, it is difficult to discern any pattern. After World War II and a period of constraint while the first few years of recovery were accomplished, direct investment emerged as the most important form of international investment.

Data on international investment levels and flows suffer from two weaknesses – incomplete coverage of transactions and the problems of the valuation of existing foreign assets. Nothing can be done about the incomplete coverage of the past. The usual means of reporting the stock of foreign direct-investment assets is to add up the book values of the individual enterprises. Unfortunately, book values will tend to underestimate the value of a firm and is likely to be a more serious underestimate, the

---

Investment Abroad (Eugene, Ore.: University of Oregon Books, 1962), provides a valuable background on this period.

older is the corporation, because of the natural conservatism of accounting practices in adjusting the valuation of existing assets for any monetary inflation. Subject to these shortcomings, Table I–1 gives selected coverage on the value of the United States stock of direct investment assets.

TABLE I–I

Value of U.S. Foreign Direct Investments, Selected Coverage

(Year end book values in millions of dollars)

Year and Industry	All Areas	Canada	Latin America	Europe	Middle East	Other
1929	7,528	2,010	3,462	1,353	14	687
1950	11,788	3,579	4,445	1,733	692	1,339
1953 total	16,329	5,242	6,034	2,369	n.a.s.	2,684
mining and smelting	1,933	677	999	30	n.a.s.	227
petroleum	4,935	933	1,684	609	n.a.s.	1,709
manufact.	5,226	2,418	1,149	1,295	n.a.s.	364
other	4,235	1,214	2,202	435	n.a.s.	384
1957	25,262	8,637	7,434	4,151	1,138	3,902
1961	34,664	11,614	8,255	7,713	1,243	5,839
1965	49,328	15,223	9,391	13,985	1,536	9,193
1968 total	64,983	19,535	13,101	19,407	1,805	11,135
mining and smelting	5,435	2,638	1,930	61	3	803
petroleum	18,887	4,094	3,680	4,636	1,656	4,821
manufact.	26,414	8,568	4,005	10,796	63	2,982
other	14,247	4,235	3,486	3,914	83	2,529
1969ᵖ total	70,763	21,075	13,811	21,554	1,829	12,494
mining and smelting	5,635	2,764	1,922	72	3	874
petroleum	19,985	4,359	3,722	4,805	1,654	5,445
manufact.	29,450	9,389	4,347	12,225	80	3,409
other	15,693	4,563	3,820	4,452	922	2,766

Source: Department of Commerce data.

p – preliminary data; n.a.s. – not available separately.

The data show the evolution of United States direct investment over a period of forty years. The table does not show a *net* investment position in any sense since it does not provide data on changes in the values of portfolio investment and in government asset positions, nor in the short-term liquid asset position of the United States. Finally, there is the countervailing stock of foreign assets in the United States, which had a book value in 1969 of $11·8 billion.[1] The pattern of United States foreign investment has changed dramatically over the period. Latin America has declined in its relative importance as a recipient area from first to third place. Canada became the main investment area in the mid-fifties only to be superseded by Europe in 1969 – though on a *per capita* basis, Canada would still rank first. Since Table I–1 gives stock data, the fact that Europe, became the prime recipient on a flow basis between 1957 and 1961 is given only implicitly. The other notable feature is the growth of the relative importance of manufacturing investments. This increase in the impoitance of manufacturing is a natural development given the rise in rich nations, particularly Europe. as hosts but it does not indicate cause and effect. It can be surmised that the change in the pattern of investment from poor to rich nations and from extractive to manufacturing industries is due partly to the increased risk in investing in developing countries in the post-war era but mainly to the technological innovations in communications and management and the new higher levels of income in Canada and Europe that made manufacturing investments both practicable and potentially rewarding. The impact of the Treaty of Rome and the formation of the European Economic Community is clearly visible on the rate of investment in Europe. If the Common Market countries were recorded separately, the change would be even more dramatic because the pattern of investment changed sharply within Europe – expansions on the continent replacing investments in Great Britain.[2]

Other nations' data on their direct foreign investments are less reliable and less detailed than those of the United States. At the end of 1966, ten rich nations (Canada, Japan, Sweden, Switzerland and the United Kingdom and the five EEC nations) estimated their assets at approximately $35 billion. Of these ten, the biggest asset-holder was the United Kingdom with assets of $16 billion.[3]

[1] Department of Commerce, *Survey of Current Business* (Oct 1970) p. 23.

[2] The category 'other' includes agriculture, transportation, trade and miscellaneous.

[3] Source: OECD data given in *The Multinational Corporation in the World Economy*, ed. Sidney E. Rolfe and Walter Damm (New York: Praeger Publishers Inc., 1970) pp. 7–8.

Table I–2 shows how the increase in the stock of foreign assets of the United States has been obtained. A graphic

TABLE I–2

Sources of Funds for U.S. Direct Investment, 1950–70

(millions of dollars)

Year	International[a] Saving	Retained Profits	Portfolio[b] Investment (– = inflow)	Change in Liquid Reserves	Direct[c] Investment (inc. profits)
1950	– 2,238	475	620	– 3,479	1,096
1951	156	752	156	– 508	1,260
1952	– 305	876	676	– 1,833	1,728
1953	– 2,095	776	– 280	– 2,550	1,511
1954	– 452	644	613	– 1,732	1,311
1955	– 489	898	435	– 1,757	1,721
1956	1,544	1,000	1,134	– 1,541	2,951
1957	3,384	1,363	1,548	– 606	3,805
1958	– 155	945	2,560	– 3,876	2,126
1959	– 2,301	1,089	620	– 4,293	2,461
1960	1,834	1,266	2,699	– 2,539	2,940
1961	3,102	1,054	2,661	– 1,159	2,652
1962	2,519	1,198	2,482	– 1,617	2,852
1963	3,245	1,507	3,357	– 2,088	3,483
1964	5,846	1,431	5,181	– 1,665	3,759
1965	4,295	1,542	2,812	– 1,986	5,010
1966	2,410	1,739	465	– 1,717	5,400
1967	2,139	1,598	2,703	– 3,700	4,735
1968	– 386	2,175	– 2,477	– 1,117	5,384
1969	– 899	2,532	– 672	– 3,481	5,786
1970	444	2,500 est.	– 415	– 3,587	6,945 est.
Total	21,598	27,360	26,878	– 46,831	68,916

Source: Department of Commerce data for flows only. Changes in the valuation of existing assets are not included.

[a] International saving does *not* include profits retained abroad nor profits of foreign subsidiaries located in the United States. Retained profits data relate only to U.S. foreign subsidiaries.

[b] Portfolio investment inflows are shown with a minus sign. Thus a positive number indicates the acquisition of foreign claims by Americans. Portfolio investment is a catch-all in this table and includes foreign direct investment in America as well as government investment. It also includes some nonliquid short-term capital flows of the private sector.

[c] Direct investments include retained profits.

est. = estimated.

picture is obtainable from Chart I–1 which is based on the same data. Total acquisition of foreign assets amounts to almost $96 billion, but $47 billion of these assets have been acquired by increasing United States liquid liabilities or by the reduction

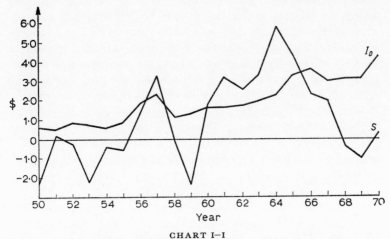

CHART I–I

Direct Investment and International Saving of the United States
1950–1970

The vertical axis is measured in billions of dollars.
The line *S* denotes international saving exclusive of retained profits.
The line *I* denotes direct international investment excluding retained profits.

in the gold stock. The increase in net worth (on a cumulative flow basis) is approximately $48 billion. There are no legitimate grounds for distributing the increases in the portfolio and the direct-investment assets between international saving and the reduction in the liquid asset position. However, it is clear that over the period as a whole, a large proportion of the increase in foreign asset holdings has not been offset by the transfer of real resources.

THE APPROACH TO THE PROBLEM

When a business expands across a national boundary there are three main sources of concern: the adjustment process that may be needed as a consequence of the foreign investment debit; the return to the investing nation in comparison with the obvious cost of diminished domestic investment in the short run; and the possibility of questioning the desirability of the entrance of the foreign concern from the host country's point of view. In addition to these aspects of the investment, there is also the possibility that the corporation's decision may be based on motives which are privately desirable but socially undesirable. Any examination of the economics of business investment abroad must consider the process from the point of view of all parties concerned. Thus, the chapters that follow comprise a sequence of what can loosely be called cost-benefit studies. Chapter II provides the tool kit in the form of a joint or double criterion based on the contribution of an investment to global economic welfare. The remaining chapters put some flesh on the bones. Chapters III, IV and VII examine the costs and benefits derived by, respectively, the investing corporation, the host country and the investing country. Chapter V provides two case studies of 'countries' that might reasonably complain of the loss of economic sovereignty because of the preponderance of foreign investment in certain sectors of the economy. Chapter VI examines the balance of payments framework in which foreign investment takes place and considers alternative adjustment possibilities. Chapter VIII examines the possible impact of growth of multinational corporations upon the world economy. Finally, Chapter IX lists some problems that remain unsolved and tries to propound some possible means of counteracting any adverse aspects that foreign investment may have.

The book must necessarily use foreign direct investment by United States corporations as its main source material if only because U.S. data are better and because the volume of foreign investment by American corporations far exceeds that of other nations. However, American investment has the additional characteristic that it is a focal point for opposition. It is the preponderance of American investment in some countries that gives rise to the opposition. While there is no reason to suppose that American business abroad is any less estimable or any less deserving of censure than the foreign subsidiaries of other nations, the use of American investment as the focus of this study necessarily brings the question of the total volume into the analysis. Failing that, there might be a tendency to concentrate upon the impact of a marginal investment.

CHAPTER II

AN ANALYTIC FRAME OF REFERENCE FOR DIRECT INVESTMENT

Direct investments that result in the creation or the expansion of a foreign subsidiary enterprise can be seen as permanent commitments of capital on the part of the investing corporation. These subsidiaries will have an impact upon the character of the host economy and upon the rate and composition of its output. Through their repatriation of profits to the parent corporation and their trading relations with the parent itself and with other related subsidiaries in third countries, a foreign subsidiary will have an enduring effect upon the host nation's international accounts and upon its pattern of trade. A third possible effect is that the subsidiary-parent relationship will expedite the transmission of technological knowhow between the two nations to the benefit of either or both. An overall assessment of the benefits that derive to both nations from the act of investment is a complicated matter – primarily because of the large number of dimensions involved in the process.

Imagine attempting to summarise the impact on the economy of the European Common Market of the introduction there of subsidiary computer plants from the United States. Equally complex would be an attempt to conjure up the benefits derived by Venezuela from the exploitation of its oil resources by a foreign corporation.

Because of the overall complexity of the process, a model of an investment and of its repercussions upon the two economies can be a valuable aid in that it simplifies the complexities of the real world, reduces them to manageable proportions and highlights (only) the most important forces and inter-relationships. Once such a frame of reference has been acquired, the temptation to omit aspects of the investment process is reduced and individual phenomena can be more easily related to the whole system. An additional advantage from such a model lies in the discipline inescapably imposed upon the analyst. He is required to make explicit any assumptions that are introduced as well as to announce the relative importance or weights that he attaches to individual items (both costs and benefits). It is in this latter aspect that the political variables can be conceptually included. The model will require that where goals are in conflict with one another, some rate of trade-off between them be established and where costs are not directly comparable, they must be made so by establishing a common denominator. However useful an abstract frame of reference may be, the possibility of its creation does not automatically mean that the costs and benefits considered in it are in any way quantifiable – either for an individual project or for an aggregate of all foreign investment. Similarly, it would be virtually impossible to achieve a general agreement on the rate of trade-off between any two conflicting variables – such as how much economic growth will compensate for a certain specified reduction in economic sovereignty.

This chapter will be divided into two main sections. The first will derive a relatively simple but highly (and tortuously) abstract criterion for the desirability of foreign investment. The second will qualify the straightforward criterion by deducing what can be expected when the investment project being considered varies by the affluence of the host country and by the type of investment involved.

I

The body of knowledge that constitutes international economics has two main branches. One concerns balance of payments forces and adjustments to changes in those forces. The other analyses gains from international trade obtainable through improved global resource allocation in line with the comparative advantages in the production of different goods enjoyed by different regions. The adaption of the first branch to the foreign investment process is carried out in Chapter VI below. This section attempts to provide a background model for analysing the effects of foreign investment on resource allocation and general economic gains. Unfortunately, the resource allocation branch of international economics is not very well suited to provide the basis of analysis: orthodox thinking on international resource allocation rests upon the desirability of the movement of goods between nations as substitutes for the movement of factors of production. In addition, the body of international trade theory is most developed in areas in which the goods traded between two nations can be produced in both countries with quite general factors of production. As will be shown below, direct investment is primarily concerned with the production of goods which are either not producible in the investing country or with the production of differentiated goods manufactured by international corporations.

There is another body of economics which deals with *criteria for investment* on a national level and this body of analysis provides a better starting point for the construction of an abstract frame of reference for the process of international investment.[1] There is, however, a fundamental difference between the basic problem which investment criteria analysis sets out to solve and that needed in this chapter. Investment criteria analysis is designed to permit selection of the best set of investment projects available to a nation from a larger population of investment projects and to provide a cut-off point which will vary according to the nation's supply of investible funds. International investment analysis needs to solve the problem – 'this investment is available from foreign sources, is it on balance beneficial to the host country?' and the obverse problem from the point of view of the investing country – 'a domestic corporation wishes to make this investment abroad, is it in our national interest to allow the export of capital and the corresponding commitment?' Domestic investment analysis is concerned with ranking competing investment possibilities by their social rates of return and establishing a cut-off point that separates the acceptable from the redundant. International analysis is concerned with a simple 'yes or no' answer. Thus, it is possible that an investment project which would not be

[1] The reader is referred to H. B. Chenery, 'The Application of Investment Criteria', *Quarterly Journal of Economics*, 67 (Feb 1953) pp. 76–96 and 'Comparative Advantage and Development Policy', *American Economic Review*, 51 (Mar 1961) pp. 18–51.

acceptable if financed out of domestic funds, is acceptable when financed by foreigners.

A simple, yes-no investment criterion can be expressed in the form of an inequality. The inequality will contain individual elements (variables) that introduce all the dimensions affecting the desirability of the investment actually being made. For example, the *simplest* criterion could require that income in the focus country (the host) increase as a result of the investment being approved and taking place. Defining income as the average product of capital (in money value) multiplied by the stock of capital (in units of a homogeneous capital good), the change in income would be approximated by the following formula and the inequality would be required to hold if the project is to be approved:

$$\Delta Y = \Delta P \cdot K + \Delta K \cdot P > 0$$

where Y stands for income P for the average product of capital and K for the stock of capital. All Δ values refer to small changes that will be achieved in some future time period when the new project would be in full operation. The criterion is satisfied if the capital stock in the focus country does increase and the *marginal* return to capital is positive. However, for an international criterion, a double criterion might be required – that both host and investing countries benefit. Then two such inequalities would jointly constitute the criterion and satisfaction of both inequalities would be necessary. This double criterion is not an unnecessary elaboration if both national governments have the power to block a corporation from carrying out an investment project.[1]

When more complex criteria are formulated, certain conceptual complications must be faced head-on. The elements can be assumed to be additive. If the series or list of elements is

[1] The existence of an alternative host country – particularly one with free rights of export to the 'first-choice' host – can severely constrain the power of the first-choice host to refuse an investment. An example might be the unwillingness of the French Government to approve the establishment in France of a wholly-owned subsidiary, being tempered by the realisation that disapproval would merely cause the same investment to take place in Belgium or in Luxembourg on a site just over the border. The choice is not a subsidiary or no subsidiary but a subsidiary *in* France or *just outside* France.

confined to purely economic dimensions, their values will all be specified in units of a national currency and will be directly comparable. If elements that are not measurable in currency units are included in an inequality, the problem of assigning relative weights or degrees of importance to the different dimensions must be solved explicitly. These complications are most likely to arise when the indirect effects of an investment are included so that it becomes necessary to attribute a numerical importance for social and political side-effects. The time element can be important since the value of individual elements in the inequality can vary according to the time horizon involved. There is no reason why the inequality for the host country should contain the same elements as the inequality for the investing country, and even if the same element appears in both parts of the criterion, the importance may vary. A basic reason for expecting that different elements or different importance for common elements will be required is that the host and investing nations are likely to have different income levels and therefore different concerns and different conceptions of what is, and is not, important (this aspect is considered in section II). Finally, there is the difficult question of considering whether or not the host country will benefit from the total amount of the capital invested. This will only happen if the investing country has real international saving (balance on current account) in the amount of the investment.[1] Whether or not this will happen depends more upon the international monetary system than upon the individual investment. It may be that the investment will use local saving in the host country and, in that way, not increase the host's total national capital stock by the amount of the subsidiary being established – local capital formation is merely diverted from one use to contributing to the foreign subsidiary.

Throughout the consideration of the criterion of social desirability for an investment project, the argument will be carried out in terms of two countries A and B. It may help to visualise the framework if the investing country A is thought of as being a rich country such as America and the host country B as being either a manufacturing country or a developing nation – Britain (or Benelux) or Brazil.

---

[1] This is the (infamous) transfer problem. It is treated in detail below in this chapter.

One of the most difficult aspects of analysing the consequences of any act of investment is the need to postulate an alternative set of circumstances as to what would have happened if the foreign investment had not taken place. If it is assumed that nothing happens, then the analysis rests on the belief that the corporation keeps the money in the bank and that these funds are not transferred through the banking system to another would-be investor or consumer. To examine the effect of a particular investment, it is necessary to establish an *alternative position* of what would happen if the projected investment were vetoed. The two positions – the investment position and the alternative – can then be directly compared. Suppose, for example, that Ford Motor Company were considering building an engine plant in Brazil. Then the investment position would depend upon the stock of capital in Brazil and in the United States (at some point in time when the investment was fully productive) and the alternative position would assume Brazil not to have the engine plant but the funds would have been spent (invested or consumed) elsewhere. The values inserted into the inequalities would be calculated from the difference between the two positions. Then, if the situation in which the investment took place is preferable to the situation in which the alternative outcome took place, the investment is desirable. The alternative position must be realistic and it must permit a fairly straightforward comparison between the two situations. In the model put forward in this chapter, it is posited that if A does not invest in B, the same amount of investment will take place domestically in A. There is no necessary presumption that the investment in A will take place in the same industry, but the assumption does allow the analyst to assume that the global stock of capital will be the same irrespective of the location of the investment.[1]

The criterion for the total desirability of a particular foreign investment can be expressed first in purely economic terms and aggregate measures of income used as measures of desirability. This procedure clearly involves the disregard of any internal

[1] Note that the text has already slipped into the easy jargon of referring to A investing in B. What actually happens is that a corporation based in A invests in B. The motivation is purely corporate and affects countries and governments only indirectly.

or income-distributional effects in the two countries and is highly aggregative. It also posits that national income data are an adequate measure of national welfare. Recently one new aspect of the weakness of national income data as measures of national improvement in material welfare has become important – the failure of national income data adequately to reflect social costs due to the worsening of the natural environment. This aspect may, in the future, become particularly important for international investment. Consider the case in which a rich country becomes concerned with its deteriorating ecology and imposes an effluent charge on all manufacturers according to the amount and potency of industrial waste that the corporation discharges. If the corporation could find a poor nation that was prepared to allow it to manufacture without an effluent charge, then there would be an advantage to the corporation to move. Since the plant was ecologically undesirable, the investing nation will have no objections to the capital export. However, if the poor nation does not allow for the damage to the natural environment in its computations, then the criterion could mislead. Developed nations afflicted with ecological problems could attempt to export their 'worst' industries to developing countries on the simple grounds that the material needs of the poor nations are too great to enable them to reject the investment. If the poor nation estimates the costs of pollution at a lower rate (as well it might) then it could still impose an effluent charge, require waste control devices and usefully host the investment. Brazil has announced a policy of seeking to attract foreign industries that are highly pollutant in order to add fuel to its industrialisation spurt – although such industries will be directed to the less-industrialised regions.

Assuming that national income data can be computed so as to include the major external costs and benefits that evade the market place, a joint criterion can be developed. However, the measure of national income used in the criterion will be slightly different from the most usual measure. The measure to be used is net national income. Ordinarily the role of international flows of factor incomes in the computation of national income is not emphasised. Since the purpose of international investment is to generate factor income abroad, the role of the international flow of factor incomes needs to be made explicit. Distinguish between net domestic product which is the value of all goods and services produced within a country's boundaries and net national product which is the value of goods and services produced by the nation's factors of production irrespective of location. For a host country, net domestic product will exceed net national product by the return flow of profits sent to the investing country. In the same way, national income in the host country will not include any savings made by nationals of the investing country whose presence is a direct consequence of the investment project. It is, in fact, easier to consider the investing country's nationals resident in the host country as still living in the investing country: in this way their consumption expenditures as well as their saving are attributed to the investing country. Any consumption goods imported from 'home' would then not figure in international trade but any expenditure on local goods and services would count as exports. (Historically, this has been important in colonial eras when settlers imported nearly all their luxuries from the home nation so that the colony benefited less than might at first be imagined from the presence of affluent settlers.)

Using asterisks to denote the values of net national income that obtain when the foreign investment is made and letting the absence of asterisks denote values that obtain under the alternative position, the criterion is met if:

$$NNP_B^* > NNP_B \quad \text{and} \quad NNP_A^* > NNP_A$$

or

$$\Delta^* NNP_B > 0 \quad \text{and} \quad \Delta^* NNP_A > 0$$

where Δ^* denotes the difference between the values when the investment is made in B and when it is made in A (under the alternative position).

The inequalities (and therefore the criterion) are clearly only as useful as the data on which they are based are accurate. Inaccuracies can take two forms. There can be holes and mis-specifications in the raw data and there can be errors in the assessment or computation of the indirect effects. The computation of an aggregate measure of national income is quite complex enough in an economy which is closed against international transactions. These difficulties are enhanced when the economy is open not only to current transactions but also to foreign investments. In addition to the basic problem of computing sets of national incomes estimates for an actual or future foreign investment position, there is the problem of estimating the national income for the alternative position. Clearly, any such computations must be aimed at achieving an order of magnitude or some idea of net increase or decrease rather than any exact number.

The problem of the valuation of international transactions is also particularly difficult. To obtain the domestic currency value of imported goods their foreign prices must be multiplied by the rate of exchange between the two currencies. If rates of exchange are flexible over time then it will be difficult to conceive of the alternative values of the exchange rates that need to be included in the computations. In any cost-benefit analysis, there is a whole group of variables which is directly influenced by the rate of exchange. The future rate of exchange would be influenced not only by the changes in the pattern of international trade of the two countries but also by the flow of foreign investment at any single period. For this reason the direction of change of the exchange rate under the two sets of circumstances must be clearly identified even if an accurate estimate is not possible.

The process of foreign investment must have an effect upon income distribution in the two nations. The possibility that the investment process will cause unemployment is examined in Chapter VI. In rich or manufacturing nations, the possibility that foreign investment – either as investor or as host – will make income distribution less equal or otherwise affect it adversely can be ignored, temporarily, by making the assumption that governments in developed nations have sufficiently flexible policies at their disposal that they can counter any adverse side effects. In poor nations in which some part of the population is chronically unemployed or underemployed and lives at a subsistence level, it is unlikely that an influx of capital will have adverse effects upon the distribution of income simply because additional capital should expand the need for labour and raise the number of employed persons.

The final factor before stating the assumptions and generating a formal criterion is the role of the transfer of international saving to the host country. It is clear that the capital stock in the host nation will only be increased on balance if the funds transferred by the parent corporation are actually matched by international saving by the investing country. Only in that way can the host nation increase its capital stock by the full amount. Alternatively, the host country will have to redirect some of its own saving to assist in the establishment of the foreign subsidiary.

Suppose that the foreign subsidiary is to involve a total investment of $1 million all of which is transferred from the parent to the subsidiary corporation. Potential expenditure in B will increase by $1 million. Total capital formation will increase by $1 million only if consumption does not increase and if the current balance with foreigners actually deteriorates by $1 million. Failure to allow the current balance to deteriorate would siphon off some of the $1 million inflow and reduce the total amount of funds available for expenditure in B. This can be seen more clearly by conceiving of three sets of (hypothetical) national income data for B.

Category of Expenditure in B	No Foreign Investment	Inadequate International Saving by A	Adequate International Saving by A
Net National Product	100	100	100
Foreign Investment Inflow	0	1	1
Domestic Investment	3	2·5	3
Consumption	97	97	97
Current Account	0	−0·5	−1
Total Capital Formation	3	3·5	4

The first column shows that capital formation in B would amount to $3 million in the absence of any foreign investment. In the second column, A does not increase its balance on current account by an amount sufficient to validate the export of funds by the corporation. A manages to increase its international saving by half a million dollars and, with consumption unaffected, this increase in international saving by A makes a positive constribution by B's rate of capital formation. In the third column, A achieves enough international saving to validate all of its corporation's transfer of funds and B's capital stock increases by the full amount. Since the subsidiary is considered to be built in column 2, the half million reduction in B's capital formation will have been devoted to the establishment of a foreign-controlled subsidiary. This is not a total loss, since the domestic saving achieved by B's citizens will earn a return from the subsidiary and will reduce the volume of profits repatriated to A. It may or may not affect the degree of control exercised over the subsidiary by the parent. If the saving were in equity rather than in debt, some governments would prefer that to a straight wholly-owned subsidiary (as is considered in Chapter IV), but what is relevant here is the *unintentional* dilution of the foreign effort because of the inability of the investing nation to validate its corporation's planned transfer of funds through increasing its exports (net) by the requisite amount.

THE ASSUMPTIONS AND THE CRITERION IN FORMAL DETAIL

The following assumptions are made. They will be relaxed later to examine their effect upon the criterion.

1. The international investment takes place in year t and is completely matched by international saving by A in the same year.
2. The achievement of the requisite amount of international saving by A does not require a depreciation of A's currency (a change in the rate of exchange) in t.
3. In year $t+1$ the new investment is fully productive and exerts its influence simultaneously on the net national product of both nations and on the rate of exchange.
4. As a result of the investment, the exchange rate turns adversely to B and remains constant thereafter.[1]
5. All profits from the foreign investment are repatriated to A in each year and the absolute amount of B's currency repatriated is constant for the life of the investment.
6. Income distribution effects are ignored.

[1] The assumption that the rate of exchange will move adversely to B after the investment is productive is probably a good one but does not follow inevitably. The rate will move against B if the repatriation of profits and increased imports jointly exceeds any exports created plus any imports displaced by the new facility.

There is one more economic element that should be included in the criterion. It will normally affect the value of the criterion only in developed countries. In a monopolistic and mono-polistically-competitive world, foreign investments can reduce the degree of monopoly exercised by the domestic industry and can add to the number of competing types of a differentiated product available to the consuming public in the host country. An increase in the number of alternatives available to the public might normally be considered a positive factor but a relatively unimportant benefit – especially as it is capable of achievement through international trade and without inter-national investment. However, it is possible that an oligopolistic industry could refrain from introducing new product types which might be greatly valued by the consuming public. An example of innovative lethargy of this kind was the unwilling-ness of the United States automative industry to introduce small cars until forced to by European competition. Similarly, a foreign corporation might be tempted to invest abroad because of the existence of monopoly profits in the industry in the host country. In the course of establishing itself in the host country's market, the foreign firm will be likely to force down the price. Foreign investment may be necessary for these inroads on monopoly profits to be made since the domestic group may well be too strong and be able to prevent a small firm from achieving entry. Thus, foreign corporations may be the only possible source of large-scale competition.[1]

The criterion in the host country is:

$$\Delta^* NDP_B = I(\Delta O/\Delta K) - \Delta T - M(\Delta r/r) + C > 0$$

where I is the actual amount of investment and $\Delta O/\Delta K$ is the marginal output-capital ratio for the specific industry. The whole expression, $I(\Delta O/\Delta K)$, measures the total increase in B's *NDP* that will follow from the location of the investment in B. While the industry may use imports in its production, these imports are excluded from the measure of output and therefore

---

[1] Note that it is definitionally impossible for a new entrant to increase the excess profit rate obtained by an oligopoly. However, if the oligopoly profit rate is reduced only temporarily, the profits will now be transferred abroad instead of being retained.

need not appear in the criterion explicitly. Both directly-employed imports and any increase in imports occasioned by the higher growth rate make their effect felt in the proportionate shift in the exchange rate or terms of trade $(\Delta r/r)$. The criterion is measured in B's currency and the rate of exchange is defined as the number of units of B's currency needed to purchase one unit of A's currency. If the effects of the investment cause the terms of trade to deteriorate, as is to be expected, $(\Delta r/r)$ will be positive. Any repatriation of profits on the investment (ΔT) will be specified in B's currency and therefore will not need to be qualified by the exchange rate, but the increase in total dividend payments must be subtracted from the increase in *NDP* in order to measure the net contribution of the investment to B's economy. In the same way, the effect of any adverse shift in the terms of trade on B's original import bill must also be deducted, $M(\Delta r/r)$. Finally, the competitive benefits from foreign investments are shown by C. According to this criterion, the location of the investment in country B rather than in country A will benefit B provided that the increase in net *domestic* product is not offset by the increase in transfers of dividends and if the increase in output is not seriously impaired by the additional cost of imports that might result from a depreciation of the host country's currency.

The criterion is exclusively economic and, except for C, is directly measurable in money terms. Political costs can be included in the criterion by requiring the $\Delta^* NNP_B$ exceed some positive value which represents in money terms the intangible and subjective costs of foreign control over domestic industry. This relationship is shown schematically in Figure II–1. The trade-off relationships are depicted, one between growth and a decrease in economic sovereignty (south-east quadrant) and the other between retrogression or negative growth and decreased dependence. The relationships are not symmetric. The growth-decreased sovereignty quadrant shows the decreasing marginal utility attached to greater income and the increasing marginal disutility of dependence or lack of sovereignty. Thus, at some point, no increase in income will compensate for further inroads being made on the nation's economic independence. The origin of the figure shows the combination of existing levels of *NNP* and independence. The north-west quadrant trade-off shows a combination of increasing disutility of retrogression[1] and diminishing marginal utility of independence. The position of the curves depends upon the existing degree of economic dependence as well as upon the

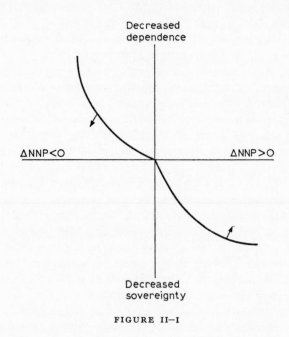

FIGURE II–I

The Trade-off between Sovereignty and Income Changes

level of income. The greater the original foreign share of the national stock of capital (the greater the degree of dependence) the more the two schedules will shift in the directions shown by the two arrows. Similarly, the position of the curve or the value on the right-hand side of the inequality might not be independent of the identity of the investing nation. Thus, Canada's trade-off between increased American investment and reduced independence would be far flatter than for, say, Dutch investment. This discrimination among investing nations

[1] Retrogression should be interpreted as a partial effect so that decreased dependence could mean a reduction in the growth rate that would otherwise be achieved rather than retrogression in the literal sense of the word.

might derive from nationalistic antipathy, from the volume of existing investment by the nation concerned or from the degree of control the government of the investing nation tries to exert over the foreign subsidiaries of its corporations.

THE A PRIORI CASE FOR FOREIGN INVESTMENT

It is the first term in the inequality, $I(\Delta O/\Delta K)$, that contains the heart of the argument for permitting international capital to flow freely among nations. In a perfectly-competitive world, capital would flow from rich, capital-plentiful regions that offered low rates of return to capital to poor, capital-short regions. The inflow of capital in the poor region would employ the local work force more effectively and, because the marginal product of capital would be greater in the poor than in the rich region, global output would be increased. Both regions could share the increase in total output.

Traditional international trade theory has shown – under quite restrictive and specific assumptions – that the gains to be derived from the international exchange of commodities are attributable to differences in the relative factor endowments in the trading regions or nations. Commodities move between nations as a substitute for the movement of factors of production. The country that is plentifully endowed with capital (relative to labour) has a comparative advantage in the production of capital-using commodities. The other country in a two-country model must be relatively plentifully endowed with labour and will enjoy a comparative advantage in the production of goods that require large amounts of labour in their production (at the going ratio of factor prices). The capital scarcity in the labour-intensive country is relieved by the importation of goods containing large amounts of embodied capital and the labour shortage in the other nation is relieved by the importation of goods with considerable labour content. In a static world, the best possible pattern of global production is achieved (if tariffs and transportation costs are disregarded) by an unhindered exchange of goods. Trade in commodities substitutes the exchange of *embodied* factors of production for the exchange of the factors *themselves*.[1]

[1] See any detailed undergraduate text in international economics.

Why, if trade is a perfect substitute for the movement of factors, is the movement of capital desirable? First, two theoretical answers can be given: a free trade (no tariff) model on which the perfect-substitute argument depends is not a stable situation since nations would always be expecting to achieve an increased gain from international trade by the imposition of a tariff; factors of production only use transportation costs once, while commodities use transportation on a continuing basis. In the real world, there are additional considerations. The theory would have factors move in both directions labour to the capital-intensive and capital to the labour-intensive country. While capital has shown itself to be quite footloose, the flow of labour out of poor countries is seriously impeded by immigration laws, languages and customs and by sheer lack of knowledge of the gains to be had from emigration. The fact that trade flows are never likely to reach the optimum rate because of tariffs and quotas, suggests that capital movements may reduce the imperfections in the system by substituting for trade flows. The pure theory pays no attention to the existence of truly immobile factors of production such as land and natural resources or to international trade in differentiated goods. These factors are likely to prevent trade from ever achieving any optimum distribution of production even in the absence of tariffs and quotas. Capital movements are necessary as a supplement to international trade in commodities especially when the immobile factors vary in quality and in relative proportion among nations.

An alternative means of demonstrating how a transfer of real capital from a rich to a poor nation will increase global output is to examine the characteristics of an average product of capital curve for two nations. The argument can be simplified, at the expense of some realism, by assuming that the technology in both countries is the same and that the supplies of labour and other co-operating factors of production are identical in both quality and quantity. The two nations are therefore *identical* except for their stocks of capital. Under these circumstances the average product of capital curve will be the same for both nations and the distinction in income levels will derive only from the position on the curve. Since the labour force is the same in both countries, the population may also be assumed to be identical and the ratio of national income in A to national income in B will be the same as the ratio of the *per capita* incomes. Figure II–2 shows the average product of capital curve for the two nations. The schedule slopes downward

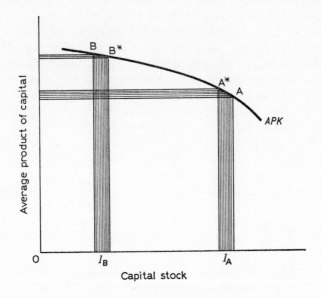

FIGURE II–2

The Effect on Output of Investment with different Original
Amounts of Capital

because the law of diminishing returns is inexorable: each additional unit of capital will add less to total output than its predecessor. The law does not ensure that the *APK* curve will be concave to the origin as drawn but this seems a probable shape: a linear curve would be adequate for the following argument. Total output for the nation is given by the area under that point on the *APK* curve corresponding to the total capital stock available in each country (capital being measured in physical units). The addition to total output resulting from an addition to the capital stock in either country can be calculated by subtracting the area under the original point (old capital stock) from the area under the new point on the curve corresponding to the larger capital stock. In Figure II–2 an increment to the capital stock of B in the amount I_B and starting from the quantity corresponding to B on the curve will increase B's total output by the vertically-shaded area minus the horizontally-shaded area. The vertically-shaded area shows the product of the new capital multiplied by the average product of capital that corresponds to the new capital stock. The horizontally-shaded area represents the loss of output due to the decline in the average product of capital. Using the asterisks once more to denote investment in B and the lack of an asterisk to denote the alternative position, the global benefit from investing in B rather than in A can be clearly seen. The gain in total output is the difference between the sum of the two areas under A* and B* and the sum of the two areas under A and B: I_A being equal to I_B by definition. Not only does the capital have a higher average product when invested in B but, in addition, the decline in the average product of capital is less in B than in A. If the assumptions of two nations identical in all features except the stock of capital were dropped, then the probability that the average product of capital will be greater in the poor country is very high since, in all likelihood, full employment will characterise the rich country while B will have unemployed or underemployed labour to work with the new capital. Parallel reasoning would apply to the possibility of technology being transferred to B with the foreign investment.

It is instructive to consider how the effects of foreign ownership as opposed to the transfer of real international saving affect the criterion. Consider an 'aid donation' from A to B that is fully matched by international saving by A. Assume that the output-capital ratio for the aid project is the same as that applying to the foreign investment. Then the difference in B's NNP would be the absence of transfer payments to A in the form of repatriated profits ($\Delta T = 0$) and a consequently smaller adverse change in the rate of exchange against B's currency. It would still be possible for the host nation to prefer foreign investment to aid if the foreign investment will transmit technology into the host economy more effectively.[1]

[1] See Chapter IV, pp. 125–30.

THE CRITERION FOR THE INVESTING NATION

The equivalent to B's inequality criterion for the investing nation is:

$$\Delta^* NNP_A = -I \cdot (\Delta O/\Delta K) + \Delta T \cdot \frac{1}{r} + M \cdot \frac{\Delta r}{r} - T \cdot \frac{\Delta r}{r} > 0$$

where I is the value of the capital export. The receipt of dividends in A's currency is shown by $+\Delta T/r$ – the value of dividends being specified originally in B's currency, needs dividing by the rate of exchange in order to transform the flow into A's currency. The proportionate change in the rate of exchange is positive and will reduce the cost of the original import bill. In the same way, the benefits from earlier receipts of dividends and interest are reduced by the depreciation of B's currency. The inequality is expressed in A's currency and therefore its numerical value is not directly comparable with the inequality of the host nation.

Provided that the effect of a foreign investment by A rather than a domestic investment in A has no overall cost to the investing country A, the total criterion can collapse into a single inequality – that of the host nation. If it suffices that $\Delta^* NNP_A$ be non-negative, any benefits that accrue to A become irrelevant and the criterion can be simplified.[1] Benefits can be put on one side of the inequality sign and costs put on the other. For the criterion to be satisfied, it is sufficient that the international benefits accruing from investment in B exceed the output lost by the failure to invest domestically. The revised inequality can be expressed as:

$$I(\Delta O/\Delta K) < \Delta T \cdot \frac{1}{r} + (M - T) \cdot \frac{\Delta r}{r}$$

The term on the left of the inequality sign is positive and represents the increment to A's national income that would have been forthcoming had the investment been made in A. Since it is a reasonable assumption that A is fully-employed, the marginal output-capital ratio will be quite small. On the right-hand side of the inequality are the returns from the investment

[1] Any adverse distributional effects have been assumed to be offset: see Chapter VII for consideration of this assumption.

and what may be called the terms-of-trade effect. The terms-of-trade effect could be negative if dividend receipts exceeded imports prior to the act of investment.

There is a strong *a priori* assumption that this inequality will hold. There is a virtual assurance that the investing corporation will have contrasted the return to capital from the foreign and best domestic investment outlets. If the investment is to be made abroad, then the foreign rate of return must exceed the domestic return – always assuming that profit expectations are justified in practice. The inequality, as written, will fail to hold only if $-T(\Delta r/r)$ were sufficiently negative to offset the net gains accruing from foreign investment. The smaller are the net gains, the more easily could they be offset by externalities of this or any other kind. But, if the investing firm's expectation about the alternative rates of return is borne out, the firm's investment margin – the difference between the rate of return on the foreign and the domestic investments – is unlikely to be small since the decision to invest abroad will only be taken if there exists some safety margin against foreign interference with the subsidiary.[1] If, on the other hand, the firm's expectations are not justified, the investment is likely to prove a bad decision from both points of view – the corporation's and the investing country's.

The larger the flow of profits as a proportion of invested capital, the more likely is an investment to be beneficial to the investing nation. Thus, if a foreign subsidiary can effect an entry into a foreign oligopoly and, once entry has been achieved, collude with the other firms to re-establish the original level of oligopoly profits, the investing country will benefit. The host country is unlikely to benefit from such an invasion since quasi-rents that were kept in the host country are now flowing to the investing country.

The terms-of-trade effect can vary widely according to the industry in which the investment is made but, generally, it can be expected to increase the probability that the inequality will hold. In addition to imports used in the productive process, the higher rate of growth to be expected in B because of the increased rate of capital formation, and the consequently lower growth in A, will move the terms of trade in A's favour. It is

[1] Considerations of the investing corporation are taken up in Chapter III.

possible that foreign direct investment takes place in order to combine the parent company sales organisation with the foreign level and mix of factor prices. Foreign investments made to supply intermediate or finished goods to the investing country's market could increase imports and affect the terms of trade adversely for A. Direct foreign investments designed primarily to serve the U.S. market have recently antagonised U.S. labour leaders.[1]

The element C does not appear in the investing country's inequality since it is not reasonable to expect that, if the funds had actually been invested at home, that the new additions to the stock of physical capital would either have reduced the profit rates of existing oligopolies or have been innovative in product design.

The probability that foreign investments will prove detrimental to the overall interest of the investing country depends very largely upon foreign capacity being created primarily to serve markets in the investing country. If the currency of the investing country is not overvalued, such projects are not likely to occur with such frequency as to constitute an important element in foreign investment – any such investments would be required to outweigh the import-reducing propensities of other investments. Subject to that consideration and to the assumptions made, it is possible to arrive at a working hypothesis that foreign investments will be beneficial to the investing nation provided the expectations of the entrepreneurs are fulfilled.

When both host and investing countries are developed it is quite possible for direct investments to flow both ways simultaneously. Indeed, in the chemical industry in which much hinges upon the use of proprietary knowledge, two-way investment flows can take place simultaneously in the same industry. It is unlikely that the flows will balance either on a bilateral or on a multinational basis. When such two-way flows occur, there is a high probability that the exchange of investments will be favourable to both nations. Usually, the investment process will make available locally the benefits of proprietary knowledge in

---

[1] See Elizabeth Jager, 'Multinationalism and Labor: For Whose Benefit?', *Columbia Journal of World Business* (Jan–Feb 1970) pp. 56–64, and Chapter VII below.

different industries. If the two flows were equal and the marginal output-capital ratios in the industries roughly the same, then it is possible that the transfer effects and the rate-of-exchange effects would cancel each other out. At a minimum, the net-transfer effects and exchange-rate effects would be reduced. The criteria for the two nations under the equality assumptions will consist only of the positive elements of C and of the impact on output levels of the new technologies. Technological changes will shift the average product of capital curve up in the host country (in Figure II–2) and can only be beneficial. If the two flows are sizeable, it may be difficult for governments to impede individual investment projects (except in rare cases where national security or a similar issue is involved). It is, however, always possible for nations with screening devices for domestic investments to control foreign investments by discriminating use of their domestic apparatus. However, between developed countries, free flows of aggregates of direct foreign investments would be the correct basis for assessing any net cost or benefit – because of the difficulty of discriminating among projects it should not be necessary to validate that each investment fulfil both halves of the criterion of desirability.

The contention was made at the beginning of this chapter that an abstract criterion would simplify the real world. That contention might now seem unwarranted. Yet a fairly concise statement about the desirability of foreign investment can be made now that the discussion of criteria has been endured. The creation of a foreign subsidiary can be expected to increase global real income either through a better allocation of capital together with the transmission of technological knowhow or through a reduction in market imperfections. This gain in real income must be shared between the host and the investing countries. The division of these gains is brought about by the mechanism of the adjustment of the exchange rate to the pressures of international flows. The costs to the host country are likely to be found primarily, though not exclusively, in the burden of profit repatriation, adverse shifts in the exchange rate and a loss in economic sovereignty. The greater the total global gain and the greater the host country's share, the more powerful must feelings about the desirability of national sovereignty be if the host is to deny the entry to an investment.

The investing country incurs the costs of possible failure of the enterprise, of adverse income distribution effects internally and of adjustment effects involving unemployment.[1]

II

The criterion can be reduced to a relatively small number of elements:

1. The change in global output from the redistribution of the world's capital stock.
2. The change in total output achieved through the transfer of technology.
3. The flow of repatriated profits and associated payments.
4. The effect of the investment upon gains from trade and the rate of exchange.
5. The effect upon the market structure of the host country.
6. The effect of the investment upon national values and on national economic sovereignty in the host country.

The importance of these six elements may vary in some predetermined way with different characteristics of the two nations involved – such as income differentials. Equally, the factors may vary in importance when some of the underlying assumptions are released. Finally, the influence of the individual elements may be expected to vary systematically according to the type of industry involved in the direct investment. This section examines these possible relationships. Before that is done, two detours must be made. The first of these is to categorise the types of industries in which direct investment can take place and the second is to examine in some detail the transfer process whereby real international saving is transferred from the investing country to the host country.

THE TRIPARTITE CLASSIFICATION OF INDUSTRIES

The impact of the creation, expansion or acquisition of a foreign subsidiary enterprise upon the host economy is likely to vary from industry to industry. For example, the development

[1] These two potential costs are considered in Chapters VII and VI respectively.

of an electronics plant in Taiwan to feed the domestic U.S. market will have different requirements and a different impact on the general level of technological knowhow in the host country than will a decision to develop a mineral deposit in a nation situated in west Africa's equatorial region. A threefold classification of products based on their differing characteristics in international trade can be used to classify foreign investment projects. The categories are non-competitive goods, competitive homogeneous goods and differentiated goods.

Non-competitive goods are those goods imported by a nation because that nation lacks the resources necessary to satisfy its own domestic needs. Ignoring such unrealistic possibilities as the United States making itself self-sufficient in bananas or in coffee by a combination of high tariffs and hot-house cultivation, non-competitive goods are those which require a specific factor of production which is not available in the consuming country or is not available in quantities sufficient to satisfy domestic needs at or near the going price of imports. The crucial aspect of this type of good is that the specific factor is neither mobile between nations nor reproducible, so that the nation is dependent upon foreign production. Goods in this category are those requiring mineral deposits, a particular type of soil or a particular climate for their production. A second important aspect of this type of goods is that since these specific resources are not freely available, it is possible for them to command an economic rent. Economic rent is defined as the difference between the price required to allocate the resource to the use in question (its opportunity cost) and the price which that resource can earn in the market. Rent can be an important surplus element in the income of the owner of a specific factor of production – the person's or the corporation's if the end product is sold in a domestic market, and the nation's (as well as the individual owner's) if the good is exported. The scarcity that generates a rent can be absolute (Colombian emerald beds), qualitative (Kuwaiti oil *vis-à-vis* Venezuelan oil), or locational (Caribbean beaches *vis-à-vis* South American beaches).[1]

[1] Locational rent depends upon the cost of transportation. Since transporting humans is more costly than transporting commodities, locational rents are more important in the tourism industry.

Competitive goods are homogeneous goods that are sold in general markets. They can be made with general factors of production such as unspecialised land, labour and capital. Whether or not they are produced in a country or imported depends upon the relative price of the different inputs at home and abroad. These goods are the foundation for modern international trade theory.

It is worth noting at this juncture that the orthodox theory of international trade is not very useful in the analysis of international investment and international business. Orthodox trade theory assumes factors of production are not mobile between countries and international business relies quite critically upon the mobility of capital (and skilled labour). Further, international business is preponderantly involved in the production of non-competitive and of differentiated goods while international trade theory relies almost exclusively upon trade in homogeneous goods. Even in those cases in which multinational business generates international trade in intermediate products that could be produced in any country and are therefore, to some degree, competitive goods, the involvement of international business with competitive goods is built into an overall production-sales organisation which really puts the transaction outside of the framework of orthodox international trade theory.

Differentiated goods are those which are not homogeneous. They comprise mainly durable manufactured goods sold in imperfectly-competitive markets. Each particular good is or is made to appear slightly different from its competitive products through differences in design or small differences in specification. Any differences that exist will tend to be blown out of proportion by advertising and sales promotion. The sale of goods of this type requires a marketing organisation. The fact that differentiated goods are sold in imperfect markets means that any would-be newcomer to the industry has to establish his particular product in a market in which established sales organisations and relationships and known brand-names exist. Overcoming this advantage enjoyed by the established firms constitutes a barrier to entry into the industry. Consequently, the profits of existing firms can be slightly higher than those accruing to a corporation in a perfectly-competitive industry producing a homogeneous product.[1] Since differentiated goods almost definitionally involve design inputs and, only slightly less probably, research-and-development inputs, there exist potential returns to knowledge and design knowhow which can be exploited through manufacture abroad or 'exported' by means of licensing arrangements. Differentiated goods may provide a quasi-rent to the producer and the knowledge element may facilitate entry into a foreign market.

Foreign investment can be expected to reflect the threefold classification quite closely. It is likely there will be heavy investment in non-competitive goods in order to ensure a source of supply for domestic production units or even for sales outlets. Minerals might be expected to characterise the first reason and tropical fruit and produce the second. These investments offer the possibility of a rental income over and above 'normal' return to capital. The bulk of this type of investment will be located in primary-producing countries and mostly in poor countries. To the extent that capital or technology is needed to produce the specific product, investment may be necessary in a poor country while the same ends can be served through long-term contracts in a developed nation. Relatively little direct investment can be expected to take place in competitive goods industries unless there is some means of linking the products up with a sales organisation in the investing country. In the absence of any economy of operation that is internal to the firm, supplies of homogeneous goods can be imported from the most efficient (lowest price) supplier. Since any foreign investor will be at some disadvantage relative to indigenous producers because of the lack of familiarity with local customs and laws and because of the danger of unfavourable political attention by the host government, indigenous entrepreneurs can be expected to supply all the capacity that exports require. Foreign investment is attracted to differentiated goods industries because of the potential returns to proprietary knowledge and because of the prospect of quasi-rents that can be obtained once entry in the local market has been established. The presence in most European countries of subsidiaries of such well-known corporations as General Motors, Ford, Frigidaire and Westinghouse as well as the oil companies testifies to the lure of an established

[1] The difference can be referred to as a quasi-rent.

position in a market for differentiated products. Direct investments that give rise to sales-distribution organisations are
frequently forerunners of manufacturing capacity.[1] Investments
in differentiated goods industries in developing nations will
usually be made only in nations in which a sheltered position is
obtainable and in which the domestic market is expected to
achieve viable size and growth in the short run. Early investment in such markets affords the corporation a good market-
share position for the future. The best examples of such
behaviour are automotive companies operating in Latin
American countries – American Motors in central America and
Kaiser in Mexico and the Argentine.

The transfer problem underlies the crucial assumption made in
section I that the foreign investment inflow into the host
country was matched by international saving by the investing
country. Only if the international saving was generated by the
investing country was it possible for the stock of capital of the
host country to grow by the amount of the foreign investment.
The adjustments in the international markets for goods, services
and currency that are necessary for the international saving to
be transferred to the host is the subject of analysis concerned
with the transfer problem. Since the investing corporation has
made the decision to invest abroad, the necessary funds will
have been obtained either from retained profits or from a bank
loan. If the funds are derived from retained earnings they
represent saving by the corporation and if obtained from the
financial system they represent someone else's saving unless
credit is being created. These savings can only be transferred
into another currency if the domestic saving is transformed into
international saving. The non-consumption of the domestic
sector must be transformed into a surplus on current account
of equal magnitude. It is the real goods provided to the host
country without claim on current output that enables the host
country to increase its rate of capital accumulation. The easiest
way to conceptualise the process is to see the additional imports
into the host country comprising only capital goods which
represent additions to the capital stock. In practice, there will

[1] For a schematic model designed to show the inter-relationships among
imports, manufacture by indigenous firms and manufacture by foreign
subsidiaries see Appendix IIA.

be some additional imports of capital goods and some substitution of domestic production away from consumer goods
and into the production of capital goods – the consumables
being replaced by imports.

There are three possibilities: (1) that the requisite international saving will not be generated and that capital accumulation in the host nation will be less than the inflow of direct
investment; (2) that the international saving will not, under
conditions of full employment, follow automatically from the
increase in domestic saving without some assistance from a
change in the terms of trade (the exchange rate) between the
host and investing nations; and (3) that the international saving
will only be achieved by the creation or tolerance of some unemployment in the investing nation. The first possibility has
proven important in practice as can be seen from Table I–2.
The second and third possibilities represent the two different
analytic approaches to the transfer problem. In a world in
which high levels of employment are primary national economic
goals, the second possibility is the more interesting. The conditions necessary for the creation of the international saving
without a deterioration of the terms of trade of the investing
country are that the changes in spending in the two countries
directly change import demands by an amount equal to the
direct investment. Technically, the condition is that the sum of
the marginal propensities to import of the two nations equal
unity. An investing nation reduces its potential expenditure
(income) as a result of the transfer. This reduces the demand
for imports, at the going terms of trade, by an amount equal to
the change in income multiplied by the marginal propensity to
import. The rest of the increase in saving (expenditure
reduction) creates spare productive capacity. If this productive
capacity is exactly used up by the additional demand for
imports by the host country, then exports will be increased and
the change in the trade balance will exactly equal the increase
in domestic saving. The transfer will have been affected without
any deterioration in the terms of trade. The third possibility
relies analytically upon a total multiplier reaction whereby
some sort of underemployment equilibrium is attained.
Facilitating the transfer of saving by the creation of unemployment is not an efficient alternative and is unlikely to be allowed

by national authorities to attain its full force. However, to the extent that unemployment does follow from an increase in domestic saving, it will reduce income and release capacity for any increase in foreign demand for exports as well as reduce the investing country's demand for imports.

If the changes in import volume that derive directly from the saving in the investing country and the additional expenditure in the host are not enough to provide the investing country with a current account surplus equal to the transfer, the investing country will have to depreciate its currency to generate the extra export surplus that is necessary.[1] This will inflict upon the investing country a cost in addition to the foregoing of the domestic investment since it will be forced to pay more for its imports in terms of inputs of its own factors of production. It is extremely unlikely that the change in the investing country's current account surplus that will occur 'automatically' will be sufficient to effect the transfer. There are two ways of looking at the problem – a multicountry world or a two-country world. In a multicountry world the host nation will purchase its extra imports from countries other than the investing country so that only a small proportion of the increase in B's imports will accrue to country A. Since the transfer must be effected in the period in which the foreign subsidiary is created, any indirect effects through third countries will be too late. In a two-country model, the host country must be included with all other countries in the 'rest of the world'. While the reduction in A's imports will still improve its current account, the only increases in its exports that it will experience is the (presumably) small proportion of B's increased demand which comes to A directly. It is quite possible that the import demand resulting from the opening of a foreign subsidiary will be of greater intensity and differently patterned than 'ordinary imports',[2] but some depreciation of the currency by the investing country can be assumed to be necessary.[3]

The net result is that the deterioration of the exchange rate provides a temporary boost in real income to the host country and inflicts an additional cost upon the investing country. How

[1] This is, strictly, an assumption since the reverse is remotely possible.
[2] This possibility is incorporated in Appendix VIA.
[3] See Chapter VI below.

much depreciation will be necessary to effect a given transfer is a very intricate problem. Most important among the determinants will be the sensitivity of import and export demand to changes in the rate of exchange and the sensitivity of output to changes in relative prices. The greater the price sensitivities, the smaller is the depreciation necessary to effect a given transfer.

The classification of products and the brief overview of the transfer problem were necessary for the interpretation of the relationship between the inequalities and certain economic relationships. These basic relationships underlie the rest of the book which approaches direct foreign investment from the cost-benefit viewpoints of the corporation, the host and the investing nation in turn. The remainder of this section will consider the criterion in the light of four variables: industry category and expected technological transfer; income differential and expected technological transfer; the burden of profit repatriation and the inter-relationship between foreign investment flows and the rate of exchange. The first two variables are inevitably inter-related since the industry breakdown of direct investments is likely to be influenced by the level of income of the host nation.

INDUSTRY CATEGORY, TECHNOLOGICAL TRANSFER AND THE INVESTMENT CRITERION

Investment in manufacturing capacity in a foreign nation will presuppose the existence of an adequate local market or the imminent establishment of such a market for the end product. Thus, investment in manufacturing capacity will take place predominantly in developed nations or, at the least, in semi-developed countries (defined as having a *per capita* income of between $600 and $900 per annum). It is possible that there will be in poor countries some manufacturing capacity established by multinational firms seeking low cost labour to produce intermediate goods for assembly in other nations. However, the association of manufacturing capacity with an existing or incipient domestic market for the product suggests that manufacturing direct investments will be correlated by volume with the level of income of the host nation.

Investment in non-competitive goods is more likely to take

place in poor nations. It is the developed manufacturing nations that will have a need for assured sources of raw materials and that may well have exhausted their own deposits of minerals in the early days of their own industrial revolutions. Poor nations with negligible manufacturing output will not have had occasion to use up any mineral deposits that they might own. Investments in agricultural output[1] are also likely to be located in poor nations since the market for imported agricultural goods in temperate climates consists largely of tropical products. Equally, that portion of tourism imports that can be considered non-competitive will also be centred in tropical and sub-tropical latitudes as affluent Europeans and Americans seek proximate escapes from winter weather. The poorer the nation in other assets the greater its probable reliance upon tourism investments.

The degree to which the establishment of a subsidiary will transfer technology to the host economy will depend upon the degree to which the level of technology embodied in the sub-sidiary relates to the general level of technology in the host country,[2] and upon the degree to which the subsidiary is integrated into the host economy. Investments in developing nations designed to produce non-competitive goods for markets in the developed world have shown very little tendency for the operations to spread their technology into the rest of the economy.[3] The historical pattern has been for the investment to be manned by citizens of the investing country in all jobs that required technical skills. No serious attempt used to be made to train indigenous workers in the technical tasks or in any managerial roles. This pattern is tending to change in the second half of the twentieth century when host governments are requiring that indigenous workers receive technical training and be promoted to supervisory positions. On the other hand, manufacturing concerns will both 'train up' indigenous workers and raise the general level of technical knowhow by involving local supplier firms as subcontractors.

[1] See Appendix IVA.
[2] Considered in the next subsection.
[3] The classic reference to this phenomenon is Hans Singer, 'The Dis-tribution of Gains between Investing and Borrowing Countries', *American Economic Review* (May 1950) pp. 473–85.

Except where some special effort is made either by the foreign subsidiary or standards are laid down by the host government and enforced, there will be a natural tendency for investments in non-competitive industries to have small or negligible technological effect. Manufacturing investments will be more effective in raising the general level of technological expertise in the host country. To the extent that the need for technology is greater in poor nations, the natural pattern of investment is perverse.[1]

INCOME DIFFERENTIAL, TECHNOLOGICAL TRANSFER
AND THE INVESTMENT CRITERION

The *prima facie* case in favour of a transfer of capital from a rich to a poor nation depends upon the assumed consequent increase in global output. The simplest version of this argument was presented in terms of Figure II–2. The motive force that induces the transfer of capital is the profit motive of a higher rate of return to capital that will be available in the poorer nation – in this sense 'profit' would be the main planning indicator in a socialist or communist economy. It should not be interpreted from the concept of greatest gain coming from moving capital to the poorest country that the process is not constrained. Poor countries are not able to absorb much capital at any given time and, because of potential political instability, the rate of return available in such countries would have to be heavily discounted for risk. Finally, where the capital is specific to an industry, there might not be adequate demand for the product of that industry in poor countries. The argument in favour of the transfer of capital to poor countries then applies to capital which poor countries can attract on a competitive basis. Subject to that condition, the poorer the country, the greater will be the boost to income from a given inflow of capital. Equally, the greater the difference in income between host and investing country, the greater can the difference in the general levels of technological knowhow be expected to be. Thus it is conceivable that the poorer the host, the greater is the marginal efficiency of investment and the greater the spread effect to be

[1] Note that this perversity may explain the failure of the colonisation process to provide a significant positive effect to the colonies – the reasons for colonising and the philosophy were enclave-oriented.

derived from technological transfer.[1] Unfortunately, this hypothesis is neither easily substantiated nor necessarily true. The reasons for the difficulty in substantiating the hypothesis are the intangible quality of the way in which technological knowhow introduced by a specific investment is spread throughout an economy, and the fact that technological knowhow can comprise two quite separate strains that will be transmitted in different ways and at different speeds. The introduction of new machinery and processes of greater sophistication than are in use in the host country will require that workers be 'trained up' to new levels of expertise. It is arguable that it is the training that contributes to the development of the host since the human capital is a 'free good' provided to the work force by the subsidiary acting in its own self-interest. Where pure knowledge that has product independently of imported and foreign-owned real capital, is instilled, that is even more valuable. This pure knowledge might be more likely to be transmitted in the agricultural sector where such knowledge can be taken and applied independently of foreign-subsidiary operations.[2] The second effect is also a disembodied type of knowledge that can have a very large effect in the long run. This is managerial knowhow in which managerial practices of communications, scheduling, personnel management and administrative procedures are introduced. However, this type of knowledge is less easily assimilated into the society as a whole and less easily applied in small, non-foreign enclaves. These two different types of technological knowhow can spread through the economy in different amounts from different projects at different speeds.

The spread-effect is really limited to any impact of the new technology outside of the firm that introduced it since, empirically at least, it would be impossible within the firm to segregate the role of capital and technology. Thus, the spread effect is very dependent upon the type of technology used in the subsidiary and the degree to which this knowledge can be transferred. Too large a gap between the technology in the foreign

[1] A spread effect can be defined as the repercussions that follow from the introduction of a technology new to the host country over and above its effect in the firm or the industry.

[2] See Appendix IV-A for a plan to effect such a knowledge transfer in Iran.

firm and the technology in the host country may forestall any transfer at all – as for example, an oil refinery in the Trucial States might do. Equally, a highly technological production process that has been skilfully reduced to a series of simple manual operations performed on intricate machines will transmit nothing to the host unless some indigenous workers are trained as maintenance men. There is a similarity between the more technologically advanced manufacturing industry and the extractive or non-competitive enclave subsidiary. Each reserves all of the skilled tasks to foreign nationals and neither transmits any generally useful knowhow.

For poor countries the element, $(\Delta O/\Delta K)$, is likely to be the most important one in the inequality – especially if some allowance is made for any spread effect. For primary-producing nations such as Canada and Australia, the constraint on natural resource exploitation and manufacturing capacity will be exercised by real capital rather than human capital (or jointly by the two types of capital). Such countries can expect to gain less technological transfer per unit of foreign investment. For rich countries, the output-capital ratio is also likely to be smaller and therefore less important. Finally, it is by no means impossible for nations to invest in host countries that are richer than the investing country. Any gains that derive from such investments must spring from gains achieved through the exploitation of proprietary knowledge or some imperfections in the product or capital markets.

The natural perversity noted in the previous subsection whereby the type of investments that could provide the greatest impetus went to those nations which stood in less need of impetus, is repeated in this subsection. Poor nations were likely to be able to attract only enclave industries which had little spread effect potential. The ability to benefit from technological innovation in a foreign subsidiary derives largely from the ability of labour to absorb the training and to leave that employment for employment in other firms in other parts of the country. This mobility of labour is likely to be found to a much greater degree in developed than in agricultural or poor societies. Even if the poor nation can obtain an industry which would generate spread effects, the mechanism for exploiting those effects is less well developed – if only because a job in a

foreign factory will be such a good one that there will be a
tendency to stick to it as long as possible.

THE BURDEN OF PROFIT REPATRIATION

There might be some predisposition to expect that the poorer
the host, the higher will be the rate of profit per unit of foreign
capital invested and, therefore, the greater the burden – the
natural perversity recurring for a third time in the profit
rate.

There is no *a priori* way of estimating the rate of profits
earned in host countries in varying stages of development.
Enclave industries need not earn the high profit rate that might
be expected of investments in very poor countries simply because
the enclave industries are tied into developed markets and not
into the host market. If enclave and extractive industries do
earn high rates that may be because of the acquisition of a rent
through holding the mineral resources over time as much as
through a commercial profit in the ordinary sense of the word.
Specific assets can increase in value over time through means
other than the inflation of money prices as increases in world
demand for the product are not matched by increased discoveries of reserves. Thus nominally high rates of return from
countries in which the bulk of investments are extractive do not
necessarily indicate exorbitant profit rates even though they
may be interpreted as such. Further even if a foreign investment
in a poor nation did earn a high profit rate for the parent, it
may have been necessary for the host country to have paid that
rate in order to bid the investment away from another
developing nation.

Profit rates reported on foreign investments in developed
nations will probably not be significantly higher than are
reported domestically. More important than the prospect of a
higher general rate of return to capital in a less-affluent but
still developed nation is the possibility of quasi-rents from
imperfectly-competitive industries. Further, there is an accounting problem in that some of the gain from the establishment of
a foreign subsidiary may be reported as royalties, fees or even
hidden in sales to and purchases from the parent corporation.

The repatriation of profits is a transfer payment in exactly the same way that the originating inflow of capital was a transfer. The mechanics of the transfer problem are necessary ingredients to any discussion of the burden of profit repatriation. Given the uncertainty that prevails over the expected relationship between profit rates and the level of income in the host country, it is quite likely that any inequality in the burden of profit repatriation will depend more on the transfer mechanism than on profit rates themselves. It was decided that under any but extraordinary conditions, the payment of a transfer would result in an adverse movement of the terms of trade and thereby reduce the level of real income by something more than the volume of funds transferred. Thus, the sensitivity of the exchange rate to the transfer flow may be the crucial factor in determining the burden.

There are two reasons to expect that the exchange rate of poor countries will be more sensitive to an increase in transfer outpayments than the exchange rate of rich countries. Therefore, the burden on poor countries per unit of transfer flow can be expected to be greater.

The first reason centres about the sensitivity of the demand for the exports and imports of poor and rich countries respectively and can be illustrated by reference to Figure II–3. Each part of the Figure shows how a depreciation – an upward movement along the vertical axis – will alter the receipts of foreign currency. Figure A shows how depreciation will affect receipts from exports and Figure B the gain in foreign exchange (the reduction of expenditures) from imports. In Figure A, the poor country's foreign exchange earnings from exports are very insensitive to the rate of exchange and a large depreciation would be necessary to effect a small increase in receipts of foreign exchange. Rich countries can, however, expect foreign exchange earnings of their import sectors to increase from relatively small depreciations. There are two reasons for suspecting that the poor country's schedule will be steeply sloped. If the export sector is dominated by enclave industries, prices are likely to be set in foreign exchange and therefore the prices will not change for the foreign customer and receipts will be constant.[1] The demand for other exports may have some slight

[1] See Singer, ibid. – the argument becomes possibly stronger if it is assumed that revenues are fixed in foreign exchange and costs of indigenous

elasticity to price and the drop in the exchange rate will induce an increase in foreign exchange earnings. The relationship could also be perverse and the schedule have a negative slope.[1] The second reason is the anticipated price-inelasticity of foreign

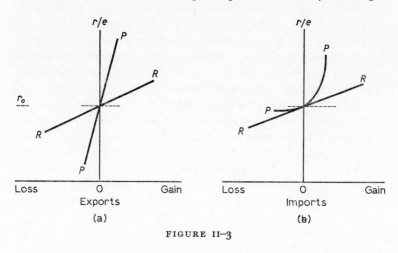

FIGURE II–3

The Sensitivity of International Markets to Changes in the
Rate of Exchange

Notes: PP denotes schedules for poor countries and RR for rich countries.
An upward movement shows a depreciation of the currency of the focus country.
To effect a transfer of a given size, the nation would be required to register a total gain in the two markets equal to that amount and would depreciate accordingly.

demand for the primary exports of a poor country. The demand for the exports of rich countries, contrarily, will be reasonably sensitive to changes in the price – particularly differentiated goods which are close substitutes for domestically-produced items. Figure B shows the same sensitive relation applies to imports of rich countries as to their exports – the substitution of domestic for foreign goods will be quite sensitive to the exchange

---

labour in domestic currency, then depreciation will increase the profits of the enclave industry and foreign currency earnings by the host will actually decline.
[1] The possibility referred to in the previous footnote will enhance the chances of a negative slope for the poor country's schedule.

rate. In poor countries, a depreciation is unlikely to permit much substitution of domestic production for imports because imports are primarily non-competitive, technologically-advanced goods. An appreciation of the currency will generate a fairly large increase in expenditures (loss of foreign exchange) as additional aggregate demand spills over into the foreign sector.

The net result of these two forces is that an increase in transfer payments will require a large depreciation of a poor country's currency to generate the international saving that is necessary and consequently a larger burden for the poor country.

The second reason for expecting that the transfer payments will require a large change in the poor country's rate of exchange is that the ratio of repatriated profits to exports will be larger in poor countries. This relationship does not follow automatically but, when applicable, would increase the burden on poor countries because the terms of trade shift would be that much greater. In a poor country, a five per cent increase in transfer outpayments will be much larger relative to the volume of foreign trade in goods and services that has to adjust to generate the saving.

INVESTMENT INFLOWS AND THE RATE OF EXCHANGE

Foreign investments may be decided upon in single discrete steps but, like domestic investments in the simple income-employment model, they aggregate into a flow of investments over time. Thus, an investment-receiving nation can expect a continuous inflow of investment from abroad for a number of consecutive years and the exchange rate which the host country experiences will depend upon the net balance between the inflow of investment funds and the outflow of dividends. Poor countries may reach a stage of development at which they become attractive locations for manufacturing investments (this stage might be identified with the stage of semi-development). When this threshold level of income is reached the host country can anticipate a net inflow of foreign capital (though not necessarily a steady inflow) for a period of years. Against this inflow must be debited an ever-increasing outflow of repatriated profits. As long as the flow is positive (investment exceeds dividends), the terms of trade will enhance disposable income. The terms of trade effect upon income becomes negative only when dividends increase to exceed any capital inflow.

It is possible to categorise nations according to their asset-liability position with other countries and according to the relationship between their balance on commodities and services and on transfer account. Thus, a young and growing debtor nation has imports greater than exports and negative international saving; a mature debtor has balanced current account (zero international saving) as its surplus on goods and services offsets exactly the deficit on transfers. A 'new creditor' nation has positive international saving and investment so that its income is reduced by the adverse exchange rate necessary to generate that international saving. Finally, a 'mature creditor' has zero international saving or dissaving but enjoys a boost to income through a more favourable exchange rate than it would enjoy in the absence of its positive international net worth as its surplus on transfers equals its deficit on goods and services.[1]

The adverse shift in the terms of trade occurs gradually as the position within each category changes but the crucial shift is from the status of young and growing debtor to mature debtor when the transfer account changes from provision of an impetus to development to a brake on development.

There is a perversity about the process by which foreign investment transmits progress to the host nations. The very poor nations gain comparatively little because of their inability to attract technology-spreading types of enterprise and because of the unsuitability of their social and economic structures for the absorption of any technology that is introduced. However, if the stage of development can be pushed to some threshold level of income at which the availability of technology in the nation, the ability to absorb it and the rate-of-exchange effect all reinforce each other, the impact of foreign investments on host country growth should be highly beneficial. This assumes that the levels of consumption are not inflated by the inflow of capital and the rate of exchange effects. When the country passes into the category of mature debtor, the net benefit to the rate of growth will decline.

[1] See Paul A. Samuelson, *Economics*, 8th ed. (New York: McGraw-Hill, 1970) pp. 636–7.

CONCLUSION

This chapter has examined sequentially and in some detail, the main mechanisms through which foreign investment flows will exert an impact upon the host and investing countries. These mechanisms can be examined in detail from the point of view of the individual interested parties. However, the basic dimensions of the problem have already been encountered.

APPENDIX II–A*

TO EXPORT GOODS
OR TO INVEST ABROAD:
AN EXPOSITORY MODEL

In traditional theory, the ability to export a commodity derives from the comparative advantage in the production of that commodity that a nation or a region enjoys. In modern analysis, the key determinants are the relative intensity of supply of the different factors of production in the country and the relative intensity of their use in the commodity. Refinements of the analysis introduce other influences such as transportation costs, tariffs and other elements of commercial policy and technological advantage.

A foreign market can be served by exporting commodities or by establishing a foreign subsidiary. The determinants that provide a firm with the ability to export can also provide the same firm with the capability to establish a successful foreign subsidiary. It is the net entrepreneurial advantage to the firm that will decide which of the two alternatives is pursued.

The many determinants that provide the sources of producer advantage can be grouped together in order to simplify the analysis. Distinguish three kinds of advantage: all forms of technological knowhow T; all conventional comparative advantage factors C; and all 'institutional' and 'natural' deter-

* This appendix is written by Professor Edwin R. Carlisle of Lowell Technological Institute.

minants unique to one region or nation N.[1] From the point of view of the domestic exporter N will work counter to C. The net comparative-national advantage $C - N$ accommodates tariffs and transport costs directly into the analysis.

From the point of view of a domestic firm considering serving a foreign market, the interactions of the three sets of determinants are shown in Figure A. Three different productive units are shown: P_D is the producer in the domestic country who will serve the market by exporting; P_S is the foreign subsidiary and P_F the indigenous foreign firm.

The salient feature of any international activity is to be found in the different characteristics or endowments of the two regions or nations. Comparative advantage C depends upon the difference in quantities and qualities of internationally immobile domestic factors of production (labour and natural resources): the other two sources of advantage are more susceptible to change in the short run – N because of its tariff component and T because technology is transferable internationally. It is only the *net* advantage between regions and firms that is important to the problem of exporting capital or goods.

Consider in further detail how the three net advantages operate. Each will give rise to a cost advantage that can be conceived of as so many cents per unit of output. Clearly C and N operate inter-regionally, that is between the producer in the domestic market, P_D, and P_S and P_F both of whom are located in the foreign market. Exportation of goods requires that P_D have an advantage over P_F – the advantage will derive from a comparative advantage (a positive C) exceeding any national advantage accorded to P_F (by commercial policy, and/or technology). The role of $C - N$ reverses in the choice of supplying the foreign market from the subsidiary, P_S. The comparative advantage enjoyed by producers in the domestic region is now a negative factor in the decision to invest abroad, but the national advantage would be circumvented by direct investment and becomes a positive factor with respect to the foreign investment decision.

The salient feature of technological knowledge is that it is proprietary to the firm. The net advantage held by a firm relates to the firm and its subsidiaries in competition with all

[1] This would allow for non-competitive goods to be produced.

other firms. Therefore, technological advantages *add* to the inducement for exportation by P_D as well as to the establishment of a subsidiary, P_S. The competing total advantages are depicted in Figure A.[1]

The condition necessary for exportation is: $T + (C - \mathcal{N}) > 0$.
The condition necessary for direct investment is:
$$T - (C - \mathcal{N}) > 0.$$
The combination of solutions of the two inequalities will yield six possible outcomes. These are shown in Figure B. The six cases are numbered *a* through *f*. Cases *c* and *d* are cases of special interest for which both exportation and direct investment are possible.

In Figure B, comparative-national advantage is measured vertically in cents per unit of output from the point of view of the firm located in the domestic region in comparison with the production units located in the foreign region. Similarly, the domestic firm's technological advantage over the firm (with the best technology) producing in the foreign market is measured horizontally in cents per unit. Since the lines dividing the areas are drawn at 45° angles, the scales on the two axes are equal.

Area *a* represents cases for which a domestic producer will supply the foreign market through exporting. The comparative-national advantage exceeds the technological advantage that foreign firms enjoy. An increase in $\mathcal{N}$ could preclude exports to the foreign market but could never induce the establishment of a foreign subsidiary.

Area *b* represents combinations of advantages in which the domestic producer enjoys advantages in both dimensions and would export to the foreign market from the domestic region. However an increase in $\mathcal{N}$ could cause the domestic producer either to license production abroad or to establish a foreign subsidiary. (An increase in $\mathcal{N}$ would result in the horizontal T axis and the two diagonals shifting upward so that points in *b* could be shifted into area *c*.)[2]

---

[1] The greater cost of doing business abroad is not included in the model but can be added fairly easily.

[2] Note that the value of C depends upon all other items in international trade and, in a very exact model, upon the decision in the industry in question to export or to manufacture abroad.

Areas *c* and *d* represent combinations of advantages which offer the domestic firm a choice between supplying the foreign market with exports or by establishing a foreign subsidiary. Both methods would be profitable. The domestic firm will prefer to supply the foreign market with exports as long as the comparative-national advantage is positive (area *c*). In *d* there

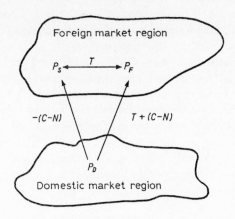

FIGURE A

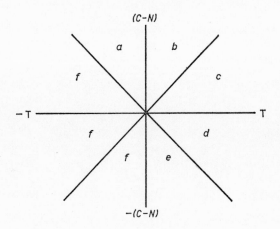

FIGURE B

is a preference for establishing a foreign subsidiary or, if satisfactory royalty rates can be negotiated, for licensing. Area d also indicates a preference for foreign manufacture for the reason that the export capability of the domestic plant is vulnerable to a loss of T.

Area e shows magnitudes of advantages for which foreign direct investment is the only means by which the domestic firm can hope to supply the foreign market. The technological advantage enjoyed by the firm will enable it to compete abroad and without the handicap of the comparative-national disadvantage suffered by the domestic region.

Because the magnitudes of $(C - N)$ cannot be assumed to be exactly equal for the reverse case – that is, the national advantages of the domestic region may differ from those of the foreign region because of different tariff rates etc. – it is not possible to include in the model the possibility of imports into the domestic region. Clearly, areas e and f all represent combinations of C, N and T that would permit importation into or the establishment of a foreign subsidiary in the domestic region.

CHAPTER III

BENEFITS AND COSTS FOR THE INVESTING CORPORATION

The act of investing assets in a foreign country exposes the parent corporation (or increases its exposure) to a wider range of business risks and competitive disadvantages. Every investment decision must take these disadvantages into account and every act of investment testifies to a belief that the expected benefits exceed the inherent disadvantages. These handicaps include: a degree of familiarity with local customs and law that is less than that of indigenous firms; the prospect of discrimination by the host government in favour of the subsidiaries' competitors; interference by the government of the investing country in profit repatriation; possible difficulties in obeying two conflicting sets of antitrust laws and the operational disadvantage of having a subsidiary and its market far removed from parental control. Even though these handicaps may vary significantly from one project to another, most of the categories of risk are self-evident. The advantages are less self-evident. It is the potential benefits that will be the deciding factors in determining the decision of whether to invest abroad or not. At the same time, a study of the potential benefits will indicate what sort of corporations in which industries will be likely to invest abroad and in what types of countries.

The publicity which the so-called multinational corporation has recently experienced and the fact that a corporation must have some subsidiary activity abroad in order to qualify for the label 'multinational', could give rise to an automatic tendency to think of the existence of foreign subsidiaries as the exclusive concern of the multinational corporation. The overlap between direct foreign investment and multinational business is large but not complete and direct foreign investment can take place without the involvement of a multinational corporation.

There is no generally accepted definition of the multinational corporation but, without question, inclusion in that category requires both some minimum size and some minimum *proportionate* involvement in foreign countries. Operations in more than two countries would seem to be a necessary attribute. Perhaps the most important qualifying characteristic is intangible: the thinking process of the top executives in a multinational corporation automatically tends toward the interlocking of all the corporation's component parts and this, in turn, enables the corporation to take advantage of any dissimilarities in costs in different countries, of any differences in tax regulations and to plan output on a global scale. One working definition of the multinational corporation is that the corporation have foreign content of 25 per cent or more – foreign content being defined as the proportion of overall sales, investment, production or employment located in foreign subsidiaries.[1] This definition very clearly requires that the multinational corporation be a large concern since only large concerns have the expertise necessary to develop foreign content of that proportion. There is no operational requirement about the degree to which the foreign subsidiary should be controlled by the parent corporation but the level of integration should be high since it is the integration that represents the main source of competitive advantage to the multinational concern.[2] There are subsidiaries which enjoy a great deal of independence from their parent but such subsidiaries do not qualify for inclusion in a multinational business *or* in an international business in any meaningful sense since, unless some control is exercised by the parent, the investment is equivalent to a portfolio investment yielding a return in the form of repatriated dividends.[3]

In addition to direct investments made abroad by fully-fledged multinational corporations, some investments are undoubtedly made by large corporations that do not meet the foreign-content criterion and some by relatively small corpora-

[1] Rolfe and Damm, *The Multinational Corporation*, p. 17.

[2] A useful study of the degree of control exercised by U.S. corporations over their French subsidiaries is: Allan W. Johnstone, *United States Direct Investment in France* (Cambridge, Mass.: M.I.T. Press, 1965). See also Chapter VIII below.

[3] Kindleberger, *American Business Abroad*, p. 4, reports the existence of such a subsidiary.

tions. Both types of business subsidiary that are not 'multi-national' are likely to follow from a corporation taking advantage of an asset that is privately held and internationally mobile or of some similar circumstance that enables the corporation to invest abroad with the expectation of increased profits but without any plan of multinational operational integration. However, foreign investment must necessarily be dominated by corporations that are generally considered as 'Big Business'. This preponderance of large companies provides a possible cause for nationalist feelings in host countries expressing opposition to foreign investment and a means by which this opposition can be encouraged. It is difficult to argue cause and effect or even the chicken and the egg in this matter, but there exists among some segments of any population a natural and understandable antipathy to big business – particularly in poor countries. In nations in which businesses that qualify as big are predominantly foreign-owned and foreign-run, antipathy toward foreign investment can grow naturally from opposition to big business. Alternatively, those forces seeking popular support in opposition to foreign investment, can expect to gain some success by merely encouraging any natural antipathy toward big business.

To avoid any possible confusion on this score, the terms 'corporation' and 'international corporation' are defined to mean a corporate enterprise with at least one subsidiary branch or company located abroad. The term 'multinational corporation' will only be used when some inclusive connotation of large size, high foreign content and multinational integration of operations is needed.

Economic analysis attributes to business the unidimensional motivation of profit maximisation. This goal or objective function is derived logically from the simple, perfectly-competitive model since profit maximisation and the internal efficiency which it requires, are vital to the survival of the firm. In the real and imperfectly-competitive world, businessmen tend to talk in terms of preservation of or maximisation of market shares, of maximising sales revenues, earnings-to-sales ratios or even growth rates rather than of maximising profits. There is a fair amount of evidence to suggest that profit maximisation is fully compatible with most of the other goals enunciated by businessmen so that analysis of corporate behaviour under the assumption that its objective is to maximise profits is realistic even though the managing director insists he is trying to maximise growth or some other dimension. For analysis of direct foreign investment, the simple objective function may not be sufficient and could mislead.

In Chapter I, three categories of motivation were given to explain direct foreign investment: subjective; aggressive and defensive. The subjective motivation is not necessarily compatible with profit maximisation. Instead a theory of profit-seeking must be used. This merely indicates the expectation of a rate of profit which is considered to be satisfactory, being achieved over a given time horizon of unspecified length.

The subjective motivation for investing abroad can be defined as putting the interests of the decision-maker as an individual into the decision-making computation. Alternatively subjective elements can become included in the decision-making process when the executive is the subject of a band-wagon effect whereby an act's desirability is increased by the fact that others are doing the same thing. Certainly, from the mid-fifties to the mid-sixties, there was in the United States an element of fashionableness in investing abroad and possession of foreign subsidiaries did enhance the aura of a corporation and of its top-level executives. Similarly, foreign investments have been made because they offered tax benefits for executives in the guise of travel expenses which had a pleasure content but which could be justified to the Internal Revenue Service as business expenses, and even because they offered a second base of operations in a more enjoyable locale. Of all of the subjective motivations for foreign investment, there is one behavioural hypothesis that both exceeds the others in importance and merits serious and detailed consideration.

If a corporation is controlled in practice by professional managers rather than by the owners of the equity, the goals of the corporation can be something other than the maximising of profits. Professor William J. Baumol has hypothesised that, for such firms in which operation and ownership are divorced, the maximisation of sales revenues subject to the achievement of an adequate profit rate, is a rational goal.[1] The subjective rationale underlying this behavioural hypothesis postulates that managers' salaries and fringe benefits are more closely determined by the size of the firm, measured by sales revenue, than by profits – provided always that stockholders are satisfied with the absolute profits earned. Maximisation of sales revenues subject to a profit constraint is an objective function which is only compatible with a differentiated product or service so that sales promotional activities can be used with effect. In a domestic firm, this policy would result in product design and sales promotion efforts which will increase sales volume at some cost to overall absolute profit. When this policy is translated into capacity terms, it may imply a greater rate or level of investment than is optimal for a policy of maximising the rate of profit achieved per unit of capital invested. In an international setting, overexpansion of capacity is still possible and the extra-marginal investments may well be located abroad as well as at home. Thus foreign direct investments might be made when the expected rate or return on the invested capital was less than the average rate of return and, possibly, less than the rate of return deemed necessary 'to keep the stockholder happy'. It is arguable, in extension of Baumol's hypothesis, that executive compensation is positively related to the number of countries in which the corporation operates a subsidiary in addition to any positive relation with sales volume. If this extension were a valid hypothesis, then there would be a bias toward investing the extra-marginal capacity by the creation of new foreign subsidiaries rather than expanding domestic capacity subject always to the constraint of an overall satisfactory level of profits. Both the original and the variant sales-revenue maximisation hypotheses are operational provided that the growth in assets that the policy entails, can be financed without undue dilution of the stockholders' existing equity through new issues and subject to the minimum profit constraint. Thus, provided that there existed a significant number of profitable ventures abroad as well as at home, the limitation of the rate of overseas investment would be a supply limitation. The determinant of foreign investment would be the availability

---

[1] *Business Behavior, Value and Growth*, rev. ed. (New York: Harcourt Brace & World, Inc., 1967) Chs. VI and VII.

of funds which would in turn depend upon the overall profit-ability of the corporation.[1] The sales-revenue maximisation hypothesis is compatible with a profit-seeking but not with a profit-maximising model of economic behaviour.

Another complication that weakens any direct reliance upon profit-maximisation as a basis for analysis of foreign investment decisions is the variability of the time horizon by which profit-ability would need to be judged for different types of foreign investment. Foreign investment can be accomplished in three basic ways: by the acquisition of an ongoing foreign enterprise, by the expansion of an existing subsidiary and by the creation of a new subsidiary. Any of these means of increasing foreign asset holdings can involve either complete ownership or control of a joint venture together with a foreign corporation. The speed with which profits will be achieved will depend upon the type of investment undertaken and, probably, the industry in which the investment is made. What may be a satisfactory performance for one corporation may not be so considered for another corporation: the discrepancy arising from different time-horizons and from different norms and opportunity costs in different industries. Professor Richard E. Caves has developed an hypothesis by which oligopolistic corporations selling differentiated products, will tend to indulge in mutual invasion of domestic markets and thereby will equalise the industry profit rate among nations – as opposed to the general concept of profit rates being equal within a country but disparate among different nations.[2]

The analysis of direct foreign investment can be based upon profit-seeking but the presence of subjective factors and the industrial organisation characteristics of business abroad preclude the analysis from being made on a basis of profit-maximisation on either an aggregate or a firm basis. Both of the other categories of motivation for direct investment are based on the need for and desirability of profits and differ only in emphasis or approach. Aggressive investments seek to

[1] Kindleberger, *American Business Abroad*, pp. 61–2, suggests that the supply model is less convincing for U.S. foreign investment in the 1970s than it was in the late fifties and early sixties.

[2] 'International Corporations: The Industrial Economics of Foreign Investment', *Economica* (Feb 1971) pp. 1–27.

increase absolute profits – with as small a diminution of the average profit rate as possible. Defensive investments are those which are made in attempts to preserve or to restore some level or rate of profit attained earlier. Any foreign investments made as a consequence of subjective motivations will also be aggressive in that the means by which such investments will be expected to return the necessary profits will be the same as those by which aggressive investors will expect to overcome the inherent disadvantages in operations located abroad. There are five basic motivations that can be considered as 'aggressive' and three as 'defensive'. They will be considered sequentially.

Aggressive Motivations

1. To realise economies that are internal to the firm.
2. To exploit a knowledge advantage.
3. To establish presence in a foreign oligopoly and to share oligopoly rents.
4. To obtain a higher rate of return to capital than is available domestically.
5. To establish a subsidiary in the expectation of earning an economic rent in the future.

Defensive Motivations

6. To establish local production in a foreign market to preserve a market share obtained by exports.
7. To acquire a sure source of raw materials to serve the domestic production complex.
8. To acquire raw material deposits to preserve a barrier to entry into a global oligopoly.

1. *Economies of internal organisation* necessarily are available only to corporations which have operations covering more than one production process under their control. These economies derive from the substitution of internal organisation for 'the cost of using the price mechanism'.[1] The costs of using the price mechanism are the costs of search, the costs of negotiation and contract, lack of precise control over the timing of shipments

---

[1] This concept of corporate economies derives from R. H. Coase, 'The Nature of the Firm', *Economica* n.s. IV (1937), 386–405, reprinted in *Readings in Price Theory*, ed. G. J. Stigler and K. E. Boulding (Homewood, Ill.: Richard D. Irwin, Inc., 1952) pp. 331–51.

and similar phenomena. These areas offer potential gains from the co-ordination of activities within a single organisation to reduce the costs of inputs, to reduce the uncertainties of scheduling and related costs and, from a sense of control over the various stages of production, to enable a corporation to plan an undertaking on a large scale that requires for its success, a compatibility of equipment and method throughout. Kindleberger cites the inefficiency that followed from the inability of the British coal and railway industries to take advantage of the economies of scale of larger coal cars because the new coal cars would have required simultaneous and co-ordinated investment in new equipment by both the mines and the railways.[1]

The secret of obtaining potential internal economies (Coase-economies) is co-ordination of different stages of treatment and the co-ordination can most easily be achieved by common executive control. This process is generally referred to as vertical integration and can involve investments that point forward to the consumer as well as backward to the crude materials.

Vertical integration is, except for the inherent costs of doing business abroad, indifferent to national boundaries. The usual way for vertical integration to involve an international investment is through the acquisition of a source of basic raw materials. To the extent that the raw material is a non-competitive good, international investment is mandatory if the firm is to acquire direct control over a source of basic raw materials. Another common form of vertical integration that involves foreign investment is the creation of a sales subsidiary in a foreign market supplied with exports from the parent company. This type of subsidiary will be created only by firms marketing a differentiated good.

Backward integration to acquire raw material sources could be avoided by normal dealings in the raw material market and/or by long-term contracts with producing companies.[2] While the acquisition of raw material sources does offer the

---

[1] *American Business Abroad*, p. 21. See also pp. 19–22 for a general discussion of these economies.

[2] See Coase, *Economica*, n.s. IV, pp. 337–8 for a discussion of long-term contracts and the problems involved.

possibility of economic rent, it is the ongoing economies of vertical integration which are the more important considerations in the decision to invest abroad. Similarly, local sales agents could be used in preference to a foreign subsidiary in the distribution of the firm's products. The incentive to prefer a sales subsidiary may derive from a special kind of internal economy – a greater sense of realisation of the importance of the product and a greater awareness of the product's advantages over its competitors. In addition to the benefits which derive from vertical integration independent of its international dimensions, international vertical integration offers a degree of flexibility which can be used to good advantage. Usually, the main reason for the creation of a foreign subsidiary involving vertical integration is the existence of an activity which is not mobile internationally. The next activity and ensuing activities in the productive sequence can be 'footloose'. The international corporation obtains in this way the possibility of additional Coase-economies if the relative national cost structures allow additional operations to be performed with profit in the foreign country as well as the main activity for which the subsidiary was established.

This ability to co-ordinate activities internationally and to locate footloose activities in that country of operation in which costs are the least, is the primary contribution to global economic efficiency of the multinational corporation. The greater the number of nations in which the multinational corporation is located, the larger the number of potential opportunities to take advantage of variations in international costs and, what may not be the same thing, of comparative advantage.[1]

A nation's price competitiveness in any particular activity does not pre-require the existence of a local subsidiary but the benefits of internal co-ordination may be sufficiently great to warrant the establishment of a subsidiary simply for the purpose of combining a small foreign cost advantage with the potential Coase-economies. This kind of foreign manufacturing operation may result in the creation of a parts-manufacturing concern in a foreign nation. It may be that the parent corporation cannot

---

[1] Where the multinational corporation achieves its international economies through playing off variations in tax regulations, the contribution to global economic efficiency is likely to be small and possibly even negative.

locate an indigenous firm with the requisite knowhow in the country in which costs are lowest. A second reason for preferring a subsidiary to a contract purchase, is the ability of the parent to set quality control and inspection standards in the wholly owned subsidiary and to combine them with domestic quality control checks. Such an investment might be induced by an increase in the ability of a developing country to produce manufactured goods, by a change in the relative cost structure between the importing and the host country or by a change in cost structure within the firm – if, for example, a labour settlement is sufficiently costly to make overseas manufacture and importation attractive even though the overall competitiveness of the investing nation has not changed.

The last area which offers the possibility of internal economies is not an aspect of integration either vertical or horizontal and is not necessarily linked to any international aspects of the corporation. A large corporation engaged in several different areas generates a large cash flow in the course of each year. This cash flow consists of both depreciation allowances and retained profits. These funds are investible wherever the parent organisation feels they can be of greatest service to the corporation. In addition to generating a sizeable annual flow of investible funds, large corporations can also derive a financing advantage through an ability to wrest better terms from lenders. To the extent that sheer size enables subsidiary corporations to expand without recourse to the local credit markets or on different terms from small competing firms, there is no difference, in the abstract, between domestic and international advantages. However, if the subsidiary of a foreign firm is able to obtain financing on more favourable terms than an indigenous competitor, nationalist antipathy to foreign investment can be fanned.

Economies of internal organisation are achieved primarily, though not exclusively, through vertical integration. There is no necessary relation between the tendency to integrate vertically and the type of product of the corporation. However, firms producing homogeneous products are unlikely to integrate forward through the establishment of sales subsidiaries. The basic industries of oil, steel, aluminium, and other metals are the prime examples of industries in which backward integration has been developed to its utmost. Other examples are in agriculture in which merchants in temperate countries (usually colonial powers) developed close links with primary sources of production through the establishment of plantations and close supervision of production through the establishment of local subsidiaries in charge of purchasing, shipping and quality control.[1] Both types of industry used foreign investment as a means of obtaining control over internationally immobile factors of production.

2. *Exploitation of a knowledge advantage* is, strictly, another form of economy internal to the firm. However, exploitation of knowledge merits separate treatment because it necessarily involves the duplication of a particular activity in a different geographic location rather than the addition of a complementary activity. Exploitation of knowledge therefore involves horizontal integration rather than vertical integration. In an international frame of reference, horizontal integration can be defined as producing abroad (usually for sale abroad) commodities which are the same as, or generically similar to, those produced by the parent corporation at home. In other words, horizontal extension takes place when a foreign subsidiary is created and its output is, actually or potentially, a source of competition with domestic production of a similar commodity. Almost necessarily, this process involves some manufacturing activity.

The fundamental reason for the creation of a manufacturing subsidiary in a foreign market is that foreign manufacture will enable the parent corporation to derive a return from an asset that exceeds the return available through other means. This asset must be privately held and unique to the investing corporation, internationally mobile and applicable in foreign nations at a return that outweighs any marginal costs by a significant margin.[2] The most common asset of this type is some element of knowledge which is either unknown to competitors or protected from imitation and which offers to the manufacturing process either a reduction in costs or a sales

[1] See Appendix IV–A on the subject of agricultural investment.

[2] This discussion draws heavily on Caves, *Economica*, Feb 1971. It is subject, to some degree, to reservations about the possibility of direct investment in manufacturing being motivated by subjective factors.

advantage. Knowledge in the form of some design experience, specific marketing knowhow, or technological device can be transferred abroad without any of the original costs being incurred for a second time.[1] Essentially, the element of knowledge offers a competitive advantage to the holder which can be transformed into additional profit through the expansion of manufacture. If there is a net advantage to the establishment of the additional capacity in a foreign country, direct investment will result.[2]

The various aspects that affect the process of exploitation of a knowledge advantage through direct investment abroad can be examined in the following sequence: the mechanics; the contributory importance of product differentiation; the alternative of licensing production by a foreign firm; the influence of the size of the parent corporation; and the influence of tariff barriers.

The mechanics rely fundamentally upon the use of the firm's asset to reduce per-unit costs of foreign manufacture below those of an indigenous entrepreneur or to reduce the firm's per-unit selling costs below those of an indigenous manufacturer. The following example assumes, for simplicity of exposition, that the return to the asset per unit of sales is computed to be equal in both the base and the host countries. This assumption has to be explicit since there is no reason to believe that such an equality exists automatically. Assume that the landed costs of exports from the base country in the country of sale are exactly equal to the costs that would be incurred in the country of sale by a foreign corporation (from a third country) with no knowledge advantage. This average total cost schedule is shown as FS_O in Figure III–1. Each export sale from the base country will provide the corporation with a quasi-rent on its knowledge asset equal to that obtained in the domestic market. The cost curve of a domestic entrepreneur will be lower than that of a foreigner with no unique asset at his disposal and is shown by DE. The difference between the two schedules, a, is the advantage derived from familiarity with the business culture of the home market. The lowest curve, FS_K, shows the average

---

[1] Minor adaptive costs could be necessary but would be negligible in comparison to the gains.

[2] A broad frame of reference for this problem is given in Appendix II–A.

total cost schedule of the foreign subsidiary endowed with the unique, cost-reducing knowledge element but with no return to the asset computed in the cost. The difference between *DE* and FS_K is *b* and shows the competitive edge which the foreign

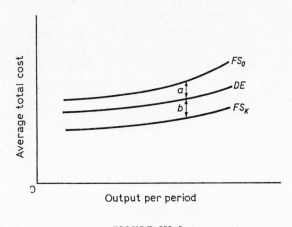

FIGURE III–I

Indigenous Advantage and the Return to Knowledge

subsidiary can achieve over the domestic entrepreneur.[1] The knowledge element reduces average costs by $a + b$ but the investing corporation can only benefit to the extent of *b* whether the local market is supplied through exports or through domestic manufacture. If the market is supplied by exports, the landed price must be shaved by *a* so that the marginal return to the knowledge element will be reduced by the advantage accruing to a local manufacturer by familiarity with the host country: if local manufacture is the means of supplying the host-country market, the return to knowledge is still only *b* per unit of sale. Under the conditions postulated, the manu-facturer would be indifferent between foreign investment and export sales. However, if there were to be another advantage to be derived from local manufacture such as a more assured source of supply to the local sales organisation, economies internal to the international manufacturing process or some

[1] Neither *a* nor *b* is drawn as independent of the rate of output.

other cause, then local manufacture becomes preferable.[1] If the disadvantage of lack of familiarity with local customs was expected to decrease with time, then local manufacture would become worth while if current factors indicated indifference or even a slight cost increase from local manufacture. If the landed cost of exports is higher than FS_O, then local manufacture is preferable. If the landed cost of exports exceeds FS_O by an amount b, then importing becomes feasible only if export prices are reduced by more than the computed return to the knowledge asset – presumably to less than average variable cost in the base country. On the other hand, local manufacture is feasible only if the cost advantage derived from the knowledge element $a + b$ exceeds the advantage derived by an indigenous entrepreneur – that is $(a + b) > a$ or $b > 0$.[2]

The magnitude of $a + b$ is determined by the knowledge element and the cost structures in the industry in the two countries. For a corporation, the crucial question is the size of a which is determined by factors outside the control of the individual firm. The major disadvantages of foreign investment have been referred to above and some additional considerations are developed at the end of this chapter. However, the advantage to the local entrepreneur can vary as a result of the behaviour of other international corporations. Another international corporation is likely to be equipped with its own set of knowledge elements which may have a total cost-effect which is greater or less than $a + b$. If the competitive corporation were to start local manufacture through a foreign subsidiary, then DE will effectively shift downwards by the excess of the competitor's knowledge advantage over his handicap from unfamiliarity with local customs. Under the original set of assumptions, the focus corporation would face an increased a and would have to shave its domestic price by a greater amount before being able to compete in the market by means of exports from the home country. If the landed price were greater than FS_O, the probability that local manufacture would have to be undertaken if the market were not to be relinquished to the competition, is enhanced. The return to the knowledge element from investing abroad would be reduced – possibly significantly – and unless the knowledge element yields a competitive (sales) advantage or cost reduction of the requisite size, local manufacture will not be undertaken.[1]

The differentiation of the product from those of its competitors is likely to be an important prerequisite for the existence of a knowledge element that can lead to foreign manufacturing facilities being established. There exist three avenues by which product differentiation can give rise to knowledge elements that will generate a competitive advantage for the potential subsidiary. A differentiated good is one that is distinguished from its competitors by design-appearance features and by performance-specification features so that individual tastes and needs influence potential buyers in addition to price.[2] The fact that design distinctions are an integral part of the production process will be likely to have created design features of proven desirability which have either been patented by the parent or which are only imitable at high cost. Long experience in the production of the commodity will have allowed the investing corporation to have acquired specialist knowhow in production management or to have evolved production processes which offer cost advantages in manufacture. Finally, the experience in the home market will have provided the corporation with a competitive advantage in marketing and sales strategy – though this latter element may not depend upon local manufacture.

Competitive advantages of this type accrue to a corporation from experience in its home country with the solution of problems in the design, manufacture and marketing of a differentiated product. The acquisition of this experience offers an indication about one influence on the pattern which foreign direct investments involving horizontal integration may be expected to follow over time. This influence suggests that the direct investment flows will obey, at least in part, the reasoning derived from simple models of international factor mobility whereby capital is expected to migrate from capital-rich to

[1] Two other factors are relevant here – the possibility of preserving the value of an extant sales organisation and the possibility of oligopoly profits being achieved in the market. They are discussed under items 6 and 3 below.

[2] See the discussion in Chapter II above.

capital-poor countries in search of the higher rate of return to capital that is available in the latter. However, any pattern that evolves from the sequence of market development is subject to the many other influences that bear upon foreign investment flows – such as the location and adaptation of technological inventions, rates of growth of domestic markets and the basic relative cost structures deriving from comparative advantage.[1] The crucial element in the process is that there exist certain commodities for which there are ranges of national, *per capita* income over which these industries will have very high rates of growth of consumption – the income elasticity of demand is very high. Goods with these requisite characteristics are likely to be differentiated commodities such as consumer durables. Historically, nations have reached these threshold levels of income sequentially. Assuming international tastes to be quite similar and that income distribution factors are negligible, the threshold levels of national income will be similar for different nations. The nation to reach that level of income first will have generated corporations to supply the domestic demand. In the process, these corporations will have acquired the knowledge elements and will have these elements available to them when other nations approach the threshold level of income. In this way, the corporations from the richest nation will be ready to invest abroad if they perceive an advantage in so doing. Given that growth rates can be expected to be high for a number of years, foreign investment may take place in anticipation of the growth period despite some temporary advantage in exporting from the home country. As other nations reach the appropriate threshold levels of income, additional foreign subsidiaries will be established. To the extent that high levels of *per capita* income and being relatively well-endowed with capital are positively related, the capital will flow from affluent to less affluent nations and in search of higher profit rates than are obtainable domestically in the way in which the simple theory would suggest. At the same time, the limitation on the body of theory imposed by the

[1] To this could be added any balance of payments strains that might inhibit capital exports – see Chapter VII below. The schema put forward here is *not* the same as Raymond Vernon's product cycle theory which is discussed below – see p. 99.

need for the host country to have achieved or to be approaching the threshold level of income, allows the market-sequence hypothesis to explain the failure of equity capital to move freely to very poor countries.

This general influence of the sequence of market development has further implications. Foreign investment flows will continue over time in three ways. Further investments will be made in existing subsidiaries as these subsidiaries grow with their local markets in 'second-generation' countries. These investments may be made out of retained profits but, if the growth rate is high, additional infusions of capital from the parent may be needed.[1] Additional investments may be made by the same parent corporations in the same industries in different, 'third-generation' countries as these countries attain threshold levels of income for these industries. Finally, additional direct investments can be made in the original, second-generation countries in different industries (and presumably by different parents) as the necessary higher levels of threshold income for new differentiated products are attained. Both the first and the third processes necessarily involve further investments by the original investing country. The second process whereby new nations attain the threshold levels of income necessary for the products in which the direct investment has already taken place in second-generation countries, may or may not involve a further outflow of investment from the original investing nation. It is possible that a second-generation nation can be a recipient of foreign investment in an industry and an investing nation in the same industry. This possibility requires that its domestic market for the product shall not have been pre-empted by foreign subsidiaries. If indigenous firms did grow to compete with the foreign subsidiaries then these firms become capable of investment abroad in other countries at some future point in time. If these firms are more aggressive and if the co-operating circumstances are favourable, it may well be these firms that invest in third-generation nations.

[1] This concept of the need for future infusions of capital from the parent is compatible with the organic theory of subsidiary growth originally put forward in Judd Polk *et al.*, *U.S. Production Abroad and the Balance of Payments*, (New York: National Industrial Conference Board, 1966) pp. 132–6.

This process suggests a policy option for the host nation.[1] Licensing may be preferable to allowing the entrance of foreign investments in that it better permits the domestic corporations to flourish and potentially allows the country to become a foreign investor on balance rather than a host. This option is circumscribed by the possibility that the licensing arrangements might prevent the use of licensed knowledge in other countries or even in exports. If licensing arrangements are constrained in this way, then it might be a better long-run strategy to forego foreign knowhow altogether and to develop the knowhow and proprietary knowledge within a protected market.

Licensing is a substitute for local manufacture for a firm possessing a unique knowledge element. Licensing will be more attractive to the corporation if exports are effectively blockaded or if exports require some shaving of landed prices so that the full return to proprietary knowledge is not gained from export sales. Clearly, licensing will also be the more attractive, the nearer the per-unit rate of royalty is to $a + b$ in Figure III–1. The reasons for choosing foreign investment in preference to a licensing agreement as a means of exploiting a knowledge element are the difficulties in the negotiation of the original royalty agreement and the difficulties of incorporating into a new agreement any new, second-generation pieces of knowledge that might be produced by the licensing corporation's research and development department. Thus, it is reasonable to expect that licensing will be a less popular technique when the proprietary knowledge is expected to be a continuous flow rather than a one-shot item. Where a one-shot knowledge element exists, licensing may be the preferred but is not the inevitable means of exploitation. It is quite possible that a one-shot piece of knowledge could be used to establish a subsidiary in a monopolistically competitive or tightly-knit oligopolistic foreign market. The per-unit cost saving derived from the piece of knowledge would offset the cost disadvantages that any subsidiary must experience and would allow the new subsidiary to enjoy the quasi-rents that follow from membership in the market structure in the foreign country. Since the cost saving would tend to attentuate over time as the original piece of knowledge is more widely known or incorporated into other firms' pro-

[1] This policy option is elaborated on below in Chapter IV.

duction processes, the firm would also be likely to experience some cost disadvantage in the long run – this might be offset by a partial reduction in the net quasi-rents or by the fact that the disadvantage of operating in a foreign country, a, may be expected to attenuate over time.

The establishment of a foreign subsidiary requires that the parent have some minimum access to capital and also imposes a high fixed cost on the investing corporation. Both of these factors will bias small firms that own proprietary pieces of knowledge to exploit them by means of licensing arrangements.

It is possible that a corporation's knowledge element may not be adequate to provide an overall cost advantage to a manufacturing subsidiary – particularly so if another international competitor has used its own knowledge elements to shift DE downward either through licensing a local entrepreneur or by establishing its own foreign subsidiary. In that case, b might be negative but the knowledge would still have potential value to another domestic firm and licensing would be the sole means of exploitation. On the other hand, certain types of knowledge are not transferable through licensing arrangements alone – such as technical processes which involve the use of the corporation's own executives – and the knowledge advantage can only be exploited through the establishment of a foreign subsidiary.

The size of the investing corporation is influenced partly by the sheer magnitude of the undertaking of the establishment of a foreign manufacturing enterprise. However, there are other factors that will tend to limit entry into the ranks of the international corporation to large firms. It is unlikely that a firm will establish a foreign manufacturing subsidiary to duplicate a domestic operation while economies of scale in production, sales or marketing strategy are still available to it in its home market. The potential gains from achieving economies of scale are likely to surpass the expected profits to be derived from foreign manufacture *plus* any return that can be obtained from licensing the use of the knowledge item. It is possible that the lack of availability of funds for diversion to a foreign enterprise can be offset by using the potential flow of return to the knowledge element (and especially if future additions are expected) to obtain a large share in a foreign firm and thereby to establish a subsidiary abroad as a joint venture. A firm that has exhausted all available economies of scale in its home market – particularly in sales – will be a large firm. It may well be established in many different product lines and is likely to be an oligopolist in at least one of them.

The rate of effective protection offered to domestic manufacture by the imposition of *tariffs* on competitive imports will affect the attractiveness of the creation of a foreign subsidiary through its impact upon the landed price of imports. Differentiated goods are likely to be fairly sensitive to tariff rates because of quite high price elasticities of demand following from the similarity between competitive products. Tariffs can therefore be expected to eliminate imports before very high rates of nominal protection have been reached unless a distinct comparative advantage in costs accrues to the exporting nation. In Figure III–1, assume that the landed price of imports is equal to DE and is equal to the costs of local manufacture. If b were to be small and positive, the market might be served by exports from the home country to a local sales subsidiary and supplemented perhaps by local ancillary purchases. An increase in the rate of tariff protection would increase landed costs of imports and leave the corporation no option but to license a local manufacturer, to establish its own local manufacturing subsidiary or to relinquish its share of the market.[1]

In conclusion, the exploitation of a knowledge advantage as an incentive to establish a foreign manufacturing, horizontally-integrated subsidiary is fundamental and is weakened only by the existence of an alternative in the form of licensing arrangements and by the disadvantage under which a foreigner operates in a host nation. The principal kind of firm which will be engaged in horizontal foreign investment is likely to be a large firm producing a differentiated product in a highly imperfect domestic market. The evidence supporting this diagnosis is impressive.[2]

Finally, horizontal integration in itself does not seem to offer multinational corporations great advantages nor does it lead to greater global economic efficiency being achieved through multinational corporations. These corporations seem to achieve

[1] See point 6 below.
[2] See Caves, *Economica*, Feb 1971, *passim*.

the bulk of their economies through vertical integration and, perhaps, through increased powers of financial manoeuvrability. Multinational corporations could gain from horizontal integration if the number of nations in which they had active production operations and their ability to effect economies internal to the corporation were positively correlated.[1]

3. *Sharing rents* available in foreign oligopolistic markets would clearly constitute a motive for investing abroad to any profit seeking firm provided that the rents would more than reimburse the costs of effecting entry into the tightly-knit market.

The establishment of a new firm in a tightly-knit oligopolistic market is an expensive proposition since existing firms are likely to employ all the tricks of imperfect competition that began in the Middle Ages and which businessmen have been busy improving ever since. To the extent that the oligopolistic market into which entry is sought is centred on a differentiated product, the establishment of a brand name through advertising and the cost of setting up a distribution organisation are costs that are additional to those imposed upon the entrant by the existing firms. The large capital outlays that are inherent in this process reinforce the supposition made in the previous section, that corporations undertaking foreign horizontal investment will be large firms with large financial resources behind them.

However, to the extent that the oligopoly profits are appreciable, their existence could influence the decision of whether to invest in local manufacture, to export or to stay out of the market. In terms of Figure III-1, the existence of a per-unit oligopoly profit in the host country, once entry had been established, would allow a corporation to establish a foreign subsidiary even though b were negative – particularly if a could be expected to diminish with time. Thus, rents available in foreign markets are a substitute for the knowledge element in inducing foreign investment. In fact, it is quite likely that rents may be more important in oligopoly than knowledge if the oligopolists have influence over the level of the

[1] The major gains would come through the existence of sales organisations in different nations.

tariff (through the political process) and are able effectively to blockade entry from foreign-based production units, then the alternative of supplying the market by exporting to the potential host country is eliminated by means of the oligopoly structure and the alternative is one of 'to invest or not to invest'. By extension, it seems probable that the higher the tariff, the greater will be the oligopoly rents and therefore the greater the incentive for entry into the market to be effected.

There will be a tendency for the rate of return to capital to be equalised in all countries in which production takes place since entry will continue to be attracted into high-yielding markets. If oligopolists ignore the transitory costs of barriers to entry, they will invest wherever in the world the return is highest and the forces of competition within the industry will tend to equalise returns in all nations. This does not necessarily result in the elimination of excess profits provided that there is some barrier to entry into the *global* industry.

Once the decision has been made to enter the market in the host country, the entrant (investing corporation) will use in the host country any knowledge elements which it possesses. Further, the interaction of global oligopolists in different nations will presumably be beneficial to the individual host nations as the entry into the market must bias the outcome toward the lowering of oligopoly rents.

The process of foreign investment involving vertical integration – particularly backwards integration – may also be due to oligopolistic market structure. Caves suggests that the reduction of uncertainty and the desire to assure a future source of supply of a raw material may be supplemented as a motivation by the hope that establishing a firm claim to a raw material source will help to preserve the existing oligopolistic structure of the industry by denying raw materials to potential entrants. This possibility has serious implications for host countries that are poor and that rely to a large extent upon the exportation of mineral deposits.

4. *Obtaining a higher rate of return* than is available domestically is almost a self-evident motivation for investing abroad. It merits special attention perhaps because the actual pattern of investment does not seem to obey this precept on a global scale.

The underlying problem is the inter-relationship between high rates of return to capital as a generic factor of production, inadequate markets, impoverished nations and political instability or nationalistic tendencies. Simple models of international trade imply that the rate of return to capital – like the price of anything else – will be highest in those places in which its relative scarcity is the greatest. However, the migration of capital involves one different dimension from most other commodities: migration of capital involves the movement of a stock for a long period of time so that considerations about the probability that the stock can be maintained, have bearing upon the desirability of investing abroad.

Some indication that horizontal investments will depend upon the existence of a viable market before they can be undertaken, has already been given. For a viable firm to exist, the demand curve facing that firm must lie above the total average cost curve. In a developing nation – even if the investing corporation would have a virtual monopoly – it is possible for the demand curve to be so far to the left and for the average cost curve to require some minimum rate of output and to fall steeply thereafter that the demand curve is never to the right of (above) the average total cost curve. This is shown schematically in Figure III–2. A certain level of local income is prerequisite to investment in manufacturing facilities of the type that will have an advantage over indigenous entrepreneurs.

The risk of expropriation or some other impairment of the value of the investment is also greater in developing nations. Political instability and poverty walk hand in hand. The more miserable is the mass of the people, the greater is the propensity to overthrow the government and even the social system. In the process, agreements with foreigners entered into by previous governments are easily disregarded for short-term political gains. There is, however, some rate of return that will attract capital into the most unstable area. Despite the threat of the takeover of Hong Kong by the mainland Chinese in the mid-sixties, profit rates in some industries there (hotels for example) were high enough that the exposure was taken.

For non-competitive goods such as ore deposits, the investor may have no choice and must compute the rate of return on the total operation of the global corporation with and without making an investment in a poor country. The preponderance of investments of this type either involves a level of technology which the host nations find difficult to engender in the short run – such as oil industry investments – or they involve a

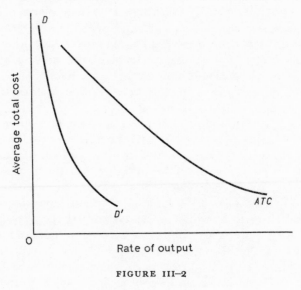

FIGURE III–2

Inadequate Demand

counter against expropriation. This counter may take the form of an assured market for the product if it is developed by the investing corporation and a difficult and possibly blockaded market for the product if the asset is expropriated because the sales outlets are dominated by the group of corporations that invest in the developing nations. Thus, expropriation would leave the country with its deposits but no market in which they could be sold – at least for a period of years. It is worth noting that the bulk of the foreign ownership of deposits of non-competitive resources can be traced back to an era prior to the awakening of the aspirations in developing nations for economic growth and independence. New discoveries of deposits are exploited by foreign corporations under very different agreements arrived at between the investing corporation and a nation state.

In addition to the expectation of acquiring a pure economic rent by investing in a natural immobile resource in a developing country, there is one other means by which international corporations may invest in developing nations. Capital will flow to poor nations in order to supply an international market when the demand is not dependent upon the income of the local residents. Examples of this are investment in tourism facilities in tropical countries and centres of touristic attraction,[1] and investment in international shipping. Investment in ocean shipping in countries that offer flag-of-convenience facilities enables a nation to combine relatively cheap labour with capital obtained at rates prevalent in developed nations.[2] Both of these investment activities are enhanced by a partial immunity of receipts to currency control by the host nation government because the funds are paid out in the investing or in other developed nations and, in the case of ocean shipping, by the fact that expropriation of the capital equipment is virtually impossible.

5. *Expectation of a future rental income* can be a factor affecting the decision to invest in either vertical-integration or horizontal-integration projects. In vertical-integration projects, the rent is expected to come from an increase in demand for a natural resource which will be in short supply in the future. If it is assumed that local deposits of some mineral are nearing exhaustion, investment in deposits of the same mineral elsewhere could generate a rent for the investing corporation. However, it is possible that the host nation perceives this rent and is misled by it. Rent may accrue to an ore deposit not because it enjoys an economic rent but because the parent corporation is able to secure preferential tariff treatment in the investing nation. Expropriation of the resource-exploiting subsidiary might result in the loss of the preferential treatment and, with it, the rent.

Horizontal-integration investments made in foreign countries

[1] The spread of American chain hotels is very obvious in any major city in Europe. In many instances, these hotels are financed locally.

[2] For a discussion of the fascinating and confusing world of international shipping, see Samuel A. Lawrence, *United States Merchant Shipping Policies and Politics* (Washington: The Brookings Institution, 1966) especially pp. 182–8.

in the expectation of some future economic rent will be made in countries in which the development of the local market to a size sufficient to support the subsidiary is expected to be forthcoming very shortly. Such investments are most likely to be located in nations which are developing quickly and which have already reached a fairly high level of income – 'semi-developed' economies. Investment in such nations in anticipation of the growth of the market can lead to two kinds of rental income. The first rental income is that which is likely to accrue to any domestic manufacturer in a nation that practices infant-industry protection or otherwise gives high rates of tariff protection.[1] This procedure will allow local manufacturers to keep their prices at the maximum level that protection affords and may therefore be expected to offer a pure rent to an efficient firm or the maximum return to a knowledge element. At the same time, the growth of the market for a differentiated good allows any existing manufacturer to maintain his share of the market merely by existing and being as efficient as the local competitors. To the extent that an ongoing sales organisation and the advantages of experience in the market and the establishment of a brand name constitute, collectively, a barrier to entry, they will earn a quasi-rent that will grow with sales volume.

6. *The preservation of a market share* only becomes a distinguishable motivation for the establishment of a foreign subsidiary when a production unit is created *in order to* prevent the value of a sales and marketing organisation being eroded. The production unit would not by itself constitute a satisfactory investment because the rate of return would not be high enough but, coupled with the gain of preserving the sales organisation, the investment becomes worth while. Equally, this procedure implies that the alternative of allowing the sales organisation to contract and to expand it again at a later date is a more costly alternative than investing in a production unit to preserve the market share.

Maintaining market share is a useful indicator of corporate performance in that it allows a direct comparison with the

[1] For a description of infant-industry arguments for tariffs, see D. Snider, *Introduction to International Economics*, 5th ed. (Homewood, Ill.: Richard D. Irwin, Inc., 1971) pp. 163–5.

performance of competitors that abstracts from any cyclical fluctuations in demand that would affect the more simple indicator of profits. The production and marketing of a differentiated good involves a concept of corporate efficiency that is a combination of effectiveness in product design, cost levels, marketing organisation, financing and sales promotion. Maintaining market share indicates that a firm is 'holding its own' with its competitors. To the extent that an established presence in the market provides an advantage in the competition for future sales and provides a quasi-rent in the form of a return on a barrier to entry, a market share represents an asset.

If there is a change in the sales market such as might occur if a new higher level of tariffs were imposed and destroyed the price competitiveness of landed imports or if a competitive international corporation established a manufacturing unit with the same result, then a firm may be faced with the choice between sacrificing its asset in its sales organisation, allowing the sales organisation to contract but still holding a token organisation, and manufacturing in the host country. If, in terms of Figure III–1, the rent accruing to the sales organisation exceeds any negative value which b may have, then a defensive subsidiary will be established. It may be that the rent accruing to the sales organisation is even a little smaller than b's negative value but that the sales organisation can be preserved on the basis that a will diminish with time (and quite quickly) and that the market is in the process of or will imminently be in the process of expansion.

Certainly, the establishment of a local subsidiary is likely to follow quickly on the perception of danger to the sales organisation. The option of allowing the sales organisation to contract but not to disappear is probably the worst of all possible worlds. The costs of local manufacture will not be likely to decrease with a delay in the establishment of the subsidiary and there must be some expectation that it is more difficult (and costly) to expand a market share to a previous level than it is to preserve that market share. If future sales which will accrue to the sales organisation, as it were automatically, are a given percentage of current sales, the process of re-establishing a lost market share will involve winning customers away from competitors. Winning customers away from competitors will involve higher per-unit sales promotional outlays or price reductions than preventing a competitor making inroads on the existing market share. If the market has expanded in the interim, the re-establishment of market share will be *pro tanto* more difficult. The disadvantage of permitting a temporary decline in market share is based on an hypothesised asymmetry between sales costs of expanding and preserving market shares not being offset by any saving made through the postponement of the establishment of a manufacturing subsidiary.

The easiest way to think of this rather complicated motivation is to think of the flow of quasi-rents that can be earned by the existing sales organisation being capitalised into an asset. This asset can be called 'goodwill'. Defensive investment is made when the value of the 'goodwill' exceeds the expected losses of the manufacturing subsidiary – losses being computed from some concept of a satisfactory rate of profit rather than from a *zero* profit rate. The problem is analogous to the question of establishing a subsidiary in a market in which oligopoly rents are potentially obtainable even though manufacturing itself is not expected to be capable of generating a satisfactory rate of return. Finally, it is clear that a decision-making process based on maximisation of sales revenues would never consider the relinquishing of an established market share even temporarily.

7. The *acquisition of an assured source of raw materials* with which to serve a domestic production complex is straightforward. The motivation can be considered subjective in that it permits executives to 'rest more easily' at night and can also be considered as a particular example of potential economies internal to the corporation.

8. The *acquisition of raw material deposits* to preserve a barrier to entry into a global oligopoly is also a straightforward motivation. However, like its predecessor, it is defensive in that the investment is not undertaken in order to enhance profit but rather to prevent the erosion of profits at some time in the future.

The motivations to establish a foreign subsidiary are seldom as clearcut as the above listing would suggest. In nearly all decisions to invest abroad, two or more of the possible motivations will be relevant. This is particularly true for corporations that are involved in many levels of production in many countries since a decision to invest in a horizontal direction in one country opens up possibilities of increased economies of internal organisation with its other activities. Similarly, a decision to invest in any country will involve the possibility of a combination of both returns to knowledge and/or internal economies with gains made from market imperfections. Minor additional possible reasons for undertaking investment abroad are failure to ignore sunk costs of seeking information and the product cycle. A failure to write off costs incurred in investigating possible foreign investments could, in marginal cases, lead to a bias toward foreign investment resulting merely from the investigative process.[1] The product cycle is an explanation of a pattern of international trade whereby the newly-developed products are exported until such time as the development of the products and their markets have grown sufficiently to warrant local manufacture.[2] It is similar to but not identical to the 'sequence of market development' motivation for foreign investment that is considered above. The emphasis of the product cycle theory is on commodity trade rather than on patterns of direct investment. It explains the way in which a product will be manufactured in and exported from the country in which it is developed in the first stage of the product cycle. In the second, maturing stage, foreign manufacture will compete with exports from the innovating nation and ultimately, the innovating nation will be a net importer of the product. Clearly, it is possible, and even probable, that foreign manufacture of the new product will be undertaken by foreign subsidiaries of the firm which originally conceived of the product since the innovating firm will have transferable knowledge assets in all aspects of distribution and production. The more quickly the foreign manufacturing process is commenced, the more likely is the foreign capacity to be a subsidiary of the innovating corporation because of the awareness of the firm of future refinements becoming available on a regular basis.

Profits in excess of some minimum level are the necessary

[1] This is found in Yair Aharoni, *The Foreign Investment Decision Process* (Boston, 1966).

[2] See Raymond Vernon, *Manager in the International Economy* (Englewood Cliffs, N.J.: Prentice Hall, Inc., 1968) pp. 77–82 and 192–3.

ingredient for any direct foreign investment. It might be expected at first blush that the rates of profit realised by foreign subsidiaries will be higher than overall domestic profit rates because of the elements of size, rents and quasi-rents that are likely to be engendered by foreign investments. Profit data are notoriously dangerous things and aggregate profit data can be even more misleading. Subject to many caveats, Table III–1

TABLE III–I

Ratios of Profits to Book Value for Selected U.S.
Foreign Investments, 1969

(in per cent)

WORLD	
All Sectors	12·24
Mining and Smelting	15·53
Petroleum	13·20
Manufacturing	12·06
Other	10·05
CANADA	
All Sectors	7·89
Manufacturing	9·41
EUROPE	
All Sectors	9·56
Manufacturing	13·54
LESS DEVELOPED COUNTRIES	
All Sectors	19·98
LESS DEVELOPED COUNTRIES (excluding the Middle East)	
All Sectors	15·31

Note: Profits are preliminary 1969 data and book values are revised with data up to the end of 1968.

Source: David T. Devlin and George R. Kruer, 'The International Investment Position of the United States: Developments in 1969', *Survey of Current Business* (Oct 1970) pp. 21–34.

gives some profit ratios for United States foreign subsidiaries. With the possible exception of profits derived from subsidiaries in less developed countries – particularly from investments in the Middle East – profit rates do not seem to be exceptionally high. This is perhaps even more surprising when it is realised that there is some element of *upward* bias in the computations.

The profit data are calculated by dividing the money profits (including retained profits) obtained by foreign subsidiaries in 1969 by the book value of subsidiaries at the end of 1968. Book values will tend to underestimate the true value of the assets of the subsidiaries because of the appreciation of assets over time due to inflation and to the increased value of ongoing industries and natural resources. The bias due to inflation is very likely to have contributed to the relatively high profit rate shown for 'mining and smelting' and may explain, because of the comparative recency of the bulk of the investments, the relatively low rates obtained from investments in Canada and Europe.

One explanation of low aggregate profit rates is the failure of some projects to achieve the success that was expected of them. Another possible factor is the 'disguising' of overall returns to the investing parent by making charges for management fees, royalties etc., and not including these data in profits. Finally, there will always be some capital investments entered in the book value which have not yet begun to yield their expected profits.

If the benefits expected from direct investment abroad can be summarised under the single heading of greater profit, the potential costs are more diverse. The costs that a corporation can experience as a result of a foreign investment are of two kinds: an opportunity cost and the many-faceted dimensions of uncertainty. The opportunity cost is self-explanatory since the act of investment abroad is likely to preclude some investment at home. Given that foreign financing may be more readily available than domestic financing, it is possible that the opportunity cost is less than a dollar for a dollar; that is, an investment abroad may not necessitate a reduction in domestic investments by an equal amount. The uncertainties that accompany a decision to invest abroad can derive from misestimation, from discrimination against foreigners by the host government, from expropriation, from profit-reducing interference by the government of the investing country and from the possible domestic repercussions of doing business abroad.

Normally a calculation is made of the expected rate of profit before any investment decision is taken. Errors from misestimation apply to foreign investments in exactly the same way as they do to domestic investments and the difference between the two is purely one of degree and/or probability. Lack of familiarity with the foreign economy will expose the investing country to a greater probability of error of any given size for a new country but extensions of existing investments should be the subject of no less accurate forecasts than domestic investments. The risk arises from a mis-estimate of market potential or acceptance and, probably more likely, a mis-estimate of costs of production. The danger of underestimating costs of production is likely to be particularly great in projects in which the new subsidiary will be required to employ labour-intensive methods of production and/or to train the local labour supply to new levels of sophistication.

There is one source of mis-estimation which is beyond the scope of the forecaster and which must be accepted as a simple risk of doing business abroad. This is the risk of the reduction of foreign profits as a result of the relative depreciation of the currency of the host country. However, the cause of such a reduction in profit rates is only likely to be due to *domestic inflation* in the host country in an indirect way. Inflation can induce generally restrictive measures in the host nation and profits of the subsidiary may suffer from fiscal and monetary restraint and, secondly, domestic inflation can reduce the effective rate of tariff protection and similar measures of commercial policy on which the anticipated profit rate (or selling price) may hinge. However, the simple act of domestic inflation (unmatched by inflation in the rest of the world) should result in a depreciation of the host currency *vis-à-vis* other currencies *and* in higher absolute profits measured in the domestic currency of the host nation. If these two forces are offsetting, as they may be expected to be in the absence of any particular sectoral effects, then the profits of the subsidiary measured in the currency of the investing country will not be affected. However, if the terms of trade move against the host country, the value in the currency of the investing country of the profits achieved in the currency of the host country will be reduced. This distinction is important and conceptually difficult. A numerical example may simplify things.

Let the rate of exchange between the currencies of the investing and host countries be one-to-one. Let the foreign subsidiary be expected to sell goods worth one million pesos and to achieve a profit rate on sales of 5 per cent. Thus, if inflation in the host country or the terms of trade do not cause the depreciation of the peso against the currency of the investing country (the mark), profits of 50,000 marks will be earned. Now, let the peso suffer from a 10 per cent inflation. When the sectoral repercussions have worked themselves out, sales will be worth 1·1 million pesos, profits will be 55,000 pesos and the rate of exchange (at unchanged terms of trade) will be 1·1 pesos = 1 mark. Thus, profits are unchanged in marks. However, if the terms of trade move against the host country because of growth effects or external forces, the profits of the subsidiary will still be 50,000 pesos, but if the peso has been depreciated in terms of the mark to offset the adverse shift in the terms of trade to say 1·1 pesos = 1 mark, the value of subsidiary profits to the parent will have declined to $(50,000 \div 1 \cdot 1)$ marks or approximately 45,555 marks.

It is possible that the host government will discriminate against foreign firms located within its jurisdiction. This discrimination may stem from internal political pressures, external complications and a need to distract the domestic populace from domestic problems in other sectors – or indeed the discrimination may result from the fact that the subsidiary is pursuing policies that are not in the best interests of the people in the host country. If discrimination against the subsidiary is caused by 'antisocial' operations on the part of the subsidiary, this reflects upon the wisdom of the specific operations rather than on the wisdom of the investment – unless the specific operations were conceived of as an integral part of the subsidiary's operations prior to the investment.[1] It is always possible that the values of the host government have changed since the establishment of the subsidiary. This is a risk of doing business in any nation but it is larger when foreign subsidiaries are the subject of consideration because the element of 'foreignness' makes their actions more newsworthy. The risk is enhanced in a period of nationalism and in developing nations where values are more easily subjected to drastic change. Discrimination against a foreign subsidiary implies discrimination in favour of a competitive domestic firm *or* discrimination in favour of the

[1] If the subsidiary's operations were approved by the host government prior to the establishment of the subsidiary, then this is definitionally impossible without change of government.

consumer and foreign suppliers. Governments, particularly in developing nations, are important sources of demand for many advanced products. It is possible for these governments to discriminate against foreign subsidiaries overtly or covertly through their purchasing regulations and orders. Equally, it is possible for a government to lower the tariff protection behind which a foreign subsidiary is operating so that the anticipated profits of the subsidiary are not and cannot be realised. Finally, it is possible for foreign governments to discriminate against foreign subsidiaries in the application of their powers of taxation – either through overt discrimination by taxing foreign subsidiaries at higher rates or covertly by enforcing the rules of the game more energetically where foreign subsidiaries are concerned. These acts of hostility toward the foreign subsidiary are important costs to the profitability of the firm if they were unforeseen. The wise investor will examine the potential subsidiary's exposure to political risks and changes in the climate of opinion towards foreigners in the host country. It could be argued that some discrimination is natural and inevitable. The big danger lies in the possibility that written agreements between the investing corporation and the host government, which pertain to taxation, tariff undertakings and governmental purchases be renounced unilaterally by the host government after the investment has been made.

There is a natural appeal to governments in developing countries in favour of the expropriation of foreign businesses. This is particularly true where newly-empowered governments seek some quick and flamboyant action to justify their new status and where the foreign business represents big business belonging to a colonial-type power.

The simple arithmetic of the appeal of confiscation or expropriation as an aid to and in the process of economic development is given in Martin Bronfenbrenner's 'The Appeal of Confiscation in Economic Development'.[1] That example is conducted in terms of the confiscation of property from rich citizens rather than the confiscation of firms from foreign parent corporations. Thus, the arithmetic case that Bronfen-

---

[1] *Economic Development and Cultural Change* (Apr 1955) pp. 201–18, reprinted in *Economic Development: Evolution or Revolution?* ed. Laura Randall (Boston: D. C. Heath, 1964) pp. 55–75.

brenner makes in favour of confiscation is likely to be enhanced for expropriation of international firms – if only because of the foreign exchange benefits that follow from expropriation. The costs to the host country of expropriation lie largely in a possible inability to use the expropriated equipment, or in the inability to attract new foreign investment deemed beneficial. These costs to the host government are of little concern to the parent of the expropriated subsidiary. It is possible that the parent corporation can offset its loss in various ways – by receiving some settlement from the host government or by claiming a tax loss on its returns in the investing country. Settlements by the host governments are usually locked into local currencies – a fact which greatly reduces the value of the funds – or under-value the expropriated concern. From an economic point of view, there is little point in a host government paying the parent corporation full market value.[1] Offsetting the loss against taxation in the investing country is a second-best solution.

The United States government has given guarantees to foreign investors in developing nations that if its investments are expropriated, the investing corporation will be reimbursed. This does help reduce the risk of exposure to expropriation but is not an inducement to invest where the risk exceeds some critical value.

Finally, the investing corporation can suffer because of repercussions from the home nation. These repercussions can take two forms – interference by the home government in the operation of the foreign business and adverse publicity and customer reaction stemming from operations abroad.

Host governments can interfere with the free operation of a foreign subsidiary in that the anti-trust laws of the investing nation are visited upon the subsidiaries and possibly upon the subsidiaries' subsidiaries. Equally regulations governing trading with certain nations in certain commodities can be applied to subsidiaries located abroad. Questions such as these constitute the issue of 'extraterritoriality'. The anti-trust question could be an important deterrent – if the regulations were enforced – against attempting to seek oligopolistic or cartel profits for a

[1] See Norman N. Mintz, 'Economic Observations on Lump Sum Settlement Agreements', *Indiana Law Journal* (Summer 1968) pp. 885–98.

subsidiary.[1] The second problem is one of the prime objections to foreign subsidiaries of economic nationalists.[2]

A third way in which the government of the investing country can expose a subsidiary located abroad to risks is by impeding the free flow of capital funds from the parent to the subsidiary. A newly-established subsidiary, particularly one in a fast-growing market will need to grow with its market and may need further infusions of capital from its parent. Sudden and unexpected imposition of capital controls – possibly accentuated by mandatory rates of repatriation of profits – because of balance-of-payments constraints in the investing country, will seriously impede this flow of capital funds, will hinder the growth of the subsidiary and may cause it to lose its market share.[3]

The modern phenomenon of a concerned population – at least in some countries and in particular in the younger age groups – can lead to foreign subsidiaries having adverse effects upon the domestic sales of the parent corporation: particularly so when the parent produces consumer goods. The most clear-cut recent example of this phenomenon is the campaign launched against firms with subsidiaries in the Union of South Africa. The argument of those opposed to General Motors and Polaroid – to name only two corporations – is that the operation of subsidiaries in South Africa reinforces the strength of the government and therefore strengthens those in favour of the policy of apartheid. The argument proposes a consumer boycott of the products of these firms by those opposing apartheid in the United States and other countries in which the firms' products are sold.

A similar moral problem exists in any country in which the government is not representative of the people and particularly concerned with the welfare of the poor and the disadvantaged. Nor is the problem limited to private corporations. It is argu-able that in developing countries particularly, any measure

---

[1] See Wilbur L. Fugate, 'Antitrust Aspects of Transatlantic Investment', *Law and Contemporary Problems* (Winter 1969) pp. 142–5.

[2] See Kari Levitt, *Silent Surrender*, p. xiii.

[3] This problem is discussed in greater detail in Chapter VII below. This reliance of the subsidiary upon future injections of funds during the first years of its existence is compatible with the 'organic' theory of the firm expounded in Judd Polk *et al.*, *U.S. Production Abroad*, pp. 132–6.

designed to aid economic development strengthens the power of the incumbent government and contributes to the prolongation of life of the 'despotic' ruling oligarchy.

Two distinct questions are involved. Is it better to help the development process and in that way to contribute to the welfare of the people in the developing country even if the oligarchic government is stabilised in the process or is it better to deny help to the oligarchy so that things will get worse until eventually 'progressive' forces can take over? There is no simple answer to this problem and it depends not only on the political and moral values of the person giving an answer but also on the time horizon involved.

The second question is whether the withdrawal of *extant* corporations would benefit the people in the host country whom the opponents of apartheid, for example, would wish to help. Withdrawal of existing investments may not be the answer. It may be better for the foreign subsidiary to work toward 'moral justice' from within than to vacate the country. Additionally, the relinquishing of the fixed investments might diminish the demand for unskilled labour and thereby hurt the poorer people directly. No answer exists here either. However, the fact that there is no simple answer to the question of whether or not a corporation should withdraw does not mean that the campaign is ineffective. It may be, though, that the campaign could be better aimed. If the advisability of forcing a withdrawal is less than obvious, it could be that the campaign should be directed toward ensuring that corporations with subsidiaries in nations such as South Africa, strive for progress in these countries and follow hiring and operational policies that are as progressive as the law allows.

CONCLUSION

In this highly complex and interdependent world of the twentieth century, the benefits to the corporation and the possible costs of foreign investment will vary from country to country, from industry to industry and, even, from firm to firm. Profits are what the process is about. In a perfect world profits would represent some increase in global efficiency – distribution problems aside – and to the extent that profits testify to economies of internal organisation or returns to knowledge, they still do so. Monopoly profits have little to recommend them on a social basis. Against the expectation of future profits must be counted the costs. Costs, actual and potential, can assume a bewildering variety of forms and a discouraging range of possible likelihoods. The international corporation is the vehicle by which a market or private enterprise system carries out the *prima facie* case in favour of foreign investments. If that system is to continue, firms will continue to seek benefits and, it is to be hoped, will fulfil the social purpose in return for the return they acquire on their risk exposure and on their expertise and capital.

CHAPTER IV

BENEFITS AND COSTS FOR THE HOST COUNTRY

The final section of Chapter II hypothesised that the benefit to the host nation from the local establishment of a foreign subsidiary enterprise was likely to vary both in magnitude and in the kind of industry that was attracted according to the level of income of the host country. More precisely, it was argued that the difference between the income levels of the host and the investing nations would influence the volume, pattern and profitability of the investments as well as the benefits derived by the host. Since it may reasonably be assumed that the investing nations are developed and technologically-sophisticated economies, the question of the benefits and costs of the host nation should consider 'rich' countries and 'poor' countries separately.

I

The *prima facie* case that foreign investment is potentially globally beneficial on balance because of its effect of increasing the rate of output in the host nation is difficult to substantiate empirically because of the inherent complexity of the growth process. However, the *prima facie* case was expected to have its greatest relevance for developing countries provided that such countries were able to attract foreign investment to their shores and subject to the non-positive aspects of enclave industries. At the risk of committing an error of the *post hoc ergo propter hoc* variety, an examination of a success story in which foreign investment played a sizeable role, will provide an illustration of the positive aspects of foreign investments in a developing country.[1]

[1] Since the 'alternative position' cannot be known, it is always possible to argue that the focus country could have done as well by other policies. However neighbouring States that were ideologically opposed to foreign

The Republic of the Ivory Coast has actively encouraged direct private foreign investment. A legal code governing the conditions under which foreign direct investments would be admitted and the conditions under which they would operate was enacted in 1959 in the period of self-government before full independence was achieved in August 1960. This code is probably the most liberal toward foreign investors in all Africa. In particular, it specifies the tax relief that foreign investments may enjoy – provided they merit 'priority status' which covers investment in a wide range of industries, subsidiaries can be granted exemptions from a large number of taxes for different durations. The code also specifies that up to 80 per cent of profits may be repatriated to the investing country each year. The Government of President Felix Houphouet-Boigny has maintained close friendly ties with the former colonial power, France, as well as with the rest of the western world. The policy of 'Economic Liberalism' has been reconfirmed by the Plan for 1971–1975 which espoused the following principles:

'Fundamental belief in private enterprise.
Freedom of establishment to preserve competition.
Free circulation of goods and persons.
Special advantages for "priority" investors.
Willingness to co-operate with all other countries.'

On other occasions the Minister of Finance has emphasised these additional policy aspects:

'Participation of Ivorian capital in new enterprises.
Active promotion of Ivorian-owned enterprises.
Rapid "Ivorianisation" of management and employment.'

Manifestly, Ivory Coast is a prototypical example of a nation choosing to promote economic development in a way that would gain the approval of Adam Smith, David Ricardo or Jacob Viner or any other firm advocate of the 'market system' and 'free enterprise'. At the same time, there is an awareness of the advantage to the host nation of indulging in a little selective-

---

investment have done less well. A second rebuttal would be that foreign investment is beneficial only in the short-run of, say, 20 years and will prove a handicap thereafter.

ness and guidance to 'help' the natural order work more effectively.

Table IV–1 shows what has been achieved in the eleven years since independence. In 1971, the estimated *per capita* income in Ivory Coast was $306 – 'the most outstanding

TABLE IV–I

Selected Economic Indicators of Ivory Coast
1960, 1965 and 1970

(in billions of constant 1965 CFA francs[a])

	1960	1965	1970
Gross Domestic Product	141·7	214·0	317·4
Annual Average Rate of Growth (per cent)	8·6	8·2	
Population (millions)	3·7*	4·3	5·0
GDP *per capita* (CFA francs)	38,297	49,768	63,480
(In U.S. dollars at 1970 rate of exchange)	138	179	229
Annual Average Rate of Growth	5·4	5·0	
Gross Capital Formation	24·7	44·1	62·4
Debt Burden[b] (billions of current CFA francs)	– 1·9	– 8·5	– 15·0*
Trade Balance	+ 5·5	+ 5·8	+ 20·9

Source: Official data.

[a] $1 = 277·71 CFA francs (the CFA franc was devalued in 1968).
[b] Defined as gross outpayments of dividends and interest.
* Estimated.

achievement of any country in tropical Africa'.[1] These significant achievements cannot be attributed uniquely to the attitude toward foreign investments. They represent the product of an economic policy that has generated large investments in regional development projects which have been masterminded by the central government, a favourable set of circumstances in world trade as well as a liberal economic policy both domestically and internationally. Perhaps the most important external effect has been Ivory Coast's associate membership in the European Economic Community (EEC). The EEC enjoyed a

[1] See 'Foreign Economic Trends: Ivory Coast' (Washington: U.S. Department of Commerce, July 1971). This report gives 1970 *per capita* income as $287 so there is a lack of consistency with the data in Table IV–1.

very high rate of economic growth in the 1960s. This high rate of growth will have spilled over to the associate members in tropical Africa through their privileged position in exporting to the EEC and the EEC must have provided both a source of foreign capital as well as a large number of profitable investment opportunities that are export-oriented. The favourable aspect of associate member status applies particularly to second and third stage processing of raw materials (non-competitive materials) produced in tropical Africa. Member nations of the EEC are prohibited from levying tariffs on imports from associate member nations. There is a peculiarity of the tariff structures of developed nations that tends to place very high rates of effective (as opposed to nominal) tariff prtection on imports of processed raw materials.[1] Membership in the franc area will have accorded that access to French markets for the erstwhile French colonies but associate membership provides entrée to the much larger market of the EEC in which the domestic activities are now opened to foreign competition without high tariff protection. In this vulnerable market, associate members have a large advantage over other tropical nations that might compete in the supply of non-competitive goods and their processing.

The entrée to the EEC for exports of processed, locally-produced raw materials provides a partial explanation of the phenomenal increase in the value of manufacturing or industrial output that Ivory Coast has achieved in the eleven years of independence. Processed goods count as manufactures or industrial output and have contributed to the increase from $47 million in 1960 to $360 million in 1970 in current prices.

[1] A numerical example will make the mechanism clear. Suppose country G has a zero tariff on imported raw beans and a 20 per cent tariff on processed beans. Assume further that the processing is a simple activity so that processing in the source country will only cost f. 20 per unit. If raw beans cost f. 8o per unit and ignoring transport costs, raw beans will cost f. 80 when landed in G and processed beans will cost f. 120 duty-paid. The processing activity in G can cost up to f. 40 per unit before imports of processed beans are advantageous – an effective rate of protection of 100 *per cent* on the processing activity: (40-20)/20. The most thorough presentation which also gives examples of the effective protection enjoyed in the United States by some industries, is Harry G. Johnson, *Economic Policies Towards Less Developed Countries* (Washington: The Brookings Institution, 1967) pp. 90–4.

The Plan for 1971–75 emphasises the need for further increases in industrial output.

It would be fatuous to argue that each person in Ivory Coast has benefited materially from the economic achievements of the eleven years of independence to an equal degree – or even that every person has benefited. However, it is difficult to envisage so much real growth (about 5 per cent *per capita* per annum) not improving the lot of everyone to some small degree. Nor does it follow inevitably that the policies that worked well until 1971 will continue to work well in the next ten or twenty years. But, Ivory Coast with its very liberal policy toward foreign subsidiary operations is, in 1971, *the* success story in tropical Africa.

A second indication of support for the value of foreign investment to developing nations is the recent UNCTAD proposal for a General Scheme of Preferences.[1] This proposal was generated by the developing nations. It asks the developed nations to accord to developing nations as a group reductions in tariff rates on certain manufactured goods without according concomitant reductions in tariff rates applied to imports of the same goods from developed nations. This proposal would afford to the developing nations *as a group* a competitive advantage both by lowering the protection afforded to domestic producers and by according the developing countries an advantage over imports from developed nations. The Scheme will, when put into effect, stimulate exports of manufactured goods *and* the expansion of manufacturing capacity in developing nations. One of the big selling points made by UNCTAD, necessarily with the approval of the member (developing) nations, was the stimulation that the Scheme would afford to the creation of manufacturing facilities in the developing nations through private direct investment in labour-intensive production operations.

Both associate membership in the EEC and the General

[1] United Nations Conference on Trade and Development. UNCTAD document TD/B/AC.5/34 and Addenda 1–10 provide the actual preferences offered by the developed nations. Ratification of these offers by the legislative bodies is not yet universal. In particular the United States Congress had not received the recommendation from President Nixon at the end of 1971.

Scheme of Preferences accord competitive advantages to a group of nations rather than to a single nation. Both sets of preferences introduce once and for all shifts in the competitiveness of different industries in different countries as well as the advantages which will accrue through economic growth in the developed nations. The once and for all change opens up to the preferred group of nations at first a defined set of import demand that could, in theory, be calculated. It may well be that the first nation among the preferred group to take advantage of the new trading conditions and to establish industrial capacity equal to the potential increase in imports of the developed nations, will have a long-term advantage in the market supplied. Assume that processing raw material K were now made cheaper in the developing nations than in the developed nation. If a developing nation were to be able quickly to construct capacity equal to the volume of processed K that could be sold to the developed importers, it would be able to pre-empt the market for processed K. Other nations would have little incentive to invest in capacity in that industry unless they expected rapid further growth in processed imports (because they become cheaper in the importing country) or unless it was expected that they would enjoy a pure comparative advantage in the processed product. To the extent that being the *first* preferred nation to generate the new capacity in processing K and therefore the first to be able to offer sizeable quantities of processed K for export, does accord a long-term advantage, these advantages may be expected to accrue to those nations that provide a legal and business climate that is receptive to foreign investment. Direct foreign investments will provide not only the necessary capital but will also be likely to be made by firms with a firsthand experience in the industry and which can bring with the investment, the technological knowhow relevant to that industry. Further the direct investments are likely to be made by firms with knowledge of and access to the markets in the preference-giving countries. In terms of Appendix II–A, the preference reduces N so that $C - N$ becomes positive for the nations producing raw K in the preferred group. Private investment will also supply a positive T relative to other nations in the preferred group that attempt to take advantage of the preferences through domestic investment in the processing industry. This advantage which accrues to the nations accommodating foreign investment is a one-shot advantage that may be eroded over time. Further there is no guarantee that the foreign investor will use the factor combination that is best suited to the host nation and may instead transplant the factor mix used in the developed nation. However, if growth is a self-generating process, the initial impetus may yield to the host nation total benefits that are disproportionately great.

Given that foreign investments can be valuable adjuncts to the development process, what disadvantages can ensue that would cause governments of developing nations to spurn promising investment projects? The first and foremost reason in a world in which many African and Asian nations have only recently escaped from some sort of colonial status, is a desire to escape from European influence. Detestation of foreigners can make slower growth seem worth while and the fear of implicit economic subservience replacing the newly-discarded political subservience can deter a nation from rational, self-seeking assessments of the desirability of foreign investment projects. This antipathy may attenuate with time. An espousal of communist policies and doctrines and the consequent rejection or open discouragement (if not expropriation) of foreign investment by 'western' nations is understandable when a century or more of obedience to a colonial-inspired market system has historically failed to realise gains for the mass of the people and when the so-called free enterprise system did not, as in oligarchist Latin American republics, lead to vertical social mobility and to a wide distribution of economic gains. Foreign investment and *laissez-faire* capitalism are easily identifiable as part and parcel of the same package of economic *credos* that brought stagnation and backwardness. Since the market system did not work well for these people in the past, they have no overwhelming reason to suppose that it will work well in the future and no reason not to try a new approach that will exclude foreign direct investments.[1]

[1] The problem here is not uniquely with the market system but with the lack of the social and political dimensions that are necessary if the market system is to promote growth and also, perhaps, the absence of the autonomous economic system that may be vital.

It is necessary to distinguish between rejecting direct investment projects that do not meet the criterion of the host nation
and a developing nation assuming a stance that is inimical to
all foreign investment. Chapter II has referred to the possible
negative traits of foreign investments. These negative traits will
apply particularly to enclave industries, to investments that use
up a finite stock of resources without 'fair' payment (such as a
mineral deposit), investments that will affect local economic
sovereignty through domination and through extra-territoriality
problems. Finally, it must always be assumed (and is indeed
regarded here as mandatory) that the government of a developing nation maintain control over the inflow of direct investments – both quantitatively and qualitatively.

Economic reasons for rejecting or for failing to promote
foreign investments that appear to be desirable are four in
number:[1]

(1) The presence of foreign firms may retard the development of indigenous entrepreneurial talent.
(2) Foreign investment in an industry may forever preclude
the development of domestic firms in that industry.
(3) The cost to the host nation in the form of the inducement
to invest granted to the investing corporation may be too
great.
(4) The balance of payments costs will ultimately outweigh
the benefits received.

These arguments can be considered sequentially. It will be
seen that all of them can be valid but that none of them –
individually or collectively – precludes all foreign investment.

(1) The role of the entrepreneur in the development process
has been accorded great importance by Joseph A. Schumpeter.[2]
The creative talents that entrepreneurs possess are recognised
as scarce and in need of a sympathetic climate if they are to
flower. There can exist a legitimate fear that permitting the

---

[1] There is also the simple cause of government inefficiency and bureaucratic 'drag' that will deter investors and cause them to locate their subsidiaries in more efficient host nations. It is also possible that a ruling
oligarchy will rationally *oppose* economic development since the process
would reduce the real income of the elite.

[2] See Everett E. Hagen, *The Economics of Development* (Homewood, Ill.:
Richard D. Irwin, Inc., 1968) Ch. 10, particularly p. 219.

entry of large foreign corporations will deprive the indigenous entrepreneurial talent of the opportunity it needs to develop and that, in consequence of allowing the establishment of foreign subsidiaries, a nation can fail to realise the assets embodied in the *latent* entrepreneurial talents of its population. The thought sequence is not without foundation. The establishment of foreign firms does fill opportunities and gaps that local talent might some day have filled. However, this cost element may be smaller than the simple hypothesis implies and must always be compared with the benefit foregone. The reasons for suggesting that foreign investments may exert a less adverse influence upon indigenous entrepreneurial talent are (i) that the outlets most suitable for indigenous entrepreneurs are likely to be untouched by international business, and (ii) that by imposing on the international business the requirement that indigenous people be trained up to managerial and professional tasks, the foreign investment may have a *positive* effect on the development of indigenous entrepreneurial talent.[1]

The outlets most suitable for indigenous entrepreneurs are likely to be found in domestic industry in which a deep knowledge of the customer is necessary. No foreign business is likely to enter such a field unless it holds a technical advantage that will more than compensate for its lack of knowledge of local selling and marketing customs. Even if such a subsidiary were established, it is very probable that the international business would tend to use citizens of the host country as its marketing force and an agency marketing organisation would cultivate the entrepreneurial talents of host-country citizens. To the extent that the foreign business helped the agencies to develop sound managerial practices, the net effect of foreign business would be positive. Within its own organisation, foreign business will train potential 'professional managers' rather than Schumpeterian entrepreneurs in the purest sense. However, a corps of professional managers may spin off a few Schumpeterian entrepreneurs with a much higher level of general business expertise. Finally, it is also likely that the need for creative entrepreneurial talent in the development process may

[1] This requirement is being imposed now in many developing nations. Also, for example, see the second list of points in the Ivorian philosophy above.

be less intense in the second half of the twentieth century than in the industrial revolution and succeeding years.

(2) The possibility that foreign operations present in the host country will preclude the establishment of indigenous firms in a specific industry is significant. However, if the possibility is anticipated by the host government it can also be circumvented – at a cost. For example, the host government could *impose* a local firm upon an industry.

The possible failure of an indigenous firm to evolve naturally in a domestic market dominated by foreign subsidiaries of one or more nations can be a serious negative factor if only because it dooms the host country to an eternity of being a host without any hope of ever achieving some counterpart investor status in a specific industry.[1] However, realistically, it is unlikely that third-generation nations will ever achieve investor status.[2] Exclusion of foreign corporations and their accumulations of knowledge deprives the host country of the knowledge in the industry itself and of any spread effects that the investment might have generated. However, an indigenous firm could in theory and behind a sufficiently protective tariff wall, exist without the proprietary knowledge available abroad. It could develop its own stock of proprietary knowledge in time so that it might ultimately be able to create its own foreign subsidiary in, say, a fifth-generation country. It is more probable that the late start in the industry would never be overcome and the ultimate goal of becoming an investing nation would never be attained. Licensing is not a good alternative as a basis for ultimate foreign investment except under very unusual circumstances since licensed knowhow can seldom either be exported in an embodied form in goods or through a foreign subsidiary. The possibility exists that a firm might obtain basic original knowhow by licensing and develop its own knowhow thereafter.

Provided no ambition ultimately to become an investor nation exists, then the cost of avoiding foreign domination is not so great. The host government can deliberately create a

[1] This is the policy option referred to in footnote on p. 88.

[2] Third-generation nations in the sequence of market development pattern are those nations in which both the original developer of the industry and the first group of countries to receive foreign investments in the industry can both have subsidiaries.

duopoly situation when the foreign subsidiary is allowed in. The domestic competitor would enjoy the same tariff protection as the foreign subsidiary, could acquire licensed knowledge and could learn from its rival. The domestic firm might require some subsidy in its early years but given good oversight by the 'ministry of Economic Affairs' could achieve profitable status and could slowly evolve to face the competition of the foreign subsidiary and foreign manufacturers with a lower tariff.

The danger of exclusion of domestic firms from an industry is greatest in industries in which foreign subsidiaries enjoy a proprietary knowledge advantage – therefore predominantly in differentiated-goods industries. Provided that the nation has no ultimate ambitions to become an investor then this danger of complete exclusion of indigenous firms can be virtually eliminated by intelligent policy. The cost of refusing entry to established foreign firms or of refusing to create a local firm with licensed knowledge may be very great both because of the delays involved in acquiring knowledge and because of the very high opportunity cost of the resources (skilled workers) who are likely to be involved in the generation of that knowledge.[1]

(3) The inducement necessary to attract foreign capital into the would-be host nation may be too great to warrant allowing foreign subsidiaries to establish themselves. The inducement can take many forms and is usually needed to offset what is seen by the investor as an unsympathetic political atmosphere, a high danger of expropriation, an inadequate market or an inadequate economic base in the host country itself. The necessary inducements may vary with the cause of the un-willingness to invest. If the ability of international corporations to expand is limited by their own finances and by the availa-bility within the corporation of adequate managerial personnel, then the unwillingness to invest may derive quite simply from the availability in another developing nation of a more favour-able package. Thus what are necessary to attract the foreign

[1] What may be called follower nations always have the advantage of importing a foreign product and dissecting it – witness the great stress that both Russia and the U.S.A. put on the physical acquisition by the other side of a technologically-advanced weapon.

investment are pure economic blandishments. The inducements can take the form of a high profit rate (including royalties and all other return flows), concomitant high tariffs, and concomitant long-term tax exemptions. Another possible attraction to a foreign firm is the expectation of an economic rent which will accrue to the subsidiary through the exploitation of some resource that becomes progressively more scarce. Finally, an assured monopoly position may be required to 'guarantee' a level of profit sufficient to induce the corporation to invest in the would-be host.

The possibility of paying too high a price may not be a once and for all decision. Time may enter into the calculation as an important factor. It may be that the nation's image (and reality) may change in the near future toward one of a most hospitable location for foreign subsidiaries. It would then not be sound to yield a high price in inducements in the form of tax relief etc., to obtain a subsidiary quickly – unless the presence of the subsidiary in question was instrumental in the improvement of the image. The possibility that the first subsidiary attracted has to be offered more favourable terms than following entrants is quite realistic. It is also possible that postponing the introduction of the foreign subsidiary may cause the alternative outlets for firms in that industry to deteriorate so that the firm can be obtained on cheaper terms.

The ability of a developing country to attract a foreign subsidiary depends very largely upon the relative attractiveness of that nation as a host in comparison with other outlets. Special inducements can only be of marginal influence in changing a locational decision. To the extent that developing nations try to outcompete each other in blandishments, the only gainer will be the international corporation. This feature may be one distinct advantage to the formation of a customs union by developing nations: a customs union, especially if it allocates specific industries to specific countries, will both reduce the competition of would-be hosts and make the market a more attractive entity.[1]

(4) The contemplation of an annual drain of profits being paid to the investing corporation for an infinitely long period

---

[1] The Central American market has allocated different industries to different nations in this way.

of years can be a depressing one to the planner in a developing nation. However, if the project passes the host country's investment criterion, the adverse balance-of-payments effects will have been expected not to exceed the favourable effects of the investment. Thus a refusal to accept or to encourage foreign investment on the grounds of future balance-of-payments strains must admit the possibility of a serious *and* adverse error in forecasting. The main source of error is likely to be an underestimate of the corporate subsidiary's profits. Given the sensitivity of most foreign investments to protective tariffs and to governmental tax policies, an unusually high profit rate that is beyond recall, seems improbable.

An alternative reason for refusing to countenance foreign investment on balance-of-payments grounds is more interesting – namely that the balance of payments effects will ultimately become so severe that the benefits from any investments are outweighed. This possibility suggests very large outflows of repatriated profits and an international financial pattern that makes the terms of trade extremely sensitive to changes in the volume of transfers. Large outflows of repatriated profits imply that a large amount of investment has been received into the economy. Therefore, it follows that not all investment is bad but merely that it is possible for a developing nation to have too large a volume of foreign investment. This would argue for selectivity on the part of the host government in approving capital inflows (although the *stock* of capital indebtedness may be a holdover from colonial days), it does not argue for a blanket denial of all foreign subsidiaries. This possibility is enhanced when there are large interest payments for loans made in the past and possibly for scheduled repayments of loans. However, repayments of loans improve international net worth and, while such repayments would impose a strain, they also reduce future interest payments. A large outflow of dividends and interest will not have harmful effects unless the large outflow gives rise to a severe adverse shift in the terms of trade. This great sensitivity on the part of the terms of trade of developing nations to changes in the payments flows is part and parcel of the Prebisch hypothesis which argues that foreign demand for primary exports tends to be inelastic to price and therefore to make the terms of trade of developing countries sensitive to changes in payments flows. Note that since economic growth is itself desirable and since economic growth itself is likely to cause an adverse shift in the terms of trade with other nations, the adverse shift consequent upon growth should not be attributed to the foreign investment that gives rise to the growth. Only the 'drain' of repatriated profits etc. is ascribable purely to the foreignness of the investment. This is the essence of the logic underlying reliance upon the alternative position in the derivation of an investment criterion. Finally, to some degree, an adverse shift in the terms of trade might result from a bad mix of investments in the host nation since some portion of investments must always be directed toward export promotion or import reduction.

There is one aspect of foreign investment that does mitigate against the terms of trade of the host nation because of an asymmetry in reactions by the investing and host nations. Assuming a transfer is necessarily undereffected (i.e. some price change adverse to the transferor will be necessary to generate sufficient foreign saving), the net receipt of foreign investment funds by a developing country will turn the terms of trade in its favour. Net repayment of funds – either capital or dividends and interest – will turn the terms of trade against the developing nation. Unfortunately for the developing nation there is reason to believe that the adverse shift per dollar of repayment by a developing nation will be larger than the favourable shift per dollar of funds received. When a transfer of funds is made, the degree to which the terms of trade must shift depends upon the sensitivity of the demand for imports by the two nations to the rate of exchange and upon the amount of offsetting expenditure directly induced by the transfer. When a developing nation receives investment funds, it can be expected to spend a large proportion of the investment immediately on capital goods. What remains will leak into income and will quickly be dissipated in imports so that only a small favourable change in the rate of exchange would occur (under a system of freely fluctuating exchange rates). When the repayment is made, there is little likelihood that the developed (recipient) nation will spend much of its newly-acquired funds and in a nation concerned with the preservation of aggregate demand at a given level, the inflow might be completely offset. Thus, changes in the rate of exchange that follow on a transfer will depend almost exclusively upon the sensitivity to the transfer receipt or payment of the import demand of the developing nation. Since import demand will be instigated more by an incoming transfer than it will be reduced by an outgoing transfer, the developing nation will tend to suffer from an asymmetric terms-of-trade effect. The crucial difference lies in the proportion of a transfer receipt that is paid out for directly-induced imports. Any leakage of the remaining funds into imports will be relatively slow and will compete with any tendency of additional income to leak into hoards. When the transfer payment is made, the only force that prevents the rate of exchange from having to take up the whole burden will be any reduction in imports that follows from the reduction in income. This asymmetry will be aggravated when loans are being repaid and foreign investments received at the same time. Suppose a developing nation to be paying off an inter-governmental loan and that, at the same time, direct investment funds are flowing into the developing nation in an equal amount. If the proportion of induced imports is sizeable for the foreign investment and zero for the loan repayment (as seems reasonable), the asymmetry will produce an adverse shift in the terms of trade that would generate zero international saving by the developing nation given the flows on capital account.

Provided that worth-while 'applications' for foreign investments are forthcoming and that no non-economic factors preclude admission of foreign subsidiaries, it would appear that some foreign investments are likely to be valuable to a developing nation at some stage of its growth. Clearly, only projects that satisfy the host's criterion should be considered so that it is a necessary part of development strategy that some control be retained over investment inflows. Enclave industries and extractive investments with small spread effects are unlikely to be approved. Rejection of otherwise desirable foreign investments can be a rational policy when too large a proportion of the nation's capital stock is foreign-owned. Rejection of investment applications or a failure actively to seek foreign investments is rational if there are grounds for believing that the concessions necessary to attract the investments may diminish with time. The *prima facie* case for the advisability of developing nations making use of direct foreign investment does hold but with some reservations. Additionally, the special circumstances that surrounded the success of the Ivorian case of great liberality towards foreign investments in the 1960s may have derived from Ivory Coast's associate membership in the EEC and the once and for all character of the preferences that associate membership implied. It may be concluded then that the only insuperable obstacles to deriving benefit from foreign investments would seem to be non-economic but that the other extreme of a pure *laissez faire* system may not be without danger except in quite particular circumstances.

II

When the host country is a developed nation, the basic characteristics of the relationship between host and investing nation change. First, a larger proportion of investments are likely to be manufacturing subsidiaries in industries that produce differentiated goods and/or goods with a high research-technological content. Investments are quite likely to be two-way flows so that the feasibility of selective control over incoming investments is less easy to impose. The boost to the capital stock in the host nation is less important proportionately. The more intricate workings of economic policy in developed nations may make the whole area of national policy more sensitive to the existence of subsidiary corporations and to impingements upon sovereignty. Finally, the sensitivity of the rate of exchange to a given volume of transfers is likely to be much smaller so that flows of dividends and interest can have much less important effects on the terms of trade of the paying nation.

Just as for developing nations, an inflow of foreign investment into a manufacturing nation matched by international saving on the part of the investing nation will increase the host nation's stock of capital. Ignoring for the time being, the possibility of simultaneous inflows and outflows of private direct investment, the increment to the nation's stock of capital must increase its national product capability at full employment. However, for most developed nations the inflow of foreign investment is likely to be quite small in comparison with the nation's total capital stock[1] and the marginal product of capital will not be inordinately high. The inflow of capital is, in itself, a positive factor but of notably less importance than in a developing nation.

Two qualitative factors may increase the proportionate importance of the foreign capital inflow. Some governments, notably the British government, have desired to steer investments into regions of the country which are relatively depressed and in which the unemployment rate is higher than the national average. New projects are the only investments that can reasonably be considered footloose since expansions to existing capacity are almost inevitably tied to the existing geographic pattern of the firm. Foreign investments frequently are new projects *and* since they require the blessing of the central government are susceptible to 'locational nudging'. Investments in depressed areas can have a social product that exceeds the private return to the capital. The second aspect of foreign investment in manufacturing nations is that the capacity is predominantly invested in fast-growing industries. Thus, in return for the expected high profit rates available in fast-growing businesses, foreign investment may well relieve bottlenecks and consequent inflationary pressure and/or imports in those industries.

For developed nations, technological gains that follow from foreign investment are likely to be more important to the host than the increment to the capital stock. Technological transfer is a complex phenomenon involving several dimensions. First, it is useful to distinguish between efficiency advantages that accrue from proprietary knowledge which is the fruit of previous experience in the industry and/or of research and development expenditures, and managerial advantages that involve a superior level of achievement in managerial arts. Both kinds of knowledge can be transferred internationally and one economy can be superior to another in both aspects.

[1] To take an extreme case (outside of North America), in 1969 investment by U.S. subsidiaries in the United Kingdom amounted to 20 per cent of the national total net investment in manufacturing industry. But this would include both net inflows of funds and retained earnings. If net fixed capital formation were 10 per cent of GNP and the average capital-output ratio were 2·5:1·0, this would suggest that investment by U.S. subsidiaries amounted to less than 1 per cent of the capital stock.

However, technological knowhow is derived from a deliberately undertaken past pattern of expenditures while managerial efficiency is more likely to develop from accepted attitudinal standards within an economy and from peer-group pressures. These two kinds of knowledge advantage will be transmitted by different means and will involve different kinds of techno-logical gaps – they are sometimes referred to separately as the technological and managerial gaps. Secondly, there is gain to be achieved from assimilating as quickly as possible the flow of new knowledge items as they are achieved and become avail-able. Thirdly, there is the possibility that a technological gap will have a 'stock' dimension in that the relatively backward nation will have a backlog of technological knowhow implies that there was a period in which the nation did not keep up with new knowledge items as they became available. This back-log of technology is available to the nation to be absorbed as quickly as the economy is capable of so doing and by whatever means it finds most suitable – foreign investment, licensing or copying. A nation with a stock backlog can grow more quickly than rival nations whose economies have already embodied such technological knowledge as is available to them. This knowledge backlog has been referred to as the advantage of being underdeveloped and could explain, at least in part, the fact that latecomers tend to achieve developed status much more quickly than Great Britain and the other early developers did.[1]

The identification of a 'technological gap' as the source or an important contributor of the relative economic backward-ness of Europe *vis-à-vis* the United States was articulated most forcefully by Jean-Jacques Servan-Schreiber in *The American Challenge*.[2] The argument runs as follows: growth and techno-logy are closely linked so that the countries that lag in the production of technology must have a slower growth rate and must become increasingly 'backward' in relation to countries which generate a great deal of technical knowledge.[3] However,

---

[1] Japan is the clearest example of very fast development.

[2] New York: Atheneum, 1968.

[3] See particularly John H. Dunning, 'Technology, United States Investment and European Economic Growth', *The International Corporation*, ed. Charles P. Kindleberger (Cambridge, Mass.: The M.I.T. Press, 1970) pp. 154–60.

this is a *non sequitur*. It is not the production of technology but the rate at which the knowledge is incorporated into the production process that influences the growth rate. It is true that a nation which does not produce as much technology as it uses will have a debit on international royalty account but that net debit will affect the terms of trade and the rate of exchange rather than the rate of economic growth. It could well be that the resources of the country are so constrained that its top scientific talent is more effectively used in the production aspects of the economy than in its research endeavours.[1] Another possibility is that the nation use its highly-trained personnel for some purpose other than research and import the goods that contain the fruits of the research.

Caves has contended[2] that organisational skill or a managerial gap would be a basis for successful foreign investments by management consulting firms but not by manufacturing concerns. The contention rests on the grounds that a firm with excess managerial talent would use this talent by investing domestically rather than incur the penalties associated with foreign operations. The argument's validity may be less general than is implied. It will apply to firm's considering a horizontal foreign investment based solely on the availability of excess managerial capacity of a higher level of skill than that common to the potential host country. However, a managerial gap can be the motive power for a foreign investment (rather than a long-term contract) in a backward vertically-integrated subsidiary and for a foreign sales subsidiary in preference to an agency marketing organisation. A managerial gap can also give rise to horizontal foreign investment if a takeover of an ongoing foreign business is practicable and if the parent corporation believes that the introduction of higher quality executive talent (from the parent) will rationalise a somewhat inefficient firm. The managerial talent could earn a quasi-rent abroad. It may be inferred that investments (particularly in horizontal takeovers) based on this reasoning may be more prone to failure (i.e. inadequate or substandard profit rates) than those

---

[1] This point was made with reference to the British economy in *Britain's Economic Prospects*, ed. Richard E. Caves (Washington: The Brookings Institution, 1968) p. 15 and pp. 468–71.

[2] *Economica* (Feb 1971) p. 6.

investments motivated by a piece of proprietary knowledge whose return can be estimated with greater exactness and assurance.

A deliberate policy of importing technology would recognise the existence of a comparative disadvantage in the production of knowledge and can be quite rational. There is no reason why the gains from international specialisation and trade cannot derive from the exportation and importation of knowledge just as with any other product.[1] The 'gap' argument of national backwardness requiring the use and production of more technology would seem to be more rational when transformed into an argument for nations not necessarily generating their own knowhow but to make sure that all the potentially profitable parts of the existing body of knowledge are incorporated into their economies. The variant argument would run in terms of minimising a stock backlog of knowledge rather than assuring an equality in the flow of new knowledge. Certainly, the closing of any backlog between the amount of technology embodied in the economy and the amount of technology available globally can have spectacular effects upon the rate of growth. The admission of foreign subsidiaries equipped with proprietary knowledge is one way of reducing a backlog. Using a conceptual framework developed by E. F. Denison, Dunning has shown that the 'change in the lag in the application of knowledge' in eight European countries from 1950 to 1962 is perfectly rank-correlated with the proportionate increase in the United States capital stake in those countries.[2]

It is arguable then that the host country is more likely to benefit from an inflow of direct foreign investment the greater is the stock backlog that exists between its own economy and the level of technology embodied in the foreign investments. The more backward the host, relatively, the greater the probability that foreign investment will prove beneficial. However, the key word in the variant argument is 'profitability' and foreign investments should only be welcomed when they conform to the basic criterion and are preferable to a licensing arrangement if that can be negotiated more cheaply.

It is quite possible that the third aspect of transfer of tech-

---

[1] See Dunning, *The International Corporation*, pp. 157–8.
[2] Ibid., pp. 151–3.

nology – the absorption into the host economy's production base of the flow of newly-generated knowledge – may be more efficiently accomplished through the existence in the host of foreign subsidiaries rather than through licensing arrangements. A foreign subsidiary of a corporation that generates a new piece of knowledge is likely to receive access to that knowledge more quickly than a licensee. The reduction in the delay with which new knowledge can be embodied into the host's economy will derive from the greater awareness and *camaraderie* that will exist between the executives in parent and subsidiary compared to any relationship that exists between licensor and licensee. Other possibly retarding factors will be the decision of the firm making the discovery not to publicise its new knowledge abroad and the greater time required to negotiate a licensing arrangement between corporations that do business at arm's length.

Two other benefits may also derive from the existence of foreign subsidiaries rather than from licensing arrangements: a spillover effect and a cost effect. The spillover effect will involve the spreading of the elements of the higher level of technology of the subsidiary into other parts of the economy. While this possibility could take place from a firm using a higher level of technology through a licensing arrangement, the benefits are likely to be less broad. A foreign subsidiary may purchase inputs from local firms and in the process, pass on to those firms some of its managerial and technological knowhow. Similarly, as employees leave the foreign subsidiary and take new jobs in domestic firms they will take with them into the domestic sector, the managerial skills that they have absorbed (partly through osmosis), the human capital and the technological expertise that they have received through training and experience on the job. The cost effect can most efficiently be described by reference to Figure III–1. If the maximum benefit to a foreign subsidiary from its proprietary knowledge is $a + b$, this is also the potential value of the royalty to be paid under licensing arrangements. When a license is granted, the cost schedule of the domestic entrepreneur shifts downward only if he pays less than the full value of the royalty. If a foreign subsidiary is established, the subsidiary can earn a rent or quasi-rent on its proprietary knowledge of only b. As a second foreign investor establishes a subsidiary also equipped with a knowledge saving of $a + b$,[1] the industry supply curve will shift down and the first subsidiary will no longer command a quasi-rent of b – in fact, the quasi-rent might be eliminated. If a licensing arrangement is negotiated at this point, the cost to a domestic producer will be less than the original rate of $a + b$. If foreign subsidiaries ultimately compete to the point that the quasi-rent almost disappears, the domestic economy will obtain the knowledge for a very small proportion of its original potential cost. If a similar process is carried out purely by licensing arrangements, the cost schedules do not move down because the royalty is a variable cost. Consequently the host economy will not benefit unless its domestic entrepreneurs are able to negotiate progressively lower royalty rates.

The final, potentially beneficial aspect of direct foreign investment is peculiar to host nations that are developed, and derives from the effect exerted upon the industry's market structure in the host country by the new subsidiary. A foreign subsidiary can instigate a wider range of products being made available on the host market because the newcomer subsidiary will not be content to preserve the *status quo* but rather will be determined to disturb it. The new range of products may include only variations on a theme but could also include quite significant alternatives to products available in the host country. In any imperfect market, there is always the danger that rigidity of patterns will develop with respect to both prices and product design and range because all of the firms in the market may be afraid of disturbing a 'comfortable' equilibrium. In addition to being innovatory in products, a new foreign subsidiary is also likely to reduce the oligopolistic quasi-rent which has existed. Caves has suggested that profit rates will be equalised by foreign investments in the same industry in different countries.[2] Host nations will only attract new entrants when the quasi-rents available in their domestic markets are higher than the rate of return in other nations after allowing for the extra costs of doing business abroad. To the extent that Caves' contention is a valid pattern of organisational behaviour,

---

[1] This assumption makes the example easier. It is not assumed that the pieces of proprietary knowledge are identical.

[2] Caves, *Economica* (Feb 1971) pp. 15–17.

the tendency must always be for foreign investments to reduce prices in the host nation.

These considerations exhaust the categories of important sources of benefits to the host nation.[1] The disadvantages or costs of playing host to direct investments from abroad are direct, indirect and subjective.[2] The subjective category is mainly concerned with the preservation of national values and identity and, being non-economic, is only peripheral to the subject matter of this book. Direct costs are monetary outflows or the loss of monetary inflows. These are most easily identified with profits repatriated from the subsidiary and with other dimensions explicitly treated in the host country's investment criterion. The character of foreign investments, in particular their concentration in imperfectly-competitive industries, may tend to cause their profit rates to exceed the profit rate obtained by domestic industry in general. This 'excess' rate of return may be due in part to the return gained on the proprietary knowledge transmitted with the investment, but it is also likely to be a consequence of the quasi-rents that devolve from oligopolistic market structures. While quasi-rents of this kind are clearly an undesirable feature of all industries, the repatriation of the quasi-rents makes them doubly undesirable for foreign subsidiaries. The host government is not impotent in this matter in that anti-trust legislation, enacted and enforced, can reduce the level of quasi-rents.

The main category of costs that will cause discontent with the existence of foreign subsidiaries is the category of indirect costs. These costs are difficult to estimate *ex ante* with any accuracy for inclusion in an investment criterion. Further, it may be difficult and even undesirable for host nations to put any obstacle in the way of foreign investments when the process is a two-way flow. The benefits that accrue from

[1] The possibility of favourable changes in the exchange rate is discussed below.

[2] For a fuller treatment of the costs of direct foreign investment, see Dunning, *The International Corporation*. Dunning, 'Foreign Investments in the United Kingdom', *Foreign Investment: The Experience of Host Countries*, ed. Isaiah A. Litvak and Christopher J. Maule (New York: Praeger Special Studies, 1970) pp. 205–58, Levitt, *Silent Surrender*, and Melville H. Watkins, 'Impact of Foreign Investments: The Canadian-U.S. Case', *Columbia Journal of World Business* (Mar–Apr 1969).

simultaneous inflows and outflows of direct investments and the technology that these investments transmit, may only be achievable in a political climate that encourages the (almost) perfect freedom of movement of capital among developed nations. Equally, the free flow of capital may be almost unavoidable in that refusal by one political entity may merely divert the investment to another political entity that is a part of the same economic entity. This would occur within the European Economic Community when Belgium and the Netherlands actively seek foreign investments and France places greater emphasis on national economic independence and within Canada when one province cannot deter the establishment of a subsidiary without throwing it into the arms of the neighbouring province. The indirect costs derive from externalities. They can include such aspects of economic policy as concern with the competitiveness of small domestic firms *vis-à-vis* large foreign parents, the viability and efficiency of domestic economic policy at both the aggregate or employment level and at the resource allocation level. The indirect costs therefore tend to have a 'nationalist' rather than an 'internationalist' outlook and may overlap with the subjective costs for some people.

One source of error can exist in the estimation of the investment criterion (if it were applicable *ex ante*) when foreign corporations acquire a going concern in the host nation and, in that way, acquire some proprietary knowledge. This knowledge may now be communicated to all branches of the parent organisation without cost. It is possible that the takeover bid may not be adequate to cover both the value of the capacity and the value of the proprietary knowledge.[1] Equally, local research-and-development personnel might be transferred to the parent in the investing country or the research activity otherwise stifled. The original error is the fault of the seller in not obtaining the full value price for his asset. The error can equally well be made by the investing corporation as many investors have discovered to their chagrin. Equally, the takeover of the subsidiary may well expand the research-and-development activities in the host country if the host has a comparative advantage in that area.

[1] See Dunning, 'Technological Transfer', *The International Corporation*, pp. 160–2.

The main indirect costs reflect the broad area of the diminution of sovereignty. In addition to the problems of extraterritoriality,[1] the host's concerns can include the conflict of goals between the host nation and the parent corporation of the subsidiary, the weakening of the effectiveness of domestic economic policies and the possible usurpation of domestic resources that are scarce and in fixed supply by the foreign subsidiary. This latter concern is the developed nation's equivalent to the developing country's concern for any impediments placed in the way of the development of local latent entrepreneurial talent or for the foreign acquisition of rent-earning mineral deposits.

The goals of the parent corporation might conflict with the host government's in the realms of research and development, export performance and tax avoidance. Subsidiaries may not be as positive in their enthusiasm for research and development activities or for export promotion as the host government might wish. The former will be particularly true if the government of the host nation is afflicted with a 'technological gap' mentality. Equally, since the success of a foreign subsidiary can depend vitally upon the amiability of the host government, executives of both the parent and the subsidiary should develop their sensitivities to host nations' economic aims and co-operate with them or, in an extreme case, pander to them. Conflict of interest between host government or nation and the investing corporation is particularly likely to develop in the areas of balance of payments and taxation when the investing corporation is multinational. Multinational corporations achieve some significant portion of their increased efficiency by economising on tax payments by placing different operations in different nations according to the structure of tax regulations. Equally, multinational corporations achieve economies by allocating various elements of production among different countries according to the cost savings.[2] This allocation can take place without any concern for the economy of any particular host.

[1] See above, p. 105.

[2] The two gains can be reconciled by the rate at which goods are sold from one subsidiary to another so that all of the 'profit' accrues to a subsidiary in a nation with a low corporate profits tax. Inter-subsidiary prices are known as transfer prices. See Jack Hirschleifer, 'On the Economics of Transfer Pricing', *Journal of Business* (Apr 1957) pp. 96–108.

Foreign subsidiaries do have better access than domestic firms to foreign international capital markets if their parents are large relative to the domestic firms or are based in a nation with a more efficient capital market. The subsidiary can borrow on the parent's credit rating and in a market in which credit conditions are possibly less stringent. Through this access it becomes possible for foreign subsidiaries to escape from monetary stringency imposed by the host government and thereby to weaken the effectiveness of that policy of tight money. The subsidiaries also gain an advantage over their domestic competitors who may be completely precluded from financing their expansion. Further, to the extent that any import of capital by a subsidiary has to be offset by additional restrictiveness on the part of the central bank, all domestic firms are disadvantaged. Another source of 'unfair' competition between foreign subsidiaries and their domestic competitors is the sheer size of the organisation to which the subsidiary belongs. This is extremely important in financing and very relevant to competition between American subsidiaries in Europe and domestic European firms. For example, Fiat has yearly *sales* of the order of General Motors *profits*.

The last dimension can be either a benefit or a cost to the host nation: the balance of payments effect of a foreign subsidiary. In Chapter II it was assumed that the establishment of a subsidiary would be detrimental to the host's terms of trade *in comparison with the alternative position*. This assumption is true if the growth patterns in both investing and host country are both 'neutral' with respect to trade, but foreign investments can be located in the host in an import-competing sector and provide the host with a bias in production that will cause the terms of trade to improve. Note, however, that there is a slight change in the underlying basis of analysis. The assumption made in Chapter II compared the terms of trade if the investment was made in the host and if the investment was made in the investing country. When the terms of trade of the host country are examined by themselves, the comparison is made between investment in the host and *no* investment. This will be more likely to result in the terms of trade being favourable to the host because no consideration is given to the effect of (foregone) growth in the investing country and to the possibility that the investment might have been made in an export sector in the investing country so that the terms of trade of the host might improve.

The gains from acting as host to foreign investments are clearly visible. With the exception of the balance-of-payments debits of repatriated profits, the costs are less tangible but are very visible to those concerned with economic independence. However, the degree to which economic independence is impaired by foreign investments may derive not from foreign investments as economic phenomena but rather from the distribution of a given stock of assets among investing nations. Investments in a country by the British, Dutch or Germans are only less objectionable than investments by Americans because British, Dutch and German investments are never so pervasive as to give the impression of domination of important sectors of the economy.

APPENDIX IV–A

DIRECT FOREIGN INVESTMENT IN AGRICULTURE

Direct foreign investment in agriculture is similar to investments in mining and to other forms of vertical integration whereby corporations from developed nations sought to acquire control over a factor of production that was not available in the investing country in adequate amounts. Usually, direct investment in agriculture generated a cash crop that was marketed in the investing country. Nearly all of the direct investment in agriculture revolves around non-competitive goods and much of the investment flourished under a colonial system – either an actual colonial system in the Caribbean, or in South and South-east Asia or a form of neocolonialism in Central America. Thus, it was mainly in tropical areas that agricultural investment was direct.

While a great deal of international trade does take place in crops produced in temperate climates, little foreign investment has been involved in the process. One reason for this was that citizens of the investing country frequently settled and farmed the land themselves and became citizens of the exporting nation – as in Canada, New Zealand and Australia. In addition, there was little incentive for large corporations to become involved in direct investments in the temperate countries given the fact that domestic farmers are often protected by governments of importing nations and that agricultural markets in developed nations do not lend themselves to oligopolistic imperfections that would generate quasi-rents.

In tropical countries, direct investment in agriculture is associated with colonial status and therefore is more likely to arouse the passions of nationalism.[1] But the vehicle for direct investment in agriculture is very similar to that which gives developed nations an edge in manufacturing – the vehicle was 'industrial' in the sense that plantations used the managerial knowhow of developed nations.[2] Plantations were used to produce crops by means of highly-specialised, large-scale commercial enterprises that produced a single product. The specialisation and large scale permitted the combination of wage-labour and capital-intensive means of production. The plantation system also required highly-developed managerial skills since the whole operation was rationalised and the inputs of wage labour were tightly scheduled.

The crops that were produced under the plantation system were those that were suited to a capital-intensive manufacturing system. The plantation system had to be more efficient than the competing system of peasant production of cash crops. The root of comparative advantage lay in the access enjoyed by the investors to cheap capital in their domestic capital markets. Most of the crops were 'wood plants' as opposed to grasses. Certainly the gestation period required by tree plants needed the cheap capital whereas grasses could be and were grown by peasants. Another reason for the dominance of 'wood plants' was the ability of temperate agriculture to produce a substitute

---

[1] Note that antipathy to foreign investment in affluent nations is mainly directed toward manufacturing, and in developing nations toward agricultural and extractive investment.

[2] For an analysis of plantations, their industrial features and their impact upon their host countries, see Gunnar Myrdal, *Asian Drama* (New York: Twentieth Century Fund, 1968) pp. 442–50 and 506–10.

for most grasses – particularly the temperate cereal grains.[1] Because of their reliance upon managerial skills and the integration of the production unit with the marketing unit in the investing nation, plantations were *controlled* by foreigners and constituted typical enclave industries in which the production unit was completely export-oriented. Most of the cash received was transmitted back to the investing company in the form of dividends and profits, of savings by planters and managers, in payment for purchases of durable equipment and the luxuries from 'home' that made the expatriate's life so much more enjoyable. There were few spread effects in the host country. The technology was not easily transferable to peasant agriculture and, while the output per acre was very high compared with traditional local agriculture, the wages to native, unskilled labour were low because of the very highly elastic supply of labour.

With the breakdown of colonial empires, plantations became more vulnerable, less profitable and less common. The new independence of the developing nations has induced a large multinational company with an agricultural base to retreat to a less exposed position. Unlike the rapid changeover that took place in some newly-independent nations to the detriment of the quantity and quality of the output of traditional crops, the retreat policy of United Fruit Company has been well thought out and combines the best interests of both the Company and the host nations.[2] United Fruit Company has often been the target of political opposition in the host nations where its operations were enclave industries of perhaps a more thorough type than most of the Asian plantations. The 'Associate Producer Program' involves the sale of plantation acreage to indigenous farmers while retaining a close connection with the new farmer through the arrangement of marketing schedules, transportation schedules and through the provision of financial and technical assistance. The programme clearly benefits the

[1] An exception until the twentieth century was sugar cane – a grass crop grown on plantations. Jute has no close temperate substitute but seems to lend itself to small-scale production.

[2] This passage relies heavily on Thomas E. Sutherland, 'Foreign Trade and Foreign Policy – An Uneasy Coexistence', *Michigan Business Review* (May 1965) pp. 1–11.

Company by reducing its exposure to expropriation and by creating a body of allies in the host nations. At the same time the programme benefits the host nation through the provision of technology, the continued provision of a marketing organisation and through enabling each associate producer to achieve title to the land. The associates are financially responsible for their farms and are required to practice a very exacting type of scientific agriculture.

Finally, there is one recent example in which large-scale agribusiness has been invited into a developing nation in order to provide a showpiece for local farmers to emulate. In Iran, the Dez Irrigation Project encompasses approximately 1,000 square miles of land which is to be irrigated by the harnessing of five Khuzestan rivers. Clearly, the adoption of advanced techniques is important in so new and so large a project in a nation seeking to advance the material standard of living of its people and to improve the lot of the agricultural sector in particular. In order to accelerate the adoption of new techniques and to achieve economies of scale in agricultural production, the vehicle for agricultural development in the Dez Irrigation Project was to be the 'Farm Corporation' – a kind of co-operative-cum-corporate venture in which land owners would have shares in the profits of a farm corporation by which they were also employed. The policy decisions were to be made on a shareholder voting basis. However, even given the idea of large-scale indigenous business, the problems of transportation and marketing (particularly export marketing) required a degree of finesse and training that could hardly be expected to spring spontaneously from the farm corporations. For this reason foreign (American) large-scale agribusiness was introduced to the Dez Irrigation Project. These agribusinesses were incorporated into the overall Project Plan in order that they might apply private capital, management and marketing skills in the development of the Project lands and in farm production. The foreign businesses undertook to level and to prepare mechanically their assigned lands and to employ the latest techniques in seeding, irrigation and harvesting. The agribusiness operators will clearly provide an impetus to production from the lands in order to supply the market potential available in the urban and more prosperous areas of Iran. They will also provide a clear demonstration of new techniques and modern methods to the farm corporations in the Project area. The demonstration of a successful new approach is a good antidote to traditional peasant conservatism in agricultural methods especially when the conservatism is usually based more on a shrewd awareness of the potential cost of a crop failure to the peasant's own welfare rather than on any innate conservatism or unwillingness to enjoy higher levels of output.

CHAPTER V

TWO CASE STUDIES:
CANADA AND PUERTO RICO

No nation or semi-autonomous state has ever found that being geographically situated very close to a much larger and much more powerful state is a comfortable position or an unmixed blessing. The histories of the Austrians, the Finns, the Irish, the Poles and the Vietnamese all testify to the dangers inherent in such a situation. Similarly, in more purely economic terms, metropolises have been able to dominate their hinterlands through the concentration of financial, industrial and market power that the metropolis enjoyed. It is not surprising therefore that when nationality differences and metropolis-hinterland differences reinforce each other, the desirability of the *status quo* is questioned by the hinterland nation.

The equitableness of the distribution of gains from an economic relationship or transaction among the participants is not an area in which economic analysis has been fruitful. There are no objective criteria which can be applied other than those implicit in the criterion put forward in Chapter II, that there should be a global gain in which all participants should share. To analyse more deeply requires that the benefits accruing to one group of participants be weighted more heavily or accorded greater value than those of a second group. Nationalism involves just such an assumption. There is nothing immoral about according different weights to different elements of gain and many would argue that the economics profession has abstained from such a process for too long. The process would negate the claim to the *wertfrei* or value-free scientific status to which the discipline has traditionally aspired.[1]

---

[1] One approach which might combine the value-free aspects with the introduction of income distribution into economic analysis is to be found in Abba P. Lerner's classic work, *The Economics of Control* (New York: Macmillan and Company, 1944) Ch. 3. Lerner argues there that any movement that makes income distribution more equal has a positive external effect and *vice versa*.

Canada was first developed by colonisers from Europe seeking riches by supplying the European metropolis with non-competitive goods obtainable in North America. Over time, Canada grew and evolved from a colony of Great Britain to an independent member of the British Commonwealth enjoying preferential entry into the British market. A new manufacturing metropolis closer to Canada evolved in the late nineteenth and early twentieth centuries and the metropolis-hinterland relationship changed from a semi-political one to an economic one as Canada became a prime supplier of basic materials to American manufacturing industry. In time, large American corporations began to invest in Canada for private reasons in search of profits and internal economies. Currently, a national debate is under way in Canada that concerns the possibly overlarge role that American-controlled firms exert over the Canadian economy and culture. In essence the debate questions whether the mechanism by which the metropolis acquires an 'unfair' share of the gains from the inter-relationship is direct foreign investment.

Puerto Rico has 'commonwealth status' in the United States of America.[1] Thus, to term direct investment in Puerto Rico by corporations based on the mainland United States as 'foreign direct investment' is to take liberties with the word 'foreign'. However, since the commonwealth status accords to Puerto Rico a degree of self-government over internal affairs that exceeds that accorded to the member states and since there can be no doubt that Puerto Ricans do not identify as Americans, investment in Puerto Rico can be seen as 'foreign' by the hosts and lends itself to analysis in terms of direct foreign investment.

The two brief accounts supplied here may put some welcome flesh on the bones supplied in the preceding chapters.

I

CANADA

The concern with the volume of American direct investment in the Canadian economy is not a modern fad. What is new is the

---

[1] For a succinct discussion of the politico-economic history of Puerto Rico, see Rita M. Maldonado, *The Role of the Financial Sector in the Economic Development of Puerto Rico* (Washington, D.C.: F.D.I.C., 1970) Ch. III.

articulateness of its spokesmen and the political breadth of its support. The most quoted authors are Professors Kari Levitt and Melville H. Watkins.[1] Both of these economists are active members of the New Democratic Party and both see public ownership of the means of production in the major industries as desirable. In Europe, they would probably both be members of a socialist party. Opposition to the control of the Canadian economy by giant U.S. corporations by persons with values of this kind is not surprising in the light of the probable overlap between big business and foreign investment. However, the spectrum of support for Canadian economic nationalism is much broader and includes a former Minister of Finance in the government of Lester B. Pearson and members of the Progressive Conservative Party in the major industrial province, Ontario.

Attributing the discontent with direct investment solely to economic variables would be misleading. Canadians have long been concerned with the preservation of Canada's individual cultural heritage and of her national values. At least two thirds of the Canadian population lives within range of American television stations and Americanisation through cultural media predates television. The influence of direct investment is therefore an incremental one which brings with it its own cultural barrage through the use of merchandising techniques evolved in the United States and the adoption of American products in the Canadian market. A further blow to illusions of national identity is the relatively subservient status of Canadian labour unions to the American-based, American-staffed and American-dominated international labour unions.

Finally, the problem is confounded by the history of the Federal Government's continuous encouragement of Canada's role as a host to direct investment and as a supplier of primary materials. Ever since the achievement of dominion status in 1867, the special relationship – first with the United Kingdom and then with the United States – has been either pursued or not opposed by a variety of federal governments.

[1] The main works are Professor Levitt's *Silent Surrender* and Professor Watkins' work as head of a Government of Canada Task Force and the 'Watkins Report' – *Foreign Ownership and the Structure of Canadian Industry: Report of the Task Force on the Structure of Canadian Industry* (Ottawa: Prepared for the Privy Council Office, Queen's Printer, 1968).

There is no doubt that Canadian opposition to foreign direct investment is increasing in response to the publicity given to the matter. Two surveys were conducted in 1969 and 1970 on the question of whether 'American investment in Canada is a "good or bad thing" '. Table V–1 shows that while the absolute importance of other nations' investments may be considerable, the proportionate importance of American investment is sufficient to warrant the rather narrow direction of the surveys. There was a shift in opinion against American investment – from 43 per cent in favour as against 34 per cent opposed in 1969 to 38 per cent in favour as against 41 per cent opposed in 1970.[1]

There is a danger that, at any given time, foreign investment can be looked upon and judged not for what it has accomplished for the host country in the past and its contribution to current levels of output but rather for the monetary and indirect costs which the foreign-owned stock of capital involves at that time. There is also the danger that when passions are aroused, logic weakens. Thirdly, Canadians could tend to forget the not insignificant absolute volume of foreign investment which they have made and to think of foreign investment as a one-way street.[2]

This case study will examine the positive and negative attributes of American and other foreign capital in Canada and the concomitant 'special relationship', confront the hypothesis that foreign investment is a burden because dividend outpayments exceed investment inflows, and will then examine the options open to Canadians if they were able to reach a consensus that investments by American and other foreign corporations should be restrained.

The standard benefits that accrue to Canada are, of course, the benefits that accrue to any host: the addition to the national capital stock, the introduction of technology, and, in Canada's experience, a probable bias toward industries that are producing either export goods or import-substitutes.

[1] J. Alex Murray, 'Guidelines for U.S. Investment in Canada', *Columbia Journal of World Business* (May–Jun 1971) pp. 29–37.

[2] Canadian foreign investment is quite small relative to the volume of investment that Canada hosts – nor does Canada anywhere achieve the same proportionate importance that American capital does in Canada.

An additional and potentially important benefit to Canada from the foreign investment inflow has been the ability of Canada to attract foreign migrants without seriously impairing the capital to labour ratio in Canada (and in consequence, the wage level). This in-migration has helped to expand the Canadian market to a size at which local manufacture of consumer durables achieves nearly all of the available economies of large-scale production. It seems unlikely that Canada would have been able to attract and absorb into the productive economy, the number of new immigrants that she did after World War II without an inflow of capital and direct investment from abroad. The costs are easily seen and are now well publicised. Notable among the costs is the relatively small amount of research and development expenditures carried on in Canada and the preponderance in the existing R & D expenditures of government-instituted research.[1] Implicit in any delineation of this pattern of expenditures as a cost of foreign investment is the assumption that, in the absence of foreign investment, Canada would generate more R & D expenditures – either absolutely or as a proportion of national income. This assumption is not proven. Another major issue is that of extraterritoriality whereby subsidiaries of American firms located in Canada were prohibited from trading with nations with which Canada enjoyed full diplomatic relations.

The great volume of American investment in Canada owes its existence in large part to the absence of impediments of any kind to capital flows between the two nations – perhaps supplemented by impediments to imports of manufactured goods into Canada. This freedom of capital movements is one of the factors which underlies the 'special relationship' that exists between Canada and its neighbour to the south. This special relationship extends far beyond the realm of economics into politics, national defence and almost every facet of life. The freedom of labour to cross national boundaries is another semi-economic dimension of the relationship. However, the benefits derived also involve negative aspects. The beneficial aspects have been special treatment for Canada in restrictive international fiats imposed by the United States upon its trading partners; the tourism proposal of the Johnson Administration

[1] See Levitt, *Silent Surrender*, pp. 130–5.

in 1966 and the Interest Equalisation Tax of the Kennedy Administration in 1963 both exempted Canada. Special regulations govern imports into the United States of minerals from Canada. The 1965 balance of payments policies of the Johnson Administration with their emphasis on repatriation rates of profits by foreign subsidiaries and limitations upon direct investments were applied to Canada only in 1966 – after a delay of one year. Yet another benefit to Canada has been the automotive agreement affording free trade in automobiles and parts between the two nations. This agreement has increased efficiency in Canadian automotive production by lengthening production runs and has also benefited the Canadian balance of payments by approximately a one billion dollar increase on commodity account. This increase has borne fruit for Canadians in the form of improved terms of trade and higher employment rates.

The costs are not negligible. The most spectacular instance and one with profound cultural as well as economic implications, is the special treatment afforded to *Time* and to *Reader's Digest* in the matter of the deductibility from the base used for the computation of the Canadian profits tax of advertising in these two essentially American periodicals. Only these two of all American periodicals enjoy the deductibility privilege. Such is the domination of these two periodicals in Canada that local magazines can be economically viable only with subsidy and *Time* and *Reader's Digest* are, in this way, protected against competition from other U.S. periodicals as well.[1] In effect the Canadian periodical press was sold down the river to benefit the automotive industry since the special treatment to *Time* and to *Reader's Digest* was ceded in the midst of the negotiations of the automotive agreement. Yet another cost is alleged to be the lack of monetary sovereignty that Canada enjoys, but this is a worldwide development. It affects Canada more severely than other nations, because the larger proportionate share of U.S. ownership makes the Canadian balance of payments and rate of saving more susceptible to Washington directives to U.S. foreign subsidiaries on the

[1] A full description of this episode is given in Levitt, *Silent Surrender,* pp. 7–9. The episode is symptomatic of the cause of the new nationalism – it would be funny if it were not so tragic.

required rate of profit repatriation. This is another aspect of extraterritoriality. In fact since the late 1950s all nations have found their ability to make monetary policy more effective has been severely hindered by the internationalisation of the world's capital markets and the greater flows of international capital into and out of national capital markets.

The special relationship is a two-edged sword. Perhaps Canadian governments have grown so accustomed to the costs that they do not heed them. But at least one observer posed the problem squarely in 1961:[1]

> If Canada seriously wishes to resist and retard the process of continental integration, she should refuse to accept such discriminatory treatment when it is offered. . . . If the process is to be halted or retarded, it can only be by the sacrifice of economic advantage. Preferential access to the United States market for raw materials may be a particularly difficult lure to resist, but the preservation of a measure of economic autonomy, if this is what Canadians want, can be achieved only by hard choices of precisely this nature.

Not the least of the fruits of the special relationship and the reason for the predominantly American focus of writings on the role of foreign investment in Canada are the proportionate importance of American investment in Canada – both absolutely and relative to other foreign investment. The data are provided in Table V–1. The overall importance of American investment is the more objectionable because of its concentration in particular key sectors of the Canadian economy – particularly in manufacturing and the extractive industries. Note that non-American foreign investment is proportionately much more important in manufacturing than in the extractive industries and should be a disciplining influence upon American investments with which the subsidiaries compete. (It is unfortunate that the Petroleum and Natural Gas sector is not broken down by stage of activity so that the extractive element could be segregated from the refining and marketing processes.) Such a breakdown would permit a clearer indication of the proportionate dominance of American firms in the extractive

[1] Hugh G. J. Aitken, *American Capital and Canadian Resources* (Cambridge, Mass.: Harvard University Press, 1961) pp. 171–2.

TABLE V-I

Nationality of Control of Selected Canadian Industries

(percentages)

Industry	End of 1954			End of 1959			End of 1963ʳ			End of 1965		
	Canada	U.S.	Other	Canada	U.S.	Other	Canada	U.S.	Other	Canada	U.S.	Other
Manufacturing	49	42	9	43	44	13	40	46	14	42	46	12
Petroleum and Natural Gas	31	67	2	27	67	6	28	61	11	27	58	15
Other Mining and Smelting	49	49	2	39	53	8	41	52	7	38	53	9
Railways	98	2	0	98	2	0	98	2	0	98	2	0
Other Utilities	92	7	1	95	4	1	96	4	0	96	4	0
Merchandising and Construction	91	6	3	91	6	3	88	7	5	Not Available		
Total	72	24	4	68	26	6	66	27	7	66	27	7

Source: Canada, Dominion Bureau of Statistics, *The Canadian Balance of International Payments, 1963, 1964, and 1965 and International Investment Position*, p. 127, and 'DBS Daily', 13 February 1970.
ʳ Revised.

industries. Since extractive industries are more likely to be enclave industries with small spread effects, and since they are also likely to enjoy greater ease of adjustment of the transfer prices at which sales are made to the parent corporation so that overall tax liabilities may be minimised, the proportion of extractive industries under American ownership could be an important policy variable.

The argument that foreign investment can only be beneficial when the capital inflow exceeds repatriated dividends, and its corollary that retained earnings are *Canadian* savings, needs rebuttal.[1] The basic sources of confusion in this argument stem from the failure to treat retained profits by wholly-owned foreign subsidiaries as a current outflow in the international accounts matched by a capital inflow of equal magnitude.[2] If that accounting procedure were adopted, there could be no claim that the profits of foreign subsidiaries were an element of Canadian saving. The retained profits belong to the owner of the equity and if the owner be foreign, then the saving is foreign. Retained earnings are quantitatively more important than capital inflows as a source of the growth of U.S. subsidiaries in Canada and in this way will have contributed to the ability of the Canadian economy to increase output and to welcome immigrants. The fact that foreign subsidiaries tend to reinvest earnings at a rate significantly higher than the national average rate of profit retention by corporations shows that foreign investment is an important contributor to the high rate of saving that Canada enjoys.[3]

Despair over the gloomy prospects of servicing earlier foreign investments for an indefinite period, and perhaps for an eternity, is unwarranted. If a subsidiary is created by capital invested from abroad, the capital yields an output that contributes to the Canadian economy in exactly the same way that domestic capital does. The return to the original foreign capital may be sent out of the country and thereby impose some strain on the nation's balance of payments at the time of repatriation. However, this out-transfer reflects services rendered to the host by

---

[1] The arguments are implicit in Watkins' preface to Levitt's *Silent Surrender*, pp. xii–xiii, and in the text proper, pp. 137–40 and pp. 164–8.

[2] This point was anticipated in Chapter I above.

[3] Levitt, ibid., pp. 137–8.

a foreign factor of production located in Canada. The return to this capital is payable as long as that factor of production is maintained in Canada. There is no more reason to begrudge payment on capital to a foreigner than to a resident of the host nation. Similarly, there is no difference in concept between an infinite period of servicing due to a foreign investment and that due to a holder of a perpetual bond issued by Canadian Pacific. The distress over the prospect of an indefinite return may be aggravated by the ever increasing dollar amounts that are payable on direct investments as a result of inflation and as a result of the increased return on the larger stock of foreign owned capital due to the reinvestment of retained profits. However, to ignore the growth contributions of retained profits is to ignore the principle of compound interest. To complain that profits increase in money value with inflation, is to begrudge the direct investor a constant rate of return in real terms. Finally, there is no question that a current excess of capital inflow over dividend outflow eased any current balance of payments strain on the host nation. But any investment betokens future outflows (unless the project is a failure) and ultimately every debtor nation is likely to have to face up to the fact that the acceptance of foreign capital will ultimately have to be accounted for by a period in which returns paid out are not counterbalanced by any form of inflow. In this, with the possible exception of the rate of return earned, direct investment capital is no different from portfolio investment.

In the event that the Canadian people were able to reach a consensus that foreign capital and investments (particularly American investments) played too large a role in the Canadian economy and were to return to Ottawa a Government committed to reducing that role, the Government would have two quite distinct areas in which it could exercise its mandate. The first area concerns the possibility that the Government would discipline foreign subsidiaries of international corporations so that any practices of those subsidiaries that were not in harmony with the goals of the Canadian economy would be eliminated. The second area would involve the diminution of the importance of foreign-owned capital either absolutely or relative to the stock of domestic capital.

To discipline foreign subsidiaries, the Government would

legislate, and would enforce the resultant legislation, against practices by subsidiary corporations that were not in sympathy with a defined set of Canadian economic goals. Disciplining extant industries can take two basic forms which will vary according to the industry in which the subsidiary operates. It is quite possible that some sectors of the economy in which foreign capital was only lightly represented would not be subject to the discipline (see Table V–1). Extractive industries that have the features of an enclave industry and that sell their products mainly to or through the parent or related foreign corporations would be subject to close supervision of the transfer pricing policy and possibly to special export duties. The policy for manufacturing industries that operate in imperfectly-competitive markets would be to seek to eliminate any quasi-rents that derive from the market structure. The latter form of discipline – competition policy – is easy to theorise about, easy to enact in a parliamentary system and, judging by the lack of success in such matters by other nations, very difficult to enforce effectively. It could be that the momentum of a new Government committed to economic nationalism could achieve some success. One way might be to levy an excess profits tax on industries defined as imperfectly-competitive and to have the rate increase as the degree of market imperfection increased. Unfortunately, the definition of market concentration is not an exact science and would result in widespread injustices and difficulties.[1] However, any antitrust legislation that might be used to restrain oligopolistic practices, need not discriminate by the nationality of the parent concern, and would include Canadian corporations. To the extent that such a policy were successful in reducing the profits of foreign subsidiaries, it would tend to increase Canadian saving (properly defined) and to reduce the dividend outflow – unless foreign subsidiaries reacted to the enforcement of antitrust legislation be repatriating all available profits. Such an outcome would have the indirect effect of increasing the Canadian share of the total stock of capital in Canada.

Control over extractive industries essentially requires that Canadian minerals not be exported at below the market value

[1] See Richard E. Caves, *American Industry: Structure, Conduct and Performance*, 2nd ed. (Englewood Cliffs, N.J.: Prentice-Hall Inc., 1967) Chs. 1 and 2.

of those minerals. There may be an incentive for an international corporation to arrange the prices on intra-corporation (inter-subsidiary) transactions according to the relative profits-tax structures in the different countries. This capability is one of the private advantages enjoyed particularly by multinational corporations that yields no corresponding global social benefit. The possibility that a subsidiary could evade Canadian taxes in that manner is a legitimate concern of Canadians irrespective of the degree of nationalism that they espouse.[1] The area of intra-corporation pricing is a very difficult area to control. One of the main difficulties is there is frequently no market price for 'arm's lengths' transactions against which export prices can be judged. However, there is no reason why an attempt should not be made to estimate an appropriate price and to base the tax liabilities of foreign subsidiaries on that price rather than on the actual price used by the corporation's accountants. Another problem is the fact that a nation's mineral resources are finite. Under ordinary circumstances, this fact is recognised when the assets are purchased in the first place but there is an argument that the right to process these minerals should also be accorded to the host nation. This argument is a purely nationalistic and moral one but the export of unprocessed minerals could be seen by some as the sale of the nation's birthright.[2] This process of exporting crude or minimally-processed minerals could be offset by an export tax that varied with the stage of processing carried out in the host country. In addition to its obvious effect of increasing the incentive of nationally-owned or foreign subsidiaries further to process goods in the country of origin, the export tax could be deliberately used to offset any progressivity in foreign countries in the effective rates of protection levied on raw materials, semi-processed and finished goods.[3] In this way, an export tax could help to preserve for the host country, the employment-

[1] See the quotation, in Levitt, *Silent Surrender*, p. 86, by a former Minister of Revenue of the Province of Quebec.

[2] This applies irrespective of the nationality of the extractive corporation.

[3] For a discussion of this feature of developed nations' tariff structures, see Chapter IV, p. 112, fn. 1, and the related text. Note that the system of export taxes might contravene accepted international practice and might require a reconceptualisation of what constitutes legitimate commercial policy.

and income-producing benefits that accrue to indigenous supplies of mineral resources and other rent-earning factors of production. If the variable costs of further processing were higher in the host than in the investing nation, the export tax would detract from the asset value of the natural resource.

Any serious attempt to inaugurate programmes in either area would require action at the Federal rather than at the Provincial level. International taxes and anti-trust legislation are, by definition, national in scope. No Province could unilaterally impose a screening device on capital inflows and subsidiary expansion without the risk of seeing investments not excluded but merely diverted from its own boundaries into another Province. It is no accident that the geographic centre of Canadian opposition to foreign investment is Ontario – the Province in which the highest volume of foreign investment and the highest *per capita* income are found. The thesis that intensity of opposition to foreign control increases with income and the proportion of foreign control conforms with the argument summarised in Figure II–1.

Measures to increase the relative importance of Canadian-owned firms could involve the screening and possible veto of new investments from abroad and the expansion of capacity by extant subsidiary corporations as well as measures to increase the growth of Canadian firms. In this way the asset value of foreign direct investments would grow but would do so at a slower rate than that of Canadian firms in the different sectors of the economy. A more drastic alternative would be for the Government to attempt to reduce absolutely the volume of foreign-owned capital in Canada. This procedure would require that existing foreign subsidiaries be bought out by Canadian interests – public or private – or that subsidiaries be required to sell equity locally to Canadians up to some percentage of the subsidiaries' capital.[1]

It would be extremely difficult to determine what would constitute reasonable prices for the subsidiaries or for their stock. Many subsidiaries are wholly-owned so that there is no market value of the stock on which to base any decision to

[1] The requirement that some minimum percentage of equity be owned by citizens of the host nation is not unusual. It is not fully successful since citizens will hold stock in tacit agreement with the foreign parent.

purchase. The profitability of a subsidiary is closely intertwined with that of the parent corporation – both from the point of view of the pricing of transfer payments and from the division of gains from internal economies between parent and subsidiary. Finally, the value of a subsidiary depends upon the market conditions under which it operates. If the disciplining of foreign subsidiaries were to be undertaken prior to the nationalisation or the forced sale of equity, the 'fair value' of the subsidiary would be reduced. This poses a nice moral dilemma as to the sequence of actions.

The Government of Pierre Elliott Trudeau took little positive action in its first four years to alter either the profitability of foreign subsidiaries or their rate of growth. This apparent passivity may be natural given the inheritance from the Pearson Government of a brand new automotive agreement that encouraged increased foreign investment in Canada, bound the special relationship with the United States even tighter and deliberately rejected the advice of Aitken that favourable discriminatory treatment be refused when offered.[1] One step which may have a positive effect but which must surely be incapable of stemming the tide unless it is reinforced by supplementary measures (such as a control board), is the establishment of a Canadian Development Corporation. Such a corporation was proposed in 1971 and is designed to assist Canadian entrepreneurs in developing large-scale enterprises without the involvement of international or multinational corporations. Its purpose has been stated to be:[2]

The Corporation will help shape and secure future Canadian development. It will be a large-scale source of capital to create major new enterprises. It will join others in acquiring and rationalising existing companies where competitiveness may be improved by merger, amalgamation or other corporate arrangements. In helping to bring about these changes it will reduce the risks of an undesirable degree of foreign control of the enterprises concerned. Its activity will involve close relationships with the business and financial community.

[1] See p. 141, fn. 1.
[2] *Canadian Weekly Bulletin*, 17 February 1971.

The CDC arrives at a time when large international companies are playing an important and expanding role in the economic development of many countries, and when Canadian companies must be able to compete at home and abroad by combining management and technical skills with financial size and strength.

Able and experienced entrepreneurs will direct the Corporation's operations to areas of critical importance in economic development – to high-technology industry, to resource utilisation, to northern-oriented companies and to industries where Canada has a special competitive advantage.

Another more stringent set of legislation could grow out of the *Herb Gray Report* that was submitted to the Canadian cabinet in the spring of 1971 by a task force appointed about eighteen months earlier to consider the question of the effect of the preponderant role of foreign capital. While the *Report* has not been made public, it was 'leaked' by a Canadian magazine.[1] The *Report* allegedly supports a more interventionist philosophy and approach by government in matters of competition policy, transfer pricing, screening of investments and special safeguards over the integration of Canadian subsidiaries into world-wide planning by truly multinational corporations. The absolute reduction of the volume of foreign investments does not seem to have been considered explicitly. It does not appear that the measures that will ultimately be proposed will be particularly severe.

Abstracting from any effects that the disciplining of foreign subsidiaries might have on their profits, the costs of reducing the volume of foreign-owned capital in Canada can now be considered. Assume first that the Government would set a relatively unpretentious target whereby foreign capital would be permitted to grow absolutely but would be constrained to grow at a slower rate than domestic investment by the private sector. (This could happen without governmental interference if the inflow of foreign capital into Canada including the retained profits of foreign subsidiaries, declined sufficiently.) The cost can be defined in terms of the consumption levels that can be enjoyed by the Canadian people under alternative

[1] *The Canadian Forum* (Dec 1971).

codes of behaviour toward foreign capital. The consumption levels compatible with different policies toward foreign investment are depicted in Figure V–1. Real consumption is measured on the vertical axis and time is measured horizontally. The two

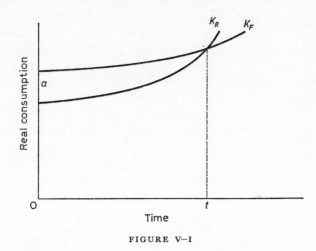

FIGURE V–I

The Cost in Consumption of Reducing Foreign Capital Inflow

schedules show the levels of consumption that can be enjoyed under conditions of full employment under a policy of completely free capital movement, K_F, and under a policy of restraint on the rate of accumulation of foreign capital permitted, K_R. The cost in year O in which the new policy is instituted will be a units of real consumption. There will also be some time, t, at which the two schedules will cross denoting that a policy of restriction on foreign capital will ultimately allow the Canadian people to consume more. The variables in the analysis are the initial cost, a, the length of time taken to achieve consumption parity, Ot, and the curvature of the two schedules. It is assumed that all factors other than those deriving from foreign investment rates, affecting the Canadian economy operate independently of the schedules and that the Canadian economy maintains its levels of aggregate demand so that employment levels will not vary under the two programmes. Under the policy of capital restraint it is necessary for Canadian saving to replace the foreign saving that manifested itself in the precluded international investment, if full employment and the total rate of investment are to be maintained. Thus the level of consumption under K_R will be less than that possible under K_F. The cost of a units of consumption will consist of the increased saving *and* the adverse shift in the terms of trade necessary to offset the effect on the balance of payments of the reduced rate of capital inflow. As the volume of foreign capital in Canada decreased under K_R relative to K_F, the rate of growth of Canadian GNP will increase as progressively smaller amounts of repatriated profits leave the country and the schedule K_R begins to slope up more quickly than K_F. Since the outflow of profits also represents international 'dissaving', the increase in the slope of K_R will benefit from a terms-of-trade effect. The length of time Ot depends upon the original cost, a, and the excess of curvature in K_R over that of K_F. The less pretentious the programme of restraint, the smaller will be a but the smaller also will be the excess of K_R's curvature over K_F's curvature. If the goal were more ambitious and involved a reduction (or zero growth) in the volume of foreign-owned business, the cost could be significantly greater. The rate of indigenous saving would have to increase both to replace the equity of foreign investors *and* to provide (without any influx from abroad) enough investment and other injections to provide the necessary high levels of aggregate demand in Canada. The change in the rate of international saving will also need to be larger and this will reinforce the unfavourable shift in the terms of trade required by the less pretentious programme. The ambitious programme would increase a but would also increase the excess of curvature of K_R over that of K_F.

This analysis, simple though it is, shows that the cost of restraining foreign investment in Canada can be heavy if the programme is ambitious and will become less burdensome as the programme becomes less restrictive. Probably the prime component of the cost would be the change in saving required of the Canadian people. There is no reason in theory why some rough calculations could not be made. The computations could allow for the loss of any proprietary knowledge through the restriction of foreign capital inflows by computing equivalent licensing costs. The analysis also shows the temporal aspects of the problem very clearly. The more ambitious the target, the greater is the burden imposed upon a single generation of Canadian consumers.

One final alternative remains. It is possible for Canada to reduce the volume of foreign *direct* investment in Canada by portfolio borrowing abroad – using the proceeds of bond floatations in the New York or some other capital market to provide the international saving. Since net worth would be unchanged, there would of course be no need to increase the rate of total saving except to replace the normal flow of investment in Canada that comes from capital inflow and subsidiary profit retention. A variant on this scheme would be to require Canadian owners of foreign assets to repatriate them as a source of foreign funds. While these owners would not be happy at such legislation, there is a sufficient volume of Canadian assets abroad to effect some small reduction in foreign ownership in key Canadian industries.

The objections of some Canadians to the preponderant role of foreign subsidiaries in certain sectors of the economy presents what is essentially a domestic, political problem. The economic policy of Canadian Governments since 1867 has been to welcome foreign businesses. In the process, Canadians have achieved a higher standard of living, have had enhanced the difficulties of maintaining an individual culture and have, to some extent, reduced (but have not abrogated) their economic sovereignty. The first question to be decided is whether or not Canadians are willing to pay the costs that a reversal of the historic policies would incur. That is a decision to be reached through the political mechanism. To some degree, the Canadian nationalists could be charged with fostering a 'generation gap' as modern people born to (relative) affluence reject the decisions made by their parents and forebears that contributed to that affluence. Put simply, the desire of the nationalists is to reduce the negative international net worth on direct investment. This is a perfectly reasonable policy but it does not follow that, had the current nationalists been making decisions in the first seventy years of Canadian independence, they would not have made the same decisions. Another possible charge against the nationalists is that they comprise mainly intellectuals who will

pay only a negligible proportion of the cost of reducing economic
dependence. It is the poor, the unemployed and the marginal
workers who are most likely to bear the brunt of any reduction
in the rate of foreign investment in Canada if only because
employment rates are likely to suffer during the period of
transition. Further, if a reduction in the rate of inflow of
foreign investment does damage the poorer sections of the
population disproportionately, the process may well exacerbate
existing political strains in Canada.

II

PUERTO RICO[1]

The purpose of the economic program of the Puerto Rico
Independence Party is not only to attain a high rate of
economic growth but also to insure that the benefits of such
growth are justly distributed among working Puertoricans,
that Puertoricans control the economic decisions of the
country and that dependence upon foreign investment is
terminated insofar as it is possible.[2]

Nationalist feeling finds its most accessible target in foreign
investment and Puerto Rico is no exception to this rule. Most
Puerto Ricans are deeply worried about the negative effects of
foreign investment. At the same time, Puerto Rico continues
to seek 'foreign' investment (mostly from the mainland United
States) in pursuit of the overall development programme and,
indeed, it is this very investment that has been significantly
responsible for the successful development of the Island's
economy in the past twenty years.

Puerto Rico has succeeded in attracting a large inflow of
foreign capital, especially since the end of World War II,
mainly – and ironically – because of the political status of the
island. As a Commonwealth of the United States,[3] it is an

[1] By Rita M. Maldonado, associate professor of economics, Brooklyn
College of the City University of New York.

[2] Taken from the *Economic Program of the Puerto Rican Independence Party*,
1971.

[3] Estado Libre Asociado ('Free Associated State') is the Spanish version
of this singular political status. It is not a Commonwealth in the British
sense of the word. Puerto Rico does not have representation in the United

integral part of the American nation and, as such, its exports to the mainland are free of duties and other restrictions. This advantage has attracted many mainland firms to Puerto Rico to conduct their manufacturing operations and to ship nearly all of the output to the mainland. Because the Island is a part of the United States, migration to and from the mainland is unrestricted – Puerto Ricans are United States citizens – and United States constitutional guarantees of civil and property rights apply. As a consequence, owners of foreign capital have no fear of expropriation of their property nor of any interference with the repatriation of profits.

The Puerto Rico Industrial Development Company (PRIDCO) is an autonomous unit under the Island's Economic Development Administration (EDA). PRIDCO has been the most active agent in soliciting foreign direct investment. It has promoted the attractiveness of Puerto Rico as a favourable industrial location, has supplied governmental financial aid to new firms and has supplied technical assistance for training personnel. Exemptions from local taxes have been granted to eligible firms for specified periods under the Industrial Incentives Act of 1947 – the duration of the exemption varied with the location of the firm. In addition, corporate profits and individual income of residents are exempt from Federal taxes unless the profits or the income are transferred to the mainland since the Island is exempt from Federal tax payments. A final and important source of attraction to locate in the Island – especially during the 1950s – was the prevailing low wage level which was substantially below that on the mainland. To advertise these attractions and to encourage business to come to Puerto Rico, PRIDCO opened industrial promotion offices in key locations on the mainland.

As Table V–2 indicates, 1,809 firms were 'promoted' during the period from 1948 to 1970. Of these firms, 64 per cent were 'foreign': and 36 per cent were 'domestic'. This was a remarkable accomplishment, given that the majority of manufacturing firms had to import most of their raw materials over large distances and had then to export most of their output just as far.

Nations nor can the Island engage in international agreements. It has the benefits accorded to the individual states of the Union although islanders do not have to pay Federal income or corporate taxes.

TABLE V-2

Firms Promoted by Economic Development Administration,
Classified by Origin of Capital, Selected Years, 1948–67

	Total No. Promoted (Cumulative)	Domestic Puerto Rico	Foreign United States	Foreign All Other	Foreign as % of Total
1948	35	7	28	0	80
1950	96	15	79	2	84
1955	328	44	275	9	87
1960	634	112	505	17	82
1965	1,055	260	714	81	75
1967	1,383	416	873	94	70
1968	1,542	486	964	92	68
1969	1,694	572	1,032	90	66
1970	1,809	644	1,075	90	64

Source: Puerto Rico Economic Development Administration, Office of
Economic Research, July 1971.

TABLE V-3

Employment and Income Attributable to Firms Promoted
by EDA, Total Employment and Income in Puerto Rico,
Selected Years, 1950–67

	Total Employment (Jobs) (thousands)	Jobs Created (thousands)	Column (2) as % of Column (1)	Total National Income ($ millions)	Income Generated ($ millions)	Column (5) as % of Column (4)
	(1)	(2)	(3)	(4)	(5)	(6)
1950	596	6·3	1·1	614	3·1	
1955	539	25·7	4·8	960	58·9	6·1
1960	542	44·3	8·2	1,355	155·4	11·5
1965	688	74·4	10·8	2,314	359·9	15·6
1967	684	84·4	12·3	2,789	491·7	17·6
1968	701	108·0	15·4	3,092	572·0	18·5
1969	722	105·2	14·6	3,422	669·2	19·6
1970	738	103·0	13·9	3,821	711·8	18·6

Source: Column (1) Puerto Rico Department of Labor, Bureau of Labor
Statistics. Column (2) Puerto Rico Economic Development Administration,
Office of Economic Research, Statistics Section, 'Working Papers on
Employment and Payroll Statistics of Fomento's Industrialization Program'
Annual Series. Column (4) for the years 1950 and 1955, working papers of
the Bureau of Economic Planning, Planning Board; for the years 1960–70,
Income and Product, 1970, p. 1. Column (5) working papers of the Bureau of
Economic Planning, Planning Board.

The proportion of total income and employment generated by these new firms increased steadily over the post-World War II period. This is shown by Table V–3. In recent years roughly 17 to 20 per cent of national income is attributable to firms promoted by EDA.

TABLE V–4

Gross National Product and Personal Income *per capita*,
Puerto Rico, 1940–70

	Gross National Product (Constant 1954 $ million)	Annual Rate of Change (per cent)	Personal Income (Constant 1954 $ million)	Population (thousands)	Personal Income per capita (Constant 1954 $)	Annual Rate of Change (per cent)
1940	499·3	—	395·7	1,859	218	—
1947	705·3	—	635·5	2,152	295	—
1948	732·3	3·8	643·9	1,175	296	0·3
1949	818·6	11·8	720·7	2,192	329	11·2
1950	878·7	7·3	763·3	2,206	347	5·5
1951	925·0	5·3	800·5	2,227	359	3·5
1952	1,015·9	9·8	875·7	2,231	393	9·5
1953	1,081·3	6·4	923·4	2,216	417	6·1
1954	1,104·4	2·1	951·8	2,209	431	3·4
1955	1,138·5	3·1	994·8	2,232	446	3·5
1956	1,185·7	4·1	1,026·6	2,250	456	2·2
1957	1,221·8	3·0	1,068·6	2,255	474	3·9
1958	1,258·4	3·0	1,087·4	2,280	477	0·6
1959	1,363·9	8·4	1,161·1	2,311	502	5·2
1960	1,475·0	8·1	1,253·8	2,325	539	7·4
1961	1,552·8	5·3	1,362·1	2,351	579	7·4
1962	1,666·1	7·3	1,500·7	2,387	629	8·6
1963	1,798·0	7·9	1,638·8	2,437	672	6·8
1964	1,910·0	6·2	1,764·6	2,485	710	5·9
1965	2,058·8	7·8	1,937·2	2,519	766	7·9
1966	2,220·0	7·8	2,101·2	2,560	821	7·2
1967	2,322·7	4·6	2,192·7	2,571	853	4·0
1968	2,479·0	6·7	2,353·7	2,587	910	6·7
1969	2,629·5	6·1	2,482·3	2,632	943	3·6
1970	2,814·0	7·0	2,660·0	2,677	994	5·4

Source: GNP, Personal Income, Population and Personal Income *per capita* for the years 1940 through 1959 come from working papers of the Bureau of Economic Planning, Puerto Rico Planning Board. For the years 1960 through 1970 the same data was obtained in *Income and Product* 1970, pp. 1, 2 and 3, Puerto Rico Planning Board.

Data on gross national product (GNP) and personal income *per capita* indicate the rapid growth that has taken place on the Island during the period where foreign investment has been actively promoted (see Table V–4). The compound annual rate of growth of GNP during the entire period was 6 per cent. Personal income *per capita* in 1940 was $218, and in 1970 it was $994, both in constant 1954 dollars. This amounts to an annual rate of growth of 5·3 per cent; since 1958 it has averaged 5·9 per cent. No other country in the Caribbean or in Central or South America has experienced as high a rate of growth, nor do any of them invest as high a percentage of their GNP as Puerto Rico does.[1]

Although economic comparisons between countries are seldom useful, it is reasonable to compare Jamaica and Israel with Puerto Rico merely because their geography, their population, and their principal economic activities and their attitudes toward foreign investment are similar. The annual rate of growth of GNP *per capita* for the period 1958–69 has been 0·1 per cent for Israel, 5·7 per cent for Jamaica, and 6·3 per cent for Puerto Rico. Even though Israel and Jamaica have actively promoted foreign investment, neither has been as successful in this endeavour as Puerto Rico, and partly for this reason neither has attained as high a growth ratio of GNP *per capita* as Puerto Rico has.

It should be pointed out that foreign investment is hardly the only reason for Puerto Rico's successful growth in the post-war period. Labour mobility between the Island and the mainland has greatly eased the unemployment problem on the Island, shifting part of it to the mainland. Net migration from Puerto Rico to the mainland amounted to over 800,000 people between 1940 and 1970. Adding to this the children born to Puerto Rican families now on the mainland roughly doubles this figure. Even so, there is still a high rate of unemployment in Puerto Rico: in 1940 it was 15 per cent, in 1970 10·8 per cent.[2] Poverty is evident when one sees about 700,000 people

---

[1] Puerto Rico's gross domestic investment was 20 per cent of GNP in 1960, 26 per cent in 1969, and 30 per cent in 1970. As of 1970 only Japan, Iceland and Norway compare with Puerto Rico in this respect.

[2] These are the official figures published by the Department of Labor. Many economists in the island consider that these figures are understated. The

out of a population of 2·7 million living in slum areas or poor conditions and receiving food from the (U.S. Federal Government) Food Program.

Nevertheless, it is hard to imagine a rate of growth as rapid as Puerto Rico has had and from the low original rate of domestic saving without substantial foreign investment. Over 55 per cent of the total gross domestic investment in Puerto Rico from 1951–70 was financed by external investment, mostly from the U.S. mainland. On the Island itself, personal saving has been negative in virtually every year since 1950. Such saving as is done on the Island is generated by the government and business sectors, and it is these two sectors that have financed that portion of domestic investment not financed by external sources.

While these facts are excellent arguments in support of foreign investment for fast economic growth, they also embody the major argument *against* foreign investment – namely, the loss of economic sovereignty. Two of the most important sectors in the economy – manufacturing and trade – appear to be coming under increasing foreign control. In trade particularly, the trend toward foreign ownership is accelerating, with the establishment on the Island in recent years of branches of almost all U.S. mainland retail chain stores. The tourist sector is largely owned by mainlanders, as are certain types of financial institutions, such as insurance companies and finance companies.

In short, foreign investment has already resulted in considerable loss of domestic control and threatens to result in more so long as a large share of gross domestic investment continues to be financed externally. But without that much foreign investment, Puerto Rico is not likely to be able to maintain anywhere near its pace of economic growth – particularly since recently there has been net migration of Puerto Ricans from the mainland back to the Island.

The Island thus faces a dilemma: foreign investment and a high growth rate but loss of economic sovereignty, or less foreign investment and possible economic stagnation. The pro-statehood elements on the Island tend to favour continued reliance on foreign funds and downgrade the significance of

economists in the Puerto Rican Independence Party quote a figure of 28 per cent as the accurate figure, including unemployment and underemployment. The consensus accurate figure is probably close to 15 per cent.

foreign ownership of assets. On the other hand, the *Independentistas* tend to advocate a sharp reduction in (or the complete elimination of) foreign funds and disregard the potential effects on economic growth. How this conflict can be resolved is the major problem facing Puerto Rico today, and is likely to remain so in the near future.

III

Host countries can and should be masters of their own fate. There is no reason why prospective hosts should not exercise some control over direct foreign investments and choose *not* to accept all or some projects. Many nations do, in fact, exert such powers either overtly or covertly through some planning commission and capital controls board. There is nothing inevitable about a policy of 'open admissions'. Puerto Rico is effectively bound by its commonwealth status to permit free movement of direct investments and other capital in exactly the same way as its people are accorded freedom to migrate to the mainland United States. However, Puerto Rico's history has been one of alluring foreign investment through subsidy and there is no statutory commitment that requires a continuation of such a policy unilaterally.

However, for many countries including both Canada and Puerto Rico, the problem is not one of reserving the operational control of a sufficient proportion of the national stock of capital for indigenous entrepreneurs but whether the existing proportion of foreign control should be reduced. The burden of making such a decision must fall upon the host governments. Electorates in host countries must reach a consensus on their own trade-offs between the prospective material gain and the prospective loss of economic sovereignty – as alluded to in Figure II–1. For nationalists to emphasise the costs of existing foreign subsidiaries while tacitly ignoring the benefits derived from their presence and the material costs of reduction in dependence, is to delude. To fail to consider the problem of the probable distribution of any adjustment costs among elements of the population is to ignore a vital aspect of that cost.

The costs of a cessation of foreign investment would be proportionately less for Canada than for Puerto Rico – as always the greater the wealth, the less the cost!

For Canada an overt policy of reducing the absolute or the proportionate stock of foreign (U.S.) investment results in a reduction in consumption (and income) – the cost being greater, the faster is the planned reduction in the rate of capital inflow. The major cost element may derive from the difficulty that might be expected in maintaining an adequate level of aggregate demand (and employment) during the initial period of adjustment – say during the first five years of the programme. To the extent that these repercussions fall unevenly on different parts of Canada, the policy could exacerbate internal political problems.

A policy worth considering, independently of whether or not there is a widespread willingness to reduce consumption levels in order to reduce Canada's domination in the manufacturing sector by foreign capital, would be to institute a set of policies that would ensure that enclave industries would not be able to avoid Canadian taxes and were disciplined to treat the extractive products as something more than an extraterritorial source of supply for a parent based in another country. Secondly, Canada could institute a screening process for new capital inflows and planned expansion of subsidiaries. The special relationship with the United States would then be renounced and the Canadian dollar kept floating free, to allow international payments and receipts to make their effects felt directly upon the level of Canadian consumption and income.[1] The failure of the Nixon Administration to exempt Canada from the 10 per cent import surcharge in August 1971, may have marked the beginning of the end of the special relationship. The Canadian dollar was not fixed in terms of the United States dollar at that time. Finally, legislation might reasonably be introduced that would require foreign subsidiaries to issue shares in their equity be traded *only on Canadian exchanges*. A large proportion of this stock might reasonably be acquired by an organisation such as the Canadian Development Corporation.

[1] Limitations on the degree to which or the rate at which the exchange rate should be allowed to change may exist. See Robert M. Dunn Jr., *Canada's Experience with Fixed and Flexible Exchange Rates in a North American Capital Market* (Montreal: Canadian-American Committee, 1971) pp. 47–53. Provided there was some awareness of the relation between an adverse shift in the terms of trade and the rate of increase of national net worth, a depreciation of the currency should not cause despair or hurt national pride.

These purchases could be financed by a one per cent increase in personal income tax rates earmarked for this purpose.

In Puerto Rico there is much less freedom of action. The mere fact that personal saving is either negative or only very slightly positive shows the dearth of saving that may be expected to be available domestically as a source of increased capital formation. Add to this, the increase in the labour force consequent upon the reduction of net out-migration and the high birth rate and there is a problem of great magnitude.[1] It is the level of employment of the work force that is the foremost determinant of economic welfare since, when unemployment is high, gains in wage rates can accrue to workers only in imperfect factor markets. Given the current high rate of unemployment in Puerto Rico, there seems to be little hope of reaching a lower level if a policy of severely reducing the rate of U.S. and other foreign investments were to be adopted. There is too the question of the reaction of the United States Government to such a policy by a commonwealth. Given the lack of any strict definition of commonwealth status, the reaction is not known. But, consider the economic repercussions for Puerto Rico if the United States Government were to argue that the failure to permit freedom of movement of one factor of production should be applied generally. In that case, the right of labour to move freely could be eliminated and the right to repatriate to Puerto Rico all of those immigrants on the mainland who had been unemployed for some specified period or were receiving welfare support could be instituted. The repatriation of such numbers as this might involve, particularly in a recession in the United States, could be a large burden on the island's already overloaded economy. Add to that burden, the prospect of a substantial decrease in tourist visits because of strained political relations and the prospect of an economy viable in the short run is small. The reduction of U.S. investment and even independence might be achieved and some might even be willing to pay that price. But the costs would be cataclysmic – particularly upon the first generation.

[1] For an analysis of the inter-relationship between population growth and economic development see *Economic Development and Population Growth: A Conflict ?*, ed. H. Peter Gray and Shanti S. Tangri (Boston: D. C. Heath and Company, 1970).

CHAPTER VI

BALANCE OF PAYMENTS PROBLEMS FROM DIRECT FOREIGN INVESTMENT

The acquisition of real foreign assets by citizens of the investing nation will exchange the national currency for foreign currencies. In this way the process involves the whole national economic unit in the need either to generate a positive rate of international saving or to permit a reduction in the nation's international liquid asset position. When liquid assets have eventually been reduced to some minimum acceptable level, the establishment or the expansion of a foreign subsidiary makes international saving mandatory. The intricacies of the international transfer process and the strains and costs that balance-of-payments considerations can impose upon the residents of the investing country are sufficiently important to warrant a chapter to themselves.

The crux of the matter is that *the balance of payments imposes a monetary constraint upon a national currency*. The acquisition of an asset abroad reduces the liquidity of the nation by paying units of domestic currency to a foreign asset holder. The asset holder will, in turn, exchange the currency for his own national currency. The net worth of the citizens of the investing country has not decreased as a result of the investment but the international liquidity of the national currency (or of the nation) has decreased. An analogy can be made by reducing the size of the economic unit that is making the investment from a nation to an individual. An individual can acquire non-monetary assets either by incurring debt or by drawing down his liquid reserves (in both of these cases there is no change in his net worth), or by purchasing assets out of the proceeds of current saving (net worth increases). It is possible for an individual to acquire liquid assets at a rate faster than he can save – his net worth will increase but his liquidity will simultaneously decrease. The individual will be able to foresee the difficulty of a future shortage of liquidity and can reduce his rate of acquisition of tangible assets (although he could still encounter severe difficulties because of a refusal on the part of any creditors to extend any loans that come due). A nation does not have complete control over the foreign investments of its citizenry in the absence of a very tight system of capital controls. In fact, capital controls are notoriously difficult to enforce equitably and loopholes nearly always exist. Thus, a nation may find itself investing abroad at a rate in excess of current international saving and with no spare liquid reserves on which it can draw.[1] Thus, it may be forced to increase its rate of international saving. The balance of payments costs of direct investment can be traced fundamentally to the costs involved in the international saving itself, and to the costs involved in adjusting to a new rate of saving under various systems of international monetary rules.

The assumption was made above that the transfer of capital from one country to another would be undereffected at constant rates of employment[2] and that the investing country would have to submit to an adverse shift in its net barter terms of trade in order to achieve the requisite increase in international saving. This adverse shift in the terms of trade will represent a cost to the investing nation that is additional to the foregoing of the equivalent domestic investment. This relationship is shown in Figure VI–1. In Figure VI–1A, the relationship between the terms of trade and the rate of international saving is shown. The terms of trade deteriorate as international saving increases in any given period: the angle θ shows the rate of deterioration. The greater is θ, the more costly is it for the nation to increase its international saving. Some of the factors that affect the magnitude of θ are known and can be analysed. Figure VI–1B shows the relationship between the terms of

[1] Another way of making this important point is to point out that an individual's liquidity is defined in terms of domestic currency. A national currency's liquidity is defined in terms of its internationally-acceptable liquid reserves. The latter are always much smaller than the total cash balances of individuals.

[2] See Chapter II, p. 55 above.

trade and real national income under conditions of full employment. Both parts of the Figure rely upon some basic and unchanging set of conditions prevailing in the international sector so that, for example, the terms of trade at zero international saving are given.

However, the mere act of foreign investment will, in time, alter that basic relationship. Thus, the position of the two

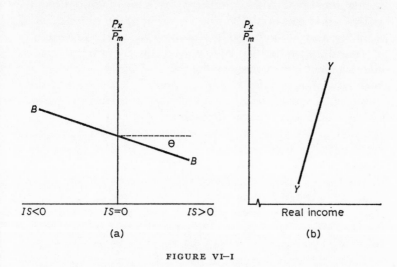

FIGURE VI–I

The Inter-relationship between International Saving, the Terms of Trade and Real Income

schedules in Figure VI–1 will shift from year to year as a result of foreign investment having taken place (including the reinvestment of profits in existing foreign subsidiaries). Figure VI–1 must be interpreted carefully and should *not* be seen as some sort of permanent relationship. The next section of this chapter considers the forces that act upon the magnitude of θ and the forces that influence the size and direction of the year-to-year shifts that will occur, in both *BB* and *YY*. By limiting the analysis to the international forces, domestic forces causing growth and external forces influencing the terms of trade, such as changing tastes and productivity, are eliminated and it is possible to focus on the impact of direct foreign investments – both those that have taken place in the past and that contribute to the nation's positive or negative international net worth and those that are currently taking place.

I

Figure VI–1(A) shows *BB* as having a negative slope indicating that the terms of trade deteriorate as the rate of international saving increases. Although there are some highly technical analyses that cast doubt on this assumption, the technical work is highly abstract and reaches its conclusions at some sacrifice of consideration of the role played by the various size of countries in a two-country model. No real world examples have been advanced in support of these doubts. If *BB* were to slope upwards, a nation wishing to achieve positive international saving would have to cut its expenditures at home to release the saving (this will be done semi-automatically), and then appreciate its currency to avoid running a balance of payments surplus.

The size of θ will be influenced by the use to which the net increase in international assets is put. Assume, temporarily, that the net increase in international assets is allotted to increasing the nation's gold stock. Then the size of θ will vary from country to country, but it will not be easily estimated because so many different factors are involved. These factors include the whole range of sensitivities to both price and income of import demand and supply, export demand and supply, and the rate at which domestic goods not involved in international trade, can be substituted at home for exports or for imports. While *BB* is drawn as a straight line there is no assurance that that is a correct assumption. However, each country will have some value for θ for each absolute amount of international saving: drawing *BB* as a straight line allows θ to be seen as a constant and independent of the volume of international saving that is being achieved. In this way, both exposition and analysis are simplified. For each country θ is determined by factors outside its control (when the international saving is being hoarded as gold) and must be accepted as a given. Call the value of θ when the proceeds of the international saving are put into the gold stock, θ_G. What is important in the study of direct foreign investment is how θ_I (the value of θ when direct foreign investment is taking place) compares with θ_G and what causes the difference. If θ_I is smaller than θ_G, the cost of the foreign direct asset is that much less.

The positive slope of YY reflects the real gain from a favourable shift in the terms of trade and *vice versa*. Like θ, the slope of YY is a complex phenomenon and it depends importantly upon the openness of the country – usually measured by the ratio of production of exports and import-substitutes as a percentage of total output. The ratio of tradable to non-tradable goods (openness) will usually be positively correlated with the size of the country. Another important factor is the ease with which the nation can switch domestic or non-tradable goods for internationally-traded goods both in production and consumption.

Excluding from consideration such unacceptable (and probably ineffective ways) of increasing international saving as the imposition of higher tariffs and/or smaller quotas on imported goods and the deliberate creation of domestic unemployment, there are two ways of generating a surplus on current account. Assuming transfer payments to be given, the rate of international saving depends upon the excess of exports over imports (the balance on goods and services). One way is to reduce the level of money prices in the investing country *relative* to the level in the rest of the world (holding rates of exchange fixed). The second way is to depreciate the currency of the investing country by increasing the number of units of domestic currency needed to buy one unit of foreign currency.[1] These two mechanisms amount to the same things in pragmatic terms since they both reduce the cost of a domestic factor of production in terms of foreign currency and thereby initiate the adverse shift in the terms of trade required to enhance the excess of exports over imports. There are, however, significant real-world differences in the mechanisms. In addition to having different wealth effects in the two countries, a decision to reduce the absolute price level will be a far slower process and

[1] The rate of exchange is defined here as the number of units of domestic currency needed to buy one unit of foreign currency so that an increase in the rate of exchange involves a depreciation of the domestic currency (the investing country's currency). Since the rate of exchange is a ratio, it could be properly expressed in either way.

will be likely to give rise to a far greater social cost of adjustment in terms of unemployment in the investing country. Since
both rising and falling prices are unpopular politically, the
analysis is conducted in terms of changes in the rate of exchange
and money prices in the two countries are assumed not to
change sufficiently to offset the currency depreciation.

In a flexible rate of exchange world, the rate of exchange is
determined in the market by the relative strengths of demand
and supply for the currency. These in turn depend upon the
demands for exports and imports at varying price levels and
upon capital flows. A capital export represents a demand for
foreign currency and will weaken the rate of exchange. The
total impact of a capital export will depend upon the sensitivity
of the market to a change in the rate of exchange (the price)
and on any offsetting forces that the capital export instigates
directly. Suppose, for example, that a capital export of $1
million was destined to set up a small manufacturing plant in a
foreign country. If the capital goods for this factory were
supplied by or through the parent corporation, were exports of
the investing country and were valued at $400,000, then the
foreign exchange market would only have to adjust to generate,
independently of investment-related transactions, a net amount
of international saving of $600,000. This is shown graphically
in Figure VI–2. The two solid schedules show the demand for
foreign exchange (import demand and capital exports) and the
supply of foreign exchange (foreigners' demand for home
exports and foreigners' own capital exports into the home
nation) as functions of the rate of exchange. An additional
capital export of $1 million shifts the demand schedule to the
right by that amount. Any induced increase in the foreign
demand for home exports (including the demand of the newly-
formed foreign subsidiary) will shift the SS schedule to the right.
The new rate of exchange, c, is less than (more favourable than)
that that would have been the ruling rate had no directly-
induced increase in the demand for exports occurred, b. This
latter rate of exchange might apply if the nation were using its
international saving to increase its gold stock. The rate of
exchange, c, is less favourable than that compatible with the
original rate of international saving, a, subsumed in the solid
schedules. The slope of SS is the functional equivalent of θ_G and

the slope of a line connecting the intersection of the two solid schedules to the intersection of the two dotted schedules is the functional equivalent of θ_I.

Given this introduction, the pattern of impact of a single direct investment upon the rate of exchange can now be

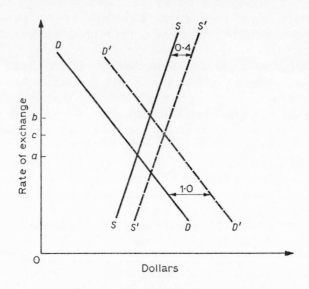

FIGURE VI-2

The Interaction of Capital Outflow and Induced Saving in the
Foreign-Exchange Market

(Note that the rate of exchange is defined such that an
upward movement denotes a depreciation.)

examined. It is assumed that the direct investment is the only influence upon the rate of exchange and that the rate of exchange reacts very quickly to net changes in the flows of credits and debits. Call any induced demand for the exports of the investing country 'induced saving'. Four types of induced saving can usefully be distinguished. (1) the direct exports of goods and services for use in the investment project – presumably predominantly capital goods; (2) the return flow of dividends and interest and other transfers such as royalties and management fees; (3) any increase in the demand for exports of the investing country net of any displacement of exports by local production; and (4) the general effect of any expansionary forces induced in either country by the investment process. Of these only the first category will take place in the same year as the capital export and serve as an offset. The other flows will exert their influences in later years. The first category is, like the capital export itself, a once and for all event. The others are flows that can be expected to continue on for a large number of years – though their total can vary from year to year. Thus, only category (1) will make θ_I smaller than θ_G and the effect of the other categories will be to shift the BB curve upward (in Figure VI–1A) once the foreign subsidiary reaches full production and profitability. The BB curve would tend then, abstracting from further changes in the system, to remain at this new higher level and to fluctuate mildly as the return flow varies over time.

It is important to master the distinction between the first category and the other categories: their effects are quite different.

Two detailed empirical studies have been made of the rates of induced saving that follow from direct foreign investment.[1] The British study provides some interesting data that tend to support the following hypotheses (though in this complex area, nothing can be proven in the full sense of the word). The first category of induced saving varied widely according to the industry involved, the stage of development of the host nation, and the type of investment made – an expansion of an existing subsidiary, a take-over of an existing enterprise or a new venture. Table VI–1 presents some of the Reddaway results. They can presumably be generalised to apply to the exports of other foreign investor nations.

The rate of induced saving as a direct offset to the capital outflow (the cause of any difference between θ_G and θ_I) will very clearly be dependent upon the mix of investment by country and the mix by industry. However, the data in Table

---

[1] W. B. Reddaway and Associates, *Effects of U.K. Direct Investment Overseas: Interim Report* and *Final Report* (Cambridge: Cambridge University Press, 1967 and 1968). G. C. Hufbauer and F. M. Adler, *Overseas Manufacturing Investment and the Balance of Payments* (Washington, D.C.: U.S. Treasury Department, 1968).

VI-1 do need to be interpreted with care since it is quite possible that the variation by industry is heavily influenced by the geographic pattern by industry or that the variation by country is heavily influenced by the industry-mix distribution across countries.

Finally, the distribution by type of subsidiary can have influenced the results given in the first two columns. The rates

TABLE VI–I

Induced Saving Rates (Category 1)
Selected Data
(per cent)

By Industry		*By Host Country*		*By Type of Subsidiary*	
Building Materials, etc.	16	Jamaica	27	New Venture	
Chemicals	15	S. Africa	18		
Textiles	20	Nigeria	39	Yr. 1	13
Food, Drink, Tobacco	7	Malaysia	35	Yr. 2	31
Vehicles and Components	21	Denmark	15	Yr. 3	21
Metals and Metal Products	10	India	20	Total 1–3	21
Electrical Engineering	3	W. Germany	2		
Paper	1	Argentina	14		
Non-electrical Engineering	11	Australia	8	Going Concern	
Total Manufacturing	10	Canada	4		
Mining	6	U.S.A.	1	Yr. 1	2
Plantations	18	Brazil	11	Yr. 2	30
		France	1	Yr. 3	18
		Italy	10	Total 1–3	4

Sources: Reddaway, *Effects of U.K. Direct Investment Overseas,* Tables XIV.1, XVI.1 and Tables XVII.2 and XVII.4 supplemented by additional information by letter. In column 3, Yr. 1 is the sum of data obtained for Yr. 0 and Yr. 1 in the original.

given for later years in column 3 denote the ratios of capital goods exports to additions to book value of the subsidiaries. The first year of a 'going concern' involves very large capital exports with negligible return flows. Going concerns are preponderantly located in developed nations.

Variation by host country and by type of subsidiary is not surprising. The more advanced the host nation, the greater is the likelihood that the new subsidiary will be able to obtain any needed capital goods from local suppliers. Whether or not it does so will depend upon the prices of local and imported goods, reliability and familiarity considerations. In a country in which capital goods are not made locally, it is more probable that goods will be exported from the parent corporation. This probability will be higher if the subsidiary is to be staffed by people from the parent company for its first few years as they will be familiar with the equipment used in the host country and will have new situations enough to cope with. When a new venture is begun, everything has to be supplied so that the potential for exports from the investing country as a proportion of the capital outflow is much greater. In contrast, when a going concern is taken over, there may be need for expansion and new equipment as new product lines are introduced, but the bulk of the capital outflows is devoted to goods previously owned and operated by someone else. The incorporation of new capital equipment in years subsequent to the take-over will explain the higher rates of induced saving for going concerns in years after year 1 (see Table VI–1).

There is a second reason for the majority of going concerns being located in developed countries in addition to the obvious one that there is a greater probability of there being a suitable firm for takeover in a developed nation. One reason for taking over a going concern is to achieve a marketing organisation and an entry into an existing market. The market in less developed nations is itself less rigidly structured and the barriers to entry are that much lower.

Nothing can be said in advance about the cost of a particularly foreign investment to the investing nation except that it will involve either a liquidity cost or a terms-of-trade cost to the nation in the short run. The larger the ratio of capital exports to capital outflow, the smaller will that cost be.

Once the foreign subsidiary is in operation, it still may not have a favourable effect on the rate of exchange of the investing nation. The net value of exports that local production displaces, may exceed the return flows of dividends etc. The question of the continuing effect of an investment on the balance on current account is an extremely complex one to which no sure overall answer can be given. The crucial question is whether the value of exports that would have been made in the absence of the foreign investment project exceeds the value of intermediate goods sold to that subsidiary plus any other return flows. The volume of exports displaced depends upon whether or not some local production would have started in the relevant industry in the host nation even if the particular investment project had not taken place. Since nature abhors a vacuum, the odds are that some aggressive (subjectively-motivated) corporation would have seen the potential available to local manufacture, though not necessarily as quickly. If exports from the investing country would have been supplanted in any case, it is better for the current account that an own-subsidiary be established since that subsidiary will probably tend to purchase inter-mediate goods from its parent corporation.

Neither the flow of intermediate goods nor the flow of dividends and interest will be likely to remain constant over time. When a subsidiary is started up in a foreign country, it is likely at first to rely only minimally on local suppliers – if only because of ignorance.[1] As the subsidiary matures and as it acquires a familiarity with the abilities and limitations of the host economy, it will arrange for local manufacture to displace imports from the investing country if there is a saving to be made in so doing. As the subsidiary changes its product mix and begins to produce new and more sophisticated goods, reliance on home-country imports will again be greater.[2]

Similarly, dividends will not be constant. They are likely to be small in the first few years of operation because only small profits will be made and because of the need to reinvest all available earnings for future expansion. As the operation matures, the dividend flow will become steadier but will be subject to fluctuation because of variation in profit levels and because of variation in the need for locally-generated investment funds.

The total effect of the investment upon net exports of goods and services and of the dividend inflow will shift the *BB* schedule in Figure VI–1A. Any effect of a higher foreign growth rates on the net demand for exports will also shift *BB*. A net increase in the demand for the currency of the investing nation will cause *BB* to shift upward and there will be a concomitant

[1] To the extent that this is true, the reliance on local suppliers will be greater for going concerns and the home country's balance on goods and services will benefit less in the very short run from this aspect.

[2] This is a variation of Vernon's product cycle.

movement upward along YY in Figure VI–1B. The Reddaway study found that, for its sample of investments, BB did shift upward.

II

A single act of direct investment is a useful basis for analysing the various forces that are exerted by it upon a nation's balance of payments. But analysis of national economies is customarily conducted on an aggregative basis with a flow model. Business investment abroad, like domestic investment, will take place every year and can be considered as a flow of investment. Flow analyses of national economies often ignore the influence of any changes in the level of stocks upon the equilibrium over time. This is really not acceptable in analysis of foreign investment since the proportionate increments to the stock of direct foreign assets from year to year can be quite substantial. Just as the one-shot investment considered in the previous section will cause BB to shift when the subsidiary becomes operative, so the aggregate flow approach must allow for the BB schedule to have its own separate existence as a result of changes over time in the stock and composition of foreign assets.

The inter-relationships among flows of direct investments, rates of induced saving and the rate of exchange can be demonstrated relatively easily provided that the variability of the position of the BB schedule is temporarily disregarded, by an equilibrium flow model. This model which is developed in greater detail in Appendix VI–A, shows the degree to which it is necessary for the investing nation to depreciate its currency (or take substitute actions) to generate the necessary surplus on current account.[1] The current account surplus consists of two kinds of international saving – feedback or induced saving S_F that is directly traceable to the direct investment and autonomous saving S_C that is achieved as a result of the competitiveness of the nation's international trading position. The flow of autonomous saving is generated by the nation reducing its own rate of absorption and by accepting less favourable terms of

[1] The model is developed in detail in my *An Aggregate Theory of International Payments Adjustment* (forthcoming).

trade than it would otherwise need to. Define the leakage from direct investments as the value of the investments less the absolute value of induced saving. The condition for equilibrium is that

$$S_C = I_I(1 - b) \quad \text{where} \quad b = S_F/I_I$$

Clearly, the larger is b, the smaller is the adverse movement of the terms of trade necessary for the requisite saving to be achieved. Equally, the more sensitive international autonomous saving is to the rate of exchange, the smaller the adverse shift in the terms of trade required per unit of investment leakage.

The applicability of such a model depends directly upon the constancy of the flows of investment and of the two types of international saving from year to year. Thus, any variability in these flows is important since it will involve frequent changes in the rate of exchange needed to generate payments balance. Most aggregate analyses of flow models rely upon individual aggregate component flows comprising a very large number of separate transactions so that the 'average transaction' is a reliable concept. The functional relationship between the average transactions and other ingredients in the model can then be considered unlikely to vary greatly. This is the essence of the belief in the comparative reliability of the consumption function in income-expenditure models. Unfortunately for analyses of models of international investments, the 'law of large numbers' is hardly applicable because of the relatively small number of decisions and projects included in the flow of direct investment in any one year. The flow of direct foreign investment hinges upon so many variables – each of which is likely to be different in different countries and for different types of subsidiary organisation – that there is no reason to expect that the flow of international investment not to change from year to year.[1] In addition, the wide variety of alternative forms of foreign subsidiaries will also imply that both the rates of induced saving and the flows of continuing saving can vary quite substantially from year to year and from project to project.

[1] This argument is developed formally in J. David Richardson, 'Theoretical Considerations in the Analysis of Direct Foreign Investment', *Western Economic Journal* (Mar 1971) pp. 87–98.

To examine the influence of foreign investment upon the balance of payments over time, the probable variability in rates of direct investment outflows and in rates of induced saving can be temporarily ignored. Assume a constant volume of capital exports and a constant rate of induced saving in the same year as well as continuing saving of a constant balance of payments effect per unit of international net worth per annum. If the outflow is constant, the return flow (and autonomous saving) will increase each year. Ultimately, proceeds from foreign investment will exceed the annual capital outflow. When this occurs, the creditor (investing) nation will have to adjust its thinking from the mentality of a transferor to that of a transferee. This concept is the *flow* equivalent of moving from a debtor to a creditor status or from an immature to a mature creditor.

Figure VI–3 shows the way in which a steady outflow of

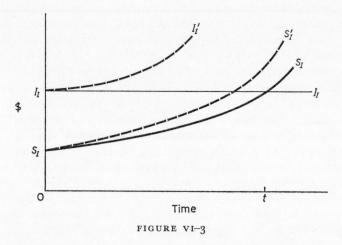

FIGURE VI–3

Direct Foreign Investments and Payments Deficits

foreign investments will affect the nation's balance of payments over time. In year O, the nation has direct foreign investment of OI_I and international saving of OS_I. There is a deficit on basic balance of $(I_I - S_I)$. It is assumed that this is financed by a reduction of non-interest bearing assets (such as gold) by the investing nation. Over time, the flow of investment remains constant but international saving increases, without any change

in the rate of exchange or any other influence affecting the rate
of international saving, as a result of the growth in the nation's
international net worth and its stock of international income-
generating assets. The maximum loss of liquid assets is shown
by the *area* between the two solid lines and the vertical axis. In
year *t* balance is achieved between international saving and
international investment. Thereafter, the problem for the
investing nation is one of the disposal of a balance of payments
surplus. This will not be a serious problem at first as the stock
of internationally-acceptable liquid assets will have been
seriously depleted and will stand in need of replenishment.
Once the stock has been brought up to the desired level, some
disposal of the surplus must then be made – if only because the
accumulation of assets beyond need reduces the standard of
living available to the people in the investing (creditor)
economy. However, if the rate of direct investment grows over
time (as shown by the dotted line I_I'), the flow of international
saving could lag behind the outflow for a very long period of
time even after allowance has been made for the consequently
steeper slope of the saving schedule (as shown by S_I'). Were the
direct investments to be financed by the national monetary
authority financing debt on long-term from foreign central
banks, the rate of increase of international saving would
decrease. For a nation whose liquid reserves are not sufficient
to finance the series of deficits, some corrective action would be
mandatory.[1]

It is worth a small digression at this point to consider the
effect of international saving upon the average consumer or the
'man in the street'. Any act of international saving will shift
the terms of trade adversely to the investing nation during the
period in which the saving is made – assuming a fully-employed
world with flexible exchange rates. If the domestic saving is
made by the investors themselves, the man in the street will
only experience the terms-of-trade effect in the form of higher
prices for imported goods – as in all analyses of direct investment, the actual situation must be compared with an alternative

---

[1] It is possible to contend that the United States did attempt to finance
her foreign investment in this way but underestimated the slope of I_I and
overestimated the slope of S_I – in addition to misconstruing competitive
trends.

position and the assumption is made here that the international saving would have resulted in increased domestic investment in the same amount. However, the average consumer will also have inherited from the past a positive international net worth which will have the opposite effect of appreciating the currency of the investing nation. Compared with a position of zero international net worth and zero international saving, the consumer will be better off if the repatriated dividends exceed the outflow of new investments. But, given the international net worth position that he has inherited, he would always be better off in the short run if he enjoyed the income from foreign investments without currently contributing anything to the international net worth. The domestic analogy is obvious.

There are four possible means at the disposal of the government of an investing country to bring international saving into equality with planned (desired) international investments in a world which precludes changes in the par values of currencies. This fixity of par values applied to the U.S. dollar except for minor infrequent revaluations by foreign nations until the strain proved too great in August 1971, when President Nixon stopped convertibility of the dollar and, effectively, set it free to find its own value in an unsupported foreign exchange market.[1] Following the Smithsonian Agreement in December of that same year, a new set of parities was created and the same set of problems can recur in the future. The problem of inequality of international saving and international investment can apply in any system other than one of perfectly flexible rates of exchange. Under the latter system, the foreign exchange markets would always clear as a result of private transactions at some rate of exchange between the two currencies. One of the problems of such a system is that there might be short-lived but large swings in rates of exchange that would be very disruptive of international commerce in goods and services and, by extension, for domestic plans for investment in industries producing internationally-tradable goods. While this possibility does exist, there is no assurance that rates of exchange would be subject to wide swings in a world in which sensible macro-

[1] See Lawrence B. Krause, *Sequel to Bretton Woods* (Washington: The Brookings Institution, 1971) Ch. 1 for a succinct description of both Nixon's policy and its implications.

stabilisation policies were followed. It may well be that any instability in exchange rates which did eventuate might be caused by fluctuations in the rate of investment or in the rate of feedback saving, rather than to destabilising speculation in currency markets.

Because both the numerator of dividends and the denominator of foreign assets are both expressed in foreign currency, the rate of return on foreign assets will be relatively unaffected by changes in rates of exchange. Thus, while investment projects may be influenced by the expected trend of the exchange rate and its impact upon the industry concerned, the decision to invest or not to invest will not be affected seriously by short-lived changes in the rate of exchange. However, the timing of the actual purchase of foreign exchange will be sensitive to variations in the exchange rate. Because the volume of planned foreign investment is unlikely to be sensitive to the exchange rate, any system of exchange-rate flexibility will tend to adjust the rate of international saving to the rate of planned direct investment rather than the reverse.

The four methods are:

(1) Finance the outflow of capital.
(2) Increase international saving by domestic deflation.
(3) Increase international saving by imposing restrictions on current-account goods.
(4) Decrease foreign investment by controls and taxes.

(1) Financing the outflow of foreign investment by drawing down the liquid and monetary reserves of the investing nation is the least painful means of all for the investing country. Unfortunately, it tends to deprive the host country of one of the main advantages of hosting foreign investments. Resource transfers that are financed do not involve a transfer of real capital and the host does not gain a net increment to its capital stock but ends up with an altered mix. The concept of financing a balance of payments deficit is normally thought of as involving a reduction in the liquid reserves of the authorities. There is another way of financing foreign investment. This method involves forcing the investing *corporation* to borrow more abroad and to export less funds from the investing country. In this way the money outflow is reduced without diminishing the volume

of foreign assets under the control of the investing nation's corporations. This shifting of the burden of financing could be accomplished by interest rate policies or by the imposition of disincentives or controls over capital exports. This policy could be countered by the banking systems in the host nations.[1]

(2) Deflation (deliberate creation of unemployment domestically) will increase international saving by an extremely costly means although there is some suggestion that concern for the balance-of-payments deficit did lead to a deliberate slowing up of the American economy in the last years of the Eisenhower Administration. Normally a deliberate policy of domestic deflation will improve the balance on current account (increase international saving) by reducing the volume of current imports. When incomes fall in a recession, total spending is reduced and, with it, the import content of the decrease in total spending. In addition to the inefficiency of the solution from a point of view of domestic economic goals, there is a danger that the increase in international saving will be transitory if other nations are themselves led into recession and reduce their purchases of the investing country's exports in consequence.

A second possible means by which a recession can increase international saving is by its effect on the domestic price level. If the recession either reduces *or* slows the rate of advance of the level of money prices, this is tantamount to a depreciation of the domestic currency. However, a relative advantage can only be achieved if the other nations offset any deflationary effects that are transmitted to their own price levels. Finally, if the subjective theory of foreign investment is valid, lower domestic profits would reduce the funds available for investment abroad by domestic corporations.

(3) Increasing international saving by the imposition of restrictions has been carried out by the Johnson Administration's controls placed on the amount of profits of foreign subsidiaries that were to be repatriated. This measure was tied in with a system whereby the volume of capital exports was also limited. The requirement that foreign subsidiaries remit some given percentage of their profits (at a minimum) was a feature of extraterritoriality that stirred great resentment in some countries.

[1] To simplify exposition, it has been assumed that the deficit equals capital outflow.

Tariffs, quotas and voluntary restrictions on imports, taxes or restrictions on foreign travel are all means by which international saving can be increased. These measures all suffer from the weakness that they may be offset by retaliation.

(4) Decreasing the outflow of foreign investments by means of controls and taxes is relatively common in Europe but unknown until recently in the United States.

Decreasing the rate of outflow of foreign investment must involve some bureaucratic supervision of international capital flows and will include portfolio as well as direct investments. Presumably, too, governmental loans will be made more selectively but since these are politically motivated, they will be only marginally affected by balance-of-payments considerations. Normally it would seem to be in the best interests of the investing nation, if it decides upon a policy of foreign-investment controls, to restrict most severely those investments that have the lowest rate of induced saving. Portfolio investments are likely to have a lower rate of induced saving than direct investments and they are likely to be more easily reduced by some objective mechanism such as a tax. The U.S. Interest Equalisation Tax in 1963 was designed expressly to make the transfer of portfolio investment abroad less attractive and to make the floating of foreign bonds on the New York market more costly.

Controls over direct capital investments were instituted in 1965 and were tightened progressively during the balance of the Johnson Administration. These measures were combined with required rates of profit repatriation from existing subsidiaries in developed nations.[1] To the extent that the controls were successful, they had the unfortunate side effects of precluding, presumably, some extremely profitable ventures, of severely stunting the growth of some immature subsidiaries that were in need of large capital transfers and they may have led to corporations using their total allotment (based on their 1962–64 investment record) irrespective of the needs of their subsidiaries.[2]

[1] Excepting developing countries did have the virtue of discriminating against areas with lower (category 1) rates of induced saving.

[2] This is yet another example of the advantages available to a multinational corporation. It has more freedom of choice in allocating its funds and a better chance of escaping control all together by allowing a subsidiary to have its own subsidiaries.

The prospect that capital controls can impair the establishment or the development of a country's corporations' subsidiaries does show a clear advantage to a nation in having a strong currency. A strong currency is one that tends to generate a surplus on the balance of payments, usually consisting of international saving exceeding positive international investment. If a country has a weak currency, some degree of discouragement of direct foreign investment will be maintained. If, as seems reasonable, there is an advantage in being able to invest abroad without let or hindrance, then corporations based in a country with a strong currency have a competitive edge. Given that competition to establish a market position in a differentiated goods market can be severe and that being first will enable the subsidiary to establish a leadership position in the market, the advantage of a strong currency is clear. It also offers a degree of protection to indigenous firms against entry by foreign competitors. It could be that this same degree of protection could be achieved by political influence exerted by the domestic oligopoly against entry by foreign firms through a Capital Control Board. However, such devices are rarely inconspicuous and can lead to retaliation. The advantages accruing to a strong currency may explain the traditional unwillingness of surplus nations to revalue their currencies upward.[1]

The balance of payments adjustment problems resulting from foreign investment flows can now be summarised. The solution is not a tidy one that fits comfortably into an equilibrium frame of reference on which economists are used to relying. Taking as the datum (see Appendix VI–A) for balanced payments, that rate of exchange that will bring international saving and international investment into equality, there are three factors which are likely to cause the 'target' rate of exchange to vary from year to year. These are: fluctuations in the volume of international investment; variation in the proportionate amount of induced saving; and changes in the

---

[1] Other reasons are the boost undervaluation gives to job creation and the adjustment problems involved in reducing production in certain basic exporting industries. Strangely enough, appreciation does not seem to give as large a boost to national egos as depreciation seems to constitute a reason for embarrassment.

amount of autonomous international saving that will occur from year to year as a result of changes in the returns from previously-made foreign investments. If the gap between investment and saving is narrowing at the going rate of exchange and if reserves are considered adequate, the investment may be financed. This is the example pictured by the solid lines in Figure VI–3. Financing is also possible if saving and investment alternate fairly frequently as to which is the greater so that payments will be more or less balanced over a period of years. Financing will not be adequate if the fluctuations in the 'target' rate of exchange are wide or if the changes in the target rate are consistently in one dimension (the latter case being illustrated by the dotted lines in Figure VI–3). There is then a serious policy question as to whether the volume of saving should be brought into equality with the volume of investment through, say, exchange depreciation, or whether the volume of investment should be brought into equality with the volume of saving through capital controls. It is worth noting that there is no such thing as a 'correct' rate of foreign investment. In the absence of capital controls, the market will determine as well as any other agency, how much foreign investment is socially desirable. Freedom to export capital from rich to less rich nations seems intuitively desirable from a global standpoint, provided that the potential host nations are willing to receive the direct investment. This philosophy would thrust upon the rich nations the task of achieving (subject to minimising any strains of over-rapid adjustment) the level of international saving required of them by the combination of investment potential and the willingness of hosts to accept the investments.

III

Since the freedom of U.S. business to invest abroad has been curtailed because of balance of payments and liquidity pressures, the corporate sector and its spokesmen have been at some pains to stress its members' divine right to export capital as they see fit. In essence, these arguments are that international saving should adjust so that planned foreign direct investments can be made. However, the arguments have never given support to the most reliable method of achieving the flexibility that would enable international saving to adjust but rather they have taken positions (1) that direct investments generate a return and that business should be free to dispose of that return, and (2) that direct investments yield a return so that corporations should be encouraged to invest in order that the return will be greater.

(1) The argument that business has some natural right to dispose of repatriated dividends and royalties takes the form of putting into juxtaposition the outflow of foreign investments and the proceeds of past foreign investment. One example of this practice is taken from a publication of the American Bankers Association and is reproduced in Table VI–2.[1]

The danger of this practice is easily apparent. Juxtaposition implies an element of immediate causality, i.e. between *current* investments and *current* returns. The immediacy of the relationship is unjustified since there is always a time lag between foreign investment and profit repatriation – even when the investment involves the expansion of an existing subsidiary.

(2) The covering letter from the United States Council of the International Chamber of Commerce to President Johnson over a Council statement on balance of payments problems and policies,[2] argued that the Voluntary Restraint Program then in force was inimical to the longer term balance-of-payments position. Greater freedom for business to invest was desirable – 'To permit the private sector to make its fullest contribution . . ., we respectfully urge that attention be focused on means by which the earnings from our foreign investments can be expanded.' The disregard of the time element still existed in

[1] An economist of the International Economic Policy Association made the following statement before a congressional committee: 'Direct investment has increasingly served as the scapegoat in the search for balance-of-payments improvement. The error of this can readily be seen from Table 7 and Chart 7, which not only show consistent excesses of inflows from income, royalties and fees over capital outflows but also the growth in the size of that excess.' See U.S. Senate, Subcommittee of the Committee on Banking and Currency, *Hearings on Balance of Payments – 1965*, Part 1, 89th Cong., 1st Sess., p. 491. A similar procedure is followed in a booklet, *U.S. Direct Investments and the Balance of Payments*, published by the International Chamber of Commerce and reprinted in U.S. House of Representatives, Committee on Ways and Means, *Hearings on Interest Equalization Tax Extension Act of 1967*, 90th Congress, 1st Session, pp. 68–78.

[2] Submitted 20 June 1967.

1970 when business and administration spokesmen were complaining in one breath of the large bilateral U.S. deficit with Japan, the large overall deficit and the desirability of Japan reducing its barriers to U.S. foreign investments in Japan. The generally evident, vague faith that international investment can come without international saving is startlingly optimistic.

TABLE VI–2

Direct Foreign Investment Outflows and Inflows from
Royalties and Fees and Repatriated Earnings, 1946–70

(millions of dollars)

	Direct Foreign Investment Outflows	*Repatriated Earnings*	*Royalties and Fees*	*Net Balance*
1946	$230	$589	$64	$423
1947	749	869	77	197
1948	721	1,064	83	426
1949	660	1,112	100	552
1950	621	1,294	126	779
1951	508	1,492	129	1,133
1952	852	1,419	130	697
1953	735	1,442	128	835
1954	667	1,725	136	1,194
1955	823	1,912	158	1,247
1956	1,951	2,171	229	449
1957	2,442	2,249	238	45
1958	1,181	2,121	246	1,186
1959	1,372	2,228	348	1,204
1960	1,694	2,355	403	1,064
1961	1,599	2,768	463	1,632
1962	1,654	3,044	580	1,970
1963	1,976	3,129	660	1,813
1964	2,435	3,674	765	1,995
1965	3,418	3,963	924	1,469
1966	3,543	4,045	1,045	1,547
1967	3,026	4,445	1,126	2,545
1968	3,209	4,973	1,546	3,310
1969	3,254	5,658	1,682	4,086
1970	4,445	6,025	1,880	3,460

Source: American Bankers Association, *The Cost of World Leadership* (New York, 1968) Table 42, p. 210. See also the relevant text on p. 209. Data were derived from Department of Commerce sources. Data for the last three years were added from the *Survey of Current Business* (June 1971).

Any programme of capital controls must presuppose some constraint upon the rate of international saving and liquidity reduction that are jointly possible. Therefore the task of capital controls is to reduce planned direct foreign investment to available international saving by eliminating the least desirable or least socially beneficial foreign investments. While in the international sector, this elimination has to be done by mechanistic formulas or by bureaucratic assessment, the process is essentially similar to that carried out by monetary policy when planned domestic investment exceeds the resources society makes domestically available for that purpose.

To argue for perfect freedom for foreign investment while acknowledging the need for a rationing device for domestic investment when planned domestic investment would push aggregate demand beyond its full-employment potential, is inconsistent. It may be that the surplus U.S. international liquidity position of the 1950s and the key currency position of the U.S. dollar in the 1960s deluded businessmen into the belief that there was always a fund of liquidity to supplement international saving. Unfortunately, any stock of international liquidity will ultimately prove to be finite.[1]

To argue for perfect freedom to invest abroad in order that international saving will ultimately be generated ignores the problem of financing. However, it does raise one point that is usually overlooked by proponents of capital control systems: an investment may not be 'paid off' within the year of investment but what matters is whether an investment will repatriate funds on balance by the time that the balance-of-payments deficit will have been eliminated. This is the crucial time dimension.

The corporate sector does not seem to have pleaded its case optimally. Provided that the host country condones the establishment of a foreign subsidiary or its expansion, business can make a good and positive argument for freedom to invest abroad. Foreign investments do help to raise the standard of living in the host nation and it is natural and inevitable that the United States should be an exporter of capital. Private direct

[1] As noted above, if capital exports are subject to surges only a perfectly flexible system of exchange rates will accomplish the necessary monetary balance – at some possibly large cost in the disruption of commodity markets.

investment is one of the main channels through which this can be accomplished.[1] Thus, an argument against controls over direct investments would be better if it were not couched in terms of offsets and ultimate return flows, if only because a weak or inexact argument tends to weaken the force of the legitimate arguments that can be made. It would be better to stress the global force for good that direct investment can serve and to recognise the international saving constraint as a fact. Then, arguments could be made in favour of means that would enable the constraint to adjust to the planned volume of investment rather than having the flow of investment conform to some immutable and artificial ratio.

DIRECT FOREIGN INVESTMENTS AND PAYMENTS BALANCE

This appendix presents a simple flow model which will delineate the inter-relationships of the flow of direct investment, the rate of induced saving, and the rate of exchange. Employment effects and changes in the flow of transfer payments that derive from increases in international net worth are added to the simple model. The analysis is, of course, subject to all the *caveats* about year-to-year variations in the individual flows and there is, therefore, no implication that any value of a policy instrument that is applicable for one year will also be the suitable value for any subsequent year.

For simplicity, it is assumed that there are no net monetary flows other than those required to fill any gap between actual

[1] It might be argued that foreign investment would help developing nations but that it is more likely to go to Canada or to E.E.C. nations. There is a growing trend in the location of manufacturing plants in developing nations (see the quotation from Mr Paul Jennings in Chapter VII, p. 201, below), and consider the possibility that it is the receipt of direct investment from the United States, *inter alia*, that enables France and other European countries to invest in developing nations with which they have close economic and cultural ties.

international investment and actual international saving. It is also assumed that there are no portfolio investments and no transfer payments other than dividends and interest receipts that derive from earlier investments. (These assumptions do not prevent the analysis from holding if such flows existed but were constant from year to year and were independent of the variables included in the model.)

Freedom to invest abroad is obtainable when actual international saving is equal to or exceeds planned direct foreign investment. The desires of corporations to acquire foreign assets are assumed to be given and are thereby assumed to be independent of any variables included in the model – particularly of the rate of exchange and the level of national income. The purpose of the model is to show the factors that bear on international saving S_I and therefore to determine the conditions and/or policies necessary for planned direct foreign investment to be realised without diminution of the national stocks of reserves.

International saving is the sum of autonomous current international saving S_C which includes dividends and the effects on trade flows of earlier direct investments, and of induced or feedback saving S_F. Induced saving is assumed equal to some proportion b of the flow of direct foreign investment I_I.

$$S_F = bI_I \qquad (0 < b < 1) \qquad (1)$$

Let there be some rate of exchange of the currency of the investing country at which payments would be balanced in the absence of any direct foreign investment. Call that rate of exchange, r_0. Assuming that absolute price levels do not change in either country except for any repercussions from changes in the rate of exchange and that these are not sufficient to counteract any change in the rate of exchange, then r_0 is that rate of exchange that corresponds to the terms of trade at which the BB schedule cuts the vertical axis in Figure VI–1A. There is also some actual rate of exchange prevailing in the world – call that r_P. Full employment is assumed in both countries.

The condition necessary for adequate international saving is:

$$I_I = S_I = (S_C + S_F) \qquad (2)$$

Autonomous saving is determined by the sensitivity of international saving to depreciation and to the difference between r_P and r_0. Thus

$$S_I = A(r_P - r_0) + b(I_I) \tag{3}$$

where A measures the change in the current balance in units of foreign currency per unit change in r_P. Both A and b are taken to be given. Setting $S_I = I_I$,

$$S_I \cdot (1 - b) = A \cdot (r_P - r_0) \tag{4}$$

$$S_I = \frac{1}{1 - b} \cdot [A(r_P - r_0)] \tag{4A}$$

The larger is the expression $A/(1 - b)$, the greater is the increase in international saving made possible by each unit increase in r_P (depreciation) and the less the terms-of-trade cost of a given volume of foreign investment. Alternatively, the larger is b (which is assumed to be independent of r_P), the greater amount of direct foreign investment that can be funded by some given volume of autonomous saving. If $r_P - r_0$ is positive, some foreign investment can be made without any additional measures being taken to increase the rate of international saving. If $r_P - r_0$ is negative then S_I can be made positive by a sufficient flow of induced investment but S_I cannot be equal to I_I.

If successful attempts are made to increase the rate of S_I through commercial policy (e.g. by means of additional tariffs on imports of commodities), then r_0 will decrease and the same volume of foreign investment can be achieved with a lower r_P. The alternative policy measures to commercial policy are depreciation, controls over direct investment or some means of increasing the value of b. The last two measures can be combined, a policy of controls over foreign investment outflows being instigated on the criterion that projects with the highest b be permitted.

It is possible to increase the flow of international saving by reducing the level of domestic employment. The social costs of such a policy are obvious. Assume that a policy of deflation of the domestic or investing nation does not affect the level of foreign employment nor the foreign demand for imports. Equations (4) and (4A) then add one element. Let Y^* represent full-employment income in the investing nation and Y the actual level of income actually achieved. Let m stand for the marginal propensity to import of the investing nation. The equilibrium condition then becomes:

$$S_I = A(r_P - r_0) + b(I_I) + m(Y^* - Y) \tag{5}$$

$$S_I = \frac{1}{1-b} \cdot [A(r_P - r_0) + m(Y^* - Y)] \tag{5A}$$

The equilibrium condition set forth in equations (4) and (4A) contains the seed of its own destruction since current international investment will, except in very unusual circumstances, increase the flow of autonomous saving in subsequent years. Letting i stand for the effect of international investment in year $t({}_t I_I)$ on the balance on current account in later years and assuming i to be a constant, it can be shown that the amount of I_I that can take place with a given value for r_P will increase annually. Alternatively, the currency can be appreciated slowly without reducing the flow of direct foreign investment.

$$_{t+1}r_0 = {}_t r_0 + \frac{{}_t I_I}{A}(i) \tag{6}$$

$$_{t+1}S_I = A(r_P - {}_{t+1}r_0) + b({}_{t+1}I_I) \tag{7}$$

The difference between the volume of I_I that can be supported in the years $t+1$ and t amounts to a multiple of the increase in autonomous saving:

$$_{t+1}I_I - {}_t I_I = \frac{1}{1-b} \cdot i \cdot {}_t I_I \tag{8}$$

In so far as the parameter b varies from year to year, the increase in the permissible outflow of direct foreign investment will vary.

CHAPTER VII

BENEFITS AND COSTS OF THE INVESTING COUNTRY

David Ricardo was a pioneer in the study of political economy and he advocated the creation of an institutional bias in favour of investment at home in preference to investment abroad.[1] Almost one hundred and fifty years later, economists were still contending that foreign investment had pronounced negative features.[2] In the interim no less a person than John Maynard Keynes argued that foreign investments involved a national cost that the investors themselves would not take into their private calculations, so that some bias in favour of domestic investment was likely to be beneficial for the investing nation.[3] The basis of these arguments is nationalistic rather than internationalistic. They were concerned that the external effects of foreign investment ran the risk of depriving the investing country of a resource that it could have used to greater advantage at home. None of the arguments denied that some foreign investment projects might be beneficial for the investing country. The thrust of the arguments must be the first concern of this chapter.

Unless the analyst is prepared to argue on the basis of some concept of global welfare and, therefore, on the inherent desirability of a transfer of capital from capital-rich to capital-poor countries, the arguments of the costs and benefits to the investing country must be nationalist as the criterion laid down in Chapter II requires. Since the assumption must be made that

---

[1] Ricardo's main work, *The Principles of Political Economy*, was published in 1817.

[2] See J. Carter Murphy, 'International Investment and the National Advantage', *Southern Economic Journal* (July 1960) pp. 11–17, and Marvin Frankel, 'Home versus Foreign Investment: A Case Against Capital Export', *Kyklos* (1965) pp. 411–31.

[3] 'Foreign Investment and the National Advantage', *The Nation and Athenaeum* (9 August 1924).

the investor regards the expected return from the foreign investment as preferable to his best domestic alternative, the argument for a net disadvantage must hinge upon external forces.

Keynes' objection was to a difference in the risk factor involved in any project from the point of view of the investing economy as a whole and from the point of view of the private entrepreneur. The specific risks were those of the economic failure of the project, loan repudiation on a bond issue or expropriation without adequate compensation of real assets located abroad. If the venture were made in a foreign country, these risks, if fulfilled, would leave both the investor and the investing country empty-handed. If a comparable investment had been made domestically, the investor would still have been left empty-handed, but the nation would have been left with the tangible assets that the investment procured.

Ricardo's complaint was that the increase in the domestic capital stock produced benefits for domestic land-owners and domestic labour. When an investment was made abroad the return to capital was the only benefit that accrued to the investing nation. It could be true that the return to the capital might be greater abroad than that available at home, but the premium would not be sufficient to outweigh the disadvantage inherent in supplying the ancillary benefits of the investment to foreign rather than to domestic, co-operating factors of production. This argument was elaborated upon by Frankel who included in his analysis the external economies that are central to the development process. These economies derive almost at zero cost from additions to the capital stock of a nation and include such considerations as scale economies, technological gains and organisational improvements. Ricardo also considered the possibility that an investment made abroad would lower the rate of return on foreign investments made in earlier years. In this way, the national (social) rate of return will be less than the private rate.

The third effect is the 'fiscal effect' which relies upon the fact that foreign governments rather than the domestic government acquire the taxes levied upon the capital and its flow of profits when it is invested abroad. However, the local or host government also supplies the services that the project uses in the form of social overhead capital and the question is not the superficial one of gross tax receipts under alternative investment decisions but the much less easily calculable one of net receipts for social goals.[1]

Keynes' argument holds at all times and nothing can make a failing project into a socially desirable investment. However, it is necessary to look at the aggregate of foreign investments rather than at a series of individual transactions. An analogy can be drawn with loan policy in a commercial bank. It is axiomatic in banking that if a loan officer has never made a bad loan, he is not maximising the profits of the bank. Thus, some losses such as Keynes was concerned about could be mere indications of a properly aggressive national attitude toward foreign investment and could provide an indication that the overall performance of funds invested abroad could be more beneficial to the investing nation than a conservative, no-loss attitude.[2]

The Ricardo-Frankel reasoning has less relevance to a developed nation in the twentieth century than it has to a developing nation now or to England at the time Ricardo was writing. It is unlikely that direct investments made now by North American or European countries or Japan either retard domestic development or seriously compete with existing foreign assets and thereby reduce their rate of return.

Still another cost of foreign investment and the consequent reduction in the domestic capital stock is the possibility of regional underdevelopment and poverty within the investing country. Thus, the foreign investments of Great Britain in the nineteenth century may have consigned parts of Wales and Scotland to a backward, rural status. The effect of this was partly counteracted by the relatively free (but not costless) mobility of labour. A similar argument could be made in the United States about Appalachia. However, there is no reason to suppose that short of some incentive-subsidy scheme or governmental dictation that the capital would have sought out the backward areas had it not been sent abroad.

[1] The question of taxation of foreign profits is discussed below.
[2] To quote Keynes: 'If a loan to improve South American capital is repudiated, we have nothing. If a Poplar housing loan is repudiated, we, as a nation, still have the houses', ibid., p. 586.

Each of these arguments emphasises the need for each project to meet the investing country's criterion of greater overall social benefit from the foreign than from any competing domestic investment. Put in terms of the inequality developed in Chapter II, the arguments would require that the number on the right-hand side of the inequality be positive rather than zero simply because of the externalities involved. In this the nationalist argument of investing nations is similar to the nationalist arguments of host nations. Together they would approve of such impediments to foreign investments as exist in the natural order of things and would add to them. There is, however, one distinction worthy of note: the investing-country arguments apply with almost equal force to direct and to portfolio investments in foreign countries. The host-nation arguments are not indifferent to the form of capital inflow. Host-nation nationalists are generally much more ready to accept portfolio investments with their absence of control than they are to accept direct investments.

If there exists a negative side to foreign investment – the possibility that entrepreneurs and investment bankers may be prone to overinvest and thereby to damage the investing economy through external effects not included in their private calculus – there is also a positive side. The return to successful direct investments is investment income, the promise of life as a *rentier* and the prospect of obtaining a sizeable portion of the national income from 'clipping coupons'. In 1970, total United States receipts from foreign investments *net* of payments to foreigners on capital owned by them amounted to $6,242 million. This was better than 12 per cent of U.S. exports of goods and services in that year and better than one half of one per cent of gross national product.[1]

NEGATIVE ASPECTS FOR LABOUR

However, the benefits of investment income are only passed on to the general economy if the immediate recipients of the income do not immediately recommit the funds abroad for further accumulations of foreign assets – unless it is argued that the

[1] Source: *Survey of Current Business* (June 1971). Exports of goods and services were computed exclusive of investment income and of exports financed by military grants. Receipts do not include profits retained abroad.

flow of foreign investment by parent corporations is independent of net receipts of investment income. The other possible problem deriving from the enjoyment of investment income is that the transfers may exert a depressant effect upon the domestic economy. If the surplus or deficit on the basic balance of payments does not vary with net investment income, then positive investment income flows will depress the balance on commodities and services. Since a receipt of a transfer adds less stimulus to a national economy than the export of a commodity or the production of an import substitute, there is a danger that ever-increasing investment income will tend to act as a drag upon aggregate demand. Provided that the rate of growth of invest-ment income is small in absolute terms, any side-effects will fall within the range of policy-making error and will not be apparent. However, one writer using 'a conservative estimate based on current trends of investment and profit' foresees a $10·2 billion increase in United States investment income between 1969 and 1980.[1] This increase in investment income is disposed of in the forecast by increasing the current account surplus by $5·9 billion and by allowing the net balance on goods and services to deteriorate by $4·3 billion. While these figures are only intended to illustrate a possible order of magnitude, they do portend a significant decrease in the number of jobs that can be attributed to the foreign trade sector.[2]

There is additional evidence that investment income can have negative aspects. In a world of flexible exchange rates, net receipts of investment income will reduce the balance on goods and services in the absence of capital movements or of money flows. The deficit balance on goods and services would equal the surplus on transfer account (investment income). The years between the two world wars were a tempestuous period in international finance that culminated in a period of com-petitive devaluations of national currencies aimed at exporting unemployment. In a depressed world in which no nation could tolerate a deficit on current account, the United States was a large creditor on investment income and suffered accord-ingly. The data on the balance on goods and services and on

[1] Lawrence B. Krause, 'Trade Policies for the Seventies', *Columbia Journal of World Business* (Mar–Apr 1971) pp. 5–14.
[2] This concept has been called 'the balance of labour'.

investment income are given in Table VII–1. Column (4) shows the dollar contribution of the foreign trade sector to employment. In 1931, the balance of labour took a sharp turn for the worse and remained at a relatively low level (with one

TABLE VII–I

U.S. 'Balance of Labor' 1922–39

(millions of dollars)

Year	Balance on Goods and Services	Net Investment Income	'Balance of Labor' (2)–(3)
(1)	(2)	(3)	(4)
1922	997	565	432
1923	842	710	132
1924	1,351	622	729
1925	1,087	742	345
1926	826	753	73
1927	1,073	741	332
1928	1,377	805	572
1929	1,148	809	339
1930	1,032	745	287
1931	516	546	– 30
1932	407	392	+ 15
1933	358	322	+ 36
1934	601	302	+ 299
1935	128	366	– 238
1936	115	299	– 184
1937	297	282	+ 15
1938	1,291	385	906
1939	1,066	311	755

Source: Department of Commerce data.

exception) until 1938. At a time when contracyclical policies were almost non-existent,[1] the decline in the employment impetus from the foreign trade sector can only have added to domestic woes. It is true that the thirties were not a period of classic exchange-rate flexibility but there were frequent re-adjustments of par values of currencies. The evidence is suggestive, though not proof, of the hypothesis that net investment income was a burden to the United States during the depression. In the modern era, the effect of a decrease in net exports could be counteracted by domestic policies – at least as far as aggregate

[1] See E. Cary Brown, 'Fiscal Policies in the 'Thirties: A Reappraisal', *American Economic Review* (Dec 1956) pp. 857–79.

demand is concerned. The sectoral mix might be less easy to adjust.

Under a regime of fixed rates of exchange among international currencies, the direct effect of the net balance on investment income is felt by the positive or negative balance on current account rather than on the demand for labour. In recent years, the net inflow of investment income will have had both a positive and a negative effect upon employment levels in the United States. The positive effect will have been that investment income allowed the authorities to maintain a more expansionary macropolicy stance in the face of deficits on international account than they would otherwise have been able to achieve. The negative aspect is that the investment income may have delayed the institution of serious measures to end the overvaluation of the dollar. President Nixon's decision in August 1971, to float the dollar as a part of a new economic package has generally been criticised as being too late in coming. The labour market in the United States has been adversely affected by the over-valuation of the dollar which made American products uncompetitive with their immediate foreign competition. Since the net balance on goods and services is a component of aggregate demand, overvaluation of the currency will depress industries manufacturing tradable goods.

In particular, organised labour has suffered from a decrease in the number of jobs available in manufacturing industries. Some of this decline can be traced to the export of capital by corporations seeking cheaper means of supplying their United States markets. A third possible reason for the decline in the demand for organised labour is the trend in the United States toward greater production and consumption of services which tend to be less-well-paid jobs and less amenable to unionisation.

The views of organised labour about the damage being done to members by the exportation of capital can be summarised from the submission of Mr Paul Jennings, President of the International Union of Electrical, Radio and Machine Workers, to the Joint Economic Committee of the U.S. Congress.[1]

[1] Joint Economic Committee, Congress of the United States, *Hearings on a Foreign Economic Policy for the 1970's, Part 4, The Multinational Corporation and International Investment* (91st Cong., 2nd Sess., 27, 28, 29 and 30 July 1970) pp. 814–16.

'The figures [on the activities abroad of U.S.-based multi-national corporations], dramatic, startling as they may be, therefore, do not fully explain what is actually occurring now. There seems to be a kind of speedup on the part of multinational firms to transfer plants, production, products and technology – and jobs – outside the borders of the United States. Entire industries, growth industries, in fact, badly needed here, and many thousands of urgently needed jobs, are exported. To many of us in the labor movement it portends a mass exodus.

'In my own industry, and in industries closely related, we have seen plant after plant shut down in recent years, their production discontinued, products, technology and jobs exported to offshore manufacturing facilities of the same multinational firms.

'Zenith, Admiral, Ford-Philco, RCA and others, for example, have recently shifted monochrome and color TV set production to Taiwan. Last year, Westinghouse closed its Edison, N.J., TV plant and transferred production to one of its Canadian facilities as well as to Japanese firms. It imports sets now for distribution under its own label.

'Emerson Radio and Phono Division of National Union Electric also discontinued production of TV sets, closing down its Jersey City, N.J. plant, and transferring production to Admiral, which, in turn, transferred production of major TV product lines to Taiwan. Warwick Electronics transferred production from its Arkansas and Illinois plants to its Mexican facility. The rush to relocate outside the United States is on. At this time, practically all radio sets, tape recorders, and casettes sold in this country are produced abroad, and before long the same may be true of black and white and color TV sets.

'Currently about half the black and white sets and about 20–25 percent of the color sets sold here are produced abroad. Some growth products, such as home video tape recorders, will not even be produced in this country because patents held by Ampex Corporation have been licensed to Japanese firms.

'About a year ago, General Instrument Corp. transferred TV tuner and other component production to its Taiwan and Portuguese plants, shutting down two New England plants and most of a third. Between 3,000 and 4,000 workers were permanently laid off. General Instrument increased its employment in Taiwan from 7,200 to over 12,000. General Instrument is that nation's largest employer, with more workers employed there than in all its U.S. operations combined. A few months ago, Motorola shut down its picture plant, selling its machinery and equipment to a General Telephone and Electronics subsidiary in Hong Kong.

'A second picture tube firm commenced operations in Mexico, taking advantage of item 807 of the Tariff Schedules. Friden, a division of Singer Corp., and Burroughs, both discontinued production of electronic desk calculators. Their desk calculators are now made for them in Japan by Hitachi and other Japanese firms. The calculators are sold in the United States by their former manufacturers under the latter's label. So, here we have another growth industry that U.S. based multinational firms have abandoned as producers – becoming importers of the products they once made.

'The household sewing machine is but one more item in the growing list of product casualties, though as a casualty, it can probably claim seniority over others. Of each three machines sold in the United States under Singer's label, two are made in its foreign based plants.

'Still another product line to be added to the casualty list is typewriters, portables and larger models. A decade ago, Sperry Rand closed out typewriter production in its Ilion, N.Y., plant, shifting production to its European plants. Now, the company's Remington typewriters are made in Japan under the Remington label by the Brothers firm. Just recently, Litton Industries shut down Royal` typewriter plants, transferring production to a Japanese firm. After acquiring Royal McBee, Litton acquired Imperial Typewriters, Ltd., in Great Britain, and, later Triumph and Adlerwerke in Germany, acquisitions the Justice Department's Antitrust Division felt merited its attention.

'These examples are proliferating and unnoticed. Names that have fixed meaning among economists and the public press alike – Sears Roebuck, Union Carbide, for example – should have new meaning as multinationals are better understood. Sears Roebuck reportedly manufactures shoes in

Spain, and Union Carbide processes shrimp in India – for sale in the U.S. market – according to a recent *Fortune* magazine story. Food processing names like H. J. Heinz and General Foods are worldwide. Genesco, Interco, and other well-known shoe industry names are not only multinational, but conglomerates. Glass manufacturing companies like Libby-Owens-Ford, Owens Corning, Pittsburgh Plate, for example, have foreign affiliates. And well-known names in the paper industry, like Kimberly Clark, have worldwide units.

'DuPont and Monsanto – chemical firms in the public eye – are makers of synthetic fibers and yarns, nylon and chemstrand. Machinery names like Cutler-Hammer, U.S. toy names like Mattel, turn out to be global conglomerate multinationals, too. Several hundred U.S. firms, it is estimated, have set up plants in Mexico, below the border under the program advertised as a 'Twin Plant' concept. Under this concept, plants on the Mexican side of the border assemble parts and components shipped to them by their U.S. parent, and then return them for final processing to a twin plant somewhere in the United States. Duty is paid only on value added.

'In actual practice, work and jobs are transferred from the United States to Mexico in order to take advantage of the cheap labor available at 30–40 cents an hour. In transferring production of TV lines from Warwick Electronic's Illinois and Arkansas plants, approximately 2,000 U.S. jobs have disappeared. Advance Ross Electronics transferred 250 jobs to Juarez, Mexico, from El Paso, then set up a U.S. facility with about 15 employees. Transitron has 1,500 workers in its Laredo, Mexico, plant and only management personnel in Laredo, Tex.'

Mr Jennings concluded with the observation that 'Capital has an enviable and increasing mobility . . . Workers, on the other hand, must usually remain in their communities . . . There is an urgent need to develop world trade on a rational basis, designed to benefit the world's people. The growth must be orderly, equitable, and must contribute to real growth in living standards. In our pursuit of this objective we cannot permit living standards already achieved – as in this country –

to be threatened or undermined. Nor can we permit our growth industries and the employment they generate to be exported at a time of substantial increases in the labor force, and at a time when we are trying desperately to find jobs for the unemployed and the underemployed poor.'[1] He consequently supplied a list of recommendations:[2]

1. Regulate and supervise export of capital to all countries.
2. Remove tax incentives now in law to spur foreign investment. This includes requiring taxation of profits wherever they are earned, at the time that they are earned.
3. Require reporting of output, employment hours, earnings by establishment by SIC numbers to a 7 digit level for foreign locations by U.S. firms, just as they are now required to report for U.S. establishments.
4. Refuse to grant new tax loopholes, such as DISC, [Domestic International Sales Corporations].
5. Require reporting of import and export data by product, not just dollar volume.
6. Require labeling of products by country of origin from any country – including U.S. brand items and all components.
7. Require uniform accounting procedures by multi-national firms as for defense contracts.
8. Tax the export of capital to create a disincentive to produce abroad.
9. Make the U.S. government-subsidized patents the property of U.S. government with royalties paid to the U.S. Treasury.

One year later, another list of recommendations was sponsored by the Director of the Department of Research, AFL-CIO:[3]

U.S. Government measures are required:
1. To stop helping and subsidizing U.S. companies in setting

---

[1] *Hearings on A Foreign Economic Policy for the 1970's, Part 4, The Multinational Corporation and International Investment* pp. 819–21.

[2] Ibid., p. 841.

[3] Nat Goldfinger, 'A Labor View of Foreign Investment and Trade Issues' in *United States International Economic Policy in an Interdependent World* (Washington: U.S. Government Printing Office, July 1971) pp. 913–28.

up and operating foreign subsidiaries – for example, to
repeal section 807 and similar provisions of the Tariff
Code, and to repeal the tax provision which permits the
deferral of U.S. taxes on income of U.S. companies from
their corporate subsidiaries.[1]

2. To supervise and curb the substantial outflows of American
    capital for the investments of U.S. companies in foreign
    operations.

3. To develop regulations covering U.S.-based multinational
    companies.

4. To press, in appropriate international agencies, for the
    establishment of international fair labor standards.

5. As a stop-gap in the face of growing unresolved problems,
    to regulate the flow of imports into the U.S. of a variety
    of goods and product lines in which sharply rising imports
    are displacing significant percentages of U.S. production
    and employment in such markets.

The problems of organised labour that begin in the international sector apply only to those workers producing goods
that can be imported or goods that are exported. Workers in
service industries and in contract construction are less vulnerable, if not completely invulnerable.

Workers employed in tradable-goods industries stand to lose
the level of affluence that they have achieved by virtue of the
high ratio of capital to labour in the United States and in those
industries in which organised labour has managed to restrict
the entry of additional labour by negotiating wage rates that
would limit demand to (approximately) the existing size of the
union concerned. The protected position of these workers is
now vulnerable as they are thrown into direct competition
with European workers and with workers in developing
countries who can now obtain physical capital and the technology at almost the same absolute cost as American industry – in
fact, as long as there are no taxes or lower taxes levied on

[1] Section 807 of the Tariff Schedule allows for import duty to be paid
only on value-added abroad. Thus, assembly in Mexico of U.S.-made parts
taxes only the assembly and not the finished value of items imported. It is,
of course, an important factor in the growth of subsidiary plants in Mexico
and in Asia and tends, by its emphasis on assembly operations, to compete
most strongly with relatively unskilled labour in the United States.

foreign subsidiaries, capital is available to co-operate with foreign workers more cheaply than in the United States. Part of this problem stems from the technological advances in communications and management that have enabled executives to contemplate multinational production schedules but another, and possibly more important aspect has been the technological gains made in the area of cybernetics. Cybernation enables management to use machinery to simplify complex tasks and to substitute unskilled or semi-skilled labour for skilled labour. If it is assumed that the general skill levels of foreign workers are less than those of American workers and that the differential can be roughly gauged by differences in *per capita* incomes in different countries, the advances in cybernetics permit machinery that is internationally mobile to be taken to cheap, unskilled labour that is not mobile. To the extent that the greatest advances in job simplification have taken place in industries in which organised labour is strongly .represented, the weakening of the position of organised labour is apparent. Given the wage rates required to hire labour in Taiwan or Mexico, the overvaluation of the U.S. dollar has little relevance for the outflow of investment designed to supply goods for the United States market.

The third reason for the weakening of the position of organised labour in the tradable-goods industries is a relative decline in their importance in *consumption* in the United States. Foreign competition merely aggravates the pain inherent in growing at less than the average rate of the national economy as a whole. Table VII–2 shows the share of the total work force employed in producing goods to have declined from approximately one half in 1947 to about 37½ per cent in 1969. The decline is projected to continue so that in 1980 the proportion of the work force employed in producing goods or commodities will amount to about one third.[1] If contract construction is excluded, the decline is even more spectacular.

Even if it is conceded that capital exports may be contributing to the weakening of the economic position and strength of organised labour in the United States, it is still not an easy matter either to allocate blame or to conceive of remedies that

[1] See Lawrence B. Krause, 'Why Exports are Becoming Irrelevant?', *Foreign Policy* (Summer 1971) pp. 62–70.

are, broadly-speaking, socially desirable. One useful way of looking at the problem is to conceive of the international flows of capital as contributing to a new 'equilibrium' distribution of wage income in the world. This new distribution will owe its

TABLE VII–2

Wage and Salary Employment in Goods-producing and Service-producing Industries, 1947 and 1969 Actual and 1980 Projected

(Employment figures in millions)

Classification and Industry	Actual 1947	Actual 1969	Pro- jected 1980	Percentage Change	
				1947–69	1969–80
Goods-producing industries	26·4	27·8	30·0	5·3	8·1
Mining	1·0	0·6	0·6	– 34·2	– 12·4
Contract construction	2·0	3·4	4·6	72·0	34·9
Manufacturing (durable and non-durable goods)	15·5	20·1	21·9	29·4	9·0
Agriculture	7·9	3·6	2·9	– 54·3	– 18·8
Service-producing industries	25·4	46·0	59·5	81·0	29·4
Transportation and public utilities	4·2	4·4	4·7	6·8	6·5
Wholesale and retail trade	9·0	14·6	17·6	63·5	20·4
Finance, insurance and real estate	1·8	3·6	4·3	102·9	19·7
General services	5·1	11·1	16·1	119·8	44·9
Federal government	1·9	2·8	3·0	45·5	9·0
State and local government	3·6	9·5	13·8	163·1	46·4
All industries	51·8	73·7	89·5	42·4	21·4

Source: U.S. Department of Labor, Bureau of Labor Statistics, *The U.S. Economy in 1980*, Bulletin 1673, Aug 1970, Table A–22, pp. 53–6. Figures are rounded and may not add to totals.

existence to the internationalisation of production and the ability of management to make use of foreign labour with relatively low skills. Prior to these innovations, the world had been in a long-lasting 'equilibrium' in which large wage differentials could be maintained between unskilled and semi-skilled labour in poor countries and the earnings and living standards of wage-earners in the United States and other developed nations. In poor countries labour is available at wage rates that offer very little above subsistence levels in those countries and that, in terms of prices and accepted standards in the developed nations, are well below subsistence levels. Not only are money wage differentials very large but labour *cost* differentials are even larger because of the absence of work rules and fringe benefits in developing countries. Differentials of the magnitudes that have existed may, because of imperfections in factor and product markets, last for quite long periods of time but the invisible hand will always be seeking ways to substitute low-cost inputs for high-cost inputs. In this way, the advantages of quasi-rents of American labour that derive from the relative international immobility of capital, from the need for human capital in the American productive process and from union bargaining gains, have always been temporary phenomena.

There are two different sets of costs that result from this problem, that should concern politicians, labour leaders and economic authorities in affluent nations. What will be the cost to organised labour in particular and to labour in general in the new equilibrium? Put another way, this question asks by how much wages and employment in the tradable-goods industries will have to fall and how much of this cost can the relevant labour unions switch from the tradable-goods industries to other segments of society. Secondly, what are the *costs of adjustment* to this new equilibrium? Certainly, the latter problem is the more immediate concern for some unions in the United States. The first impact of the technological change will reflect upon employment levels in the tradable-goods industries. Given seniority rules, the burden of unemployment will fall disproportionately heavily on the younger members of the work force.[1] An intelligent domestic policy of adjustment will be able to prevent some of the decline in the overall level of employment but the younger workers will find themselves in lower-paying jobs than they might otherwise have envisaged.

It is possible that organised labour may manage to invoke political and protective machinery that will retard the process of adjustment but, if the root cause is a structural change in the

[1] For data on this particular aspect of unemployment distribution and a critique of orthodox analysis on this subject, see Robert d'A. Shaw, 'Foreign Investment and Global Labor', *Columbia Journal of World Business* (July/ August 1971) pp. 52–62.

world economy due to technological advances, it is difficult to see how the ultimate outcome can be prevented. Early attempts by organised labour to protect themselves against the process have not met with success. Clearly, the increased vulnerability of American labour portends a permanent or long-lasting switch by labour from advocacy of low tariffs or free trade to an advocacy of high rates of tariff protection and/or quotas on imports of commodities. To the extent that this policy is inflationary, it ignores the economic interests of workers in service industries and in non-tradable-goods industries. There workers are already numerically more important in the economy and may one day become the centre of power in organised labour.[1]

One defensive measure, The Foreign Trade and Investment Act of 1972, has already been introduced into the U.S. Congress. In essence, the proposed legislation is protectionist in spirit and plans to remove a tax advantage which foreign subsidiaries enjoy relative to their domestic counterparts. The bill would limit imports of goods by category and by country to an average for the years 1965–69. It would require that U.S. corporate profits tax be paid when foreign profits were earned instead of, as now, when they are repatriated to the United States, and it would empower the President to limit capital outflows and technological outflows.

It is interesting to speculate on what would happen if this legislation were to be enacted. The fact that an adjustment caused by technological innovation or structural change is painful does not necessarily mean that offsetting it is a valid social policy – particularly if the forces set in motion by the change will inevitably prevail. It is possible to argue for a lengthening of the process of adjustment to permit a less drastic process of adaptation to take place. If the social costs of adjustment to some disturbance increase with the speed with which the adjustment must be made, then there is some social value in legislation that retards the process. Unfortunately, the steps proposed in the legislation are unlikely to achieve this goal. The imposition of quotas on specific types of imports could aid the adjustment process but would need to be in-corporated with international agreements on commercial policy

[1] Krause, *Foreign Policy* (Summer 1971).

if retaliation were to be avoided. If retaliation were instituted, the brunt of the adjustment would fall on the relatively efficient export industries. Some process of protection for dying industries might help to reduce the costs of adjustment but such policies would only escape from international censure if some explicit process of phasing out the domestic industry and the concomitant reduction of the impediments to imports were included in the measures. Secondly, there is no evidence to suggest that control over capital movements (direct investments) would prevent the transfer of the technology and the alliance of mobile capital with semi-skilled, immobile cheap labour. Finally, the arguments of organised labour do not make allowances for the job-creating potential of the additional exports that spring from the increased affluence of developing nations.

In terms of the economic theory of international resource allocation, the problem can be expressed fairly simply. As capital (and technology) moves abroad, it increases the productivity of foreign workers relative to domestic workers. Thus, foreign investment (matched by foreign saving) will decrease the relative income of domestic workers. Since, in contradiction of one of the basic assumptions of economic theory, the labour force abroad in developing countries is grievously unemployed or underemployed, the elasticity of the supply of labour to the wage rate is, to all intents and purposes, almost perfectly elastic in local currency. Thus, the money wages of American workers must fall and with them, the real wages. What the orthodox theory does not show is the concentrated sectoral impact of the change in international competitiveness. But the concentration of the sectoral impact may be due to the fact that, in the first stage of the progression, only the wage levels in specific industries are seriously inflated – in those industries that are vulnerable to foreign competition. The excess supply of labour will gradually spread its effect upon all wage rates and labour bargaining positions in the affluent nation except in so far as union monopoly positions in service and non-tradable-goods industries can withstand the pressure of an excess aggregate supply of labour.

In the new equilibrium, it may be surmised that the return to capital in general will increase relative to that paid to labour and that the decrease in real wages will be greater in vulnerable, tradable-goods industries than in other industries. It is by no means clear that the displaced workers in the United States have the option of accepting a cut in money and real wages and of thereby regaining their lost employment. The differential between foreign and domestic labour costs is simply too great. Nor is there any reasonable expectation that a sufficient depreciation of the dollar will be forthcoming because the increased demand for certain goods and the increased flow of dividends and interest will tend to maintain the value of the dollar. One question that is crucial in determining the decrease in real wages to be suffered by wage-earners is the degree to which the saving in variable costs from foreign manufacture are passed on to consumers in the United States. There is no strong evidence that the savings in costs achieved by operations abroad are being passed on to the consumer – instead the profit margins of the international corporations are being enhanced. Evidence supplied by Jennings suggests that savings are not being passed on.[1]

If the money wage rates in the vulnerable industries are not reduced, the establishment of the new set of relative wage rates is likely to engender an inflationary process. If the authorities are prevailed upon (by political pressure) to afford some measure of protection to workers in the vulnerable industries in order to ease the social costs of adaptation, then it may be possible for the authorities to ensure as a *quid pro quo* that the behaviour of the labour force in the non-vulnerable sectors should be such as to accommodate the strains – to raise wages only by an amount that would allow for some given percentage increase in the industry's employment.

Finally, to the extent that the structural change turns the terms of trade adversely to the United States, the authorities should be prepared to recognise the fact by appropriate depreciations of the dollar. The more the locus of production is switched to developing nations, the smaller will be the necessary depreciation since developing countries have an avid need for imports from technologically-advanced nations.

It is almost inevitable that exports of capital will adversely affect the interests of co-operating factors of production in the investing nation. Real wages, compared with the 'alternative

[1] *Hearings on a Foreign Economic Policy for the 1970's* pp. 841–2.

position', will be lower. However, it is important to distinguish between the effect of an export of capital as a single phenomenon and the effect of a structural change in the world economy which is facilitated by international capital mobility. When technological change and capital mobility combine to inflict a cost upon the labour force in the investing nation, the attendant redistribution of income can be serious but it may also be inevitable. If the change in income distribution is inevitable in the long run, the prime concern should be with the speed of adjustment. Attempts to prevent the structural change from occurring are often pointless and socially costly. The inhibiting of direct investments then becomes useful only if it can prevent the structural change from taking place and given the mobility of capital in other developed nations and under the control of multinational corporations, complete prevention is an impracticable target.

THE INFLUENCE OF TAXATION

The influence of the structure of taxes upon income of all kinds is great. It is then not surprising that an internationally-mobile factor of production that can earn roughly the same pre-tax rate of return in any country, is profoundly influenced in its choice of location by alternative tax considerations. In this way the relative dispensations and regulations by the government of the investing country can influence the attractiveness of foreign *vis-à-vis* domestic investment. If foreign tax rates levied on corporate profits are lower than those levied in the investing country, then the investing country is vulnerable to a tax-induced outflow of capital. Such an outflow could lead to a reduction in government revenues that might otherwise be allocated to social goals and to a balance of payments deficit. A rich nation might encourage foreign investment by its tax policy. By so doing the authorities would effectively substitute a negative number in place of the zero on the righthand side of the inequality of the investing country in Chapter II.

A tax system is neutral if it does not influence economic decision-making.[1] Where foreign investment and the global

---

[1] This section relies heavily on Lawrence B. Krause and Kenneth W. Dam, *Federal Tax Treatment of Foreign Income* (Washington: The Brookings Institution, 1964).

distribution of capital are concerned, two sets of neutrality must exist if the world stock of capital is to aim at distribution according to the real rates of return that are available in different locations.[1] These two sets are the taxation neutrality of the investing country and the taxation neutrality of the host country. The first implies no distinction between entrepreneurs investing at home and those investing abroad, and the second implies equal tax treatment in the host country of foreign subsidiaries and indigenous firms. It is at once clear that tax neutrality is an ideal that cannot be fully attained in an imperfect world. However, the degree of departure from tax neutrality will determine to what degree foreign investments are encouraged or penalised. There is no reason why a nation could not attempt to achieve tax neutrality for investments in developed nations but reckon to assist developing nations by encouraging investment in those nations. Similarly, the authorities might reasonably argue that backward vertical-integration investments (in minerals for example) would warrant different tax treatment from horizontal-integration (manufacturing) investments.

The most important departure from tax neutrality on investment is the combination of the deferral privilege and the tax credit. The tax credit allows a credit (not a deduction!) against U.S. income tax or profits tax in the amount of foreign taxes paid on dividends and profits remitted to the United States. Not to allow a credit would discriminate against foreign investment and institute a process of 'double taxation' on investment income. Of course, the credit cannot (and does not in the United States) provide full neutrality if the foreign rate of taxation exceeds that levied in the investing country. Assuming host country rates are less than investing country rates, the tax credit would achieve domestic tax neutrality if there were no deferral privilege. But, the deferral privilege requires that the U.S. tax (less the credit) be paid only when the dividends etc. are actually remitted so that holding the income in a foreign

---

[1] If tax neutrality prevailed, a free self-seeking global distribution of the world stock of capital would maximise economic welfare in its static definition – that income distribution among nations and among people is irrelevant and the degrees of income inequality are irrelevant. Perfect competition is also assumed throughout.

country provides a temporary and possibly permanent means of escaping the additional U.S. tax levy. If the income is ultimately to be repatriated, the deferral privilege supplies an interest-free loan.

It is the deferral privilege that is important to foreign investors.[1] They argue, correctly, that to deny foreign investors the deferral privilege in the name of tax neutrality in the investing country is to contravene tax neutrality in the foreign (host) country. If the profits of U.S. subsidiaries located abroad were taxed at U.S. rates when earned, the subsidiaries would be taxed at a higher rate than their indigenous and non-American competitors (always assuming that the host rate of tax is less than the U.S. rate). At the same time, the deferral privilege may be necessary to compensate for the lower level of government services or for higher rates of indirect taxation abroad.

The main advantage that the deferral privilege accords to international and to multinational business is the ability to manoeuvre the location of their profits through judicious transfer pricing. Prior to 1962, there was also the problem of tax havens – nations with negligible rates of taxation and in which dummy corporations could be set up to receive the profits of a large corporation.[2] The benefit that can be derived from the privilege depends upon the lowest tax rate in a country in which the multinational corporation has a subsidiary. By virtue of selective transfer pricing, a corporation can allow all of the profit to accumulate in that country and can effectively establish that subsidiary as a second financial headquarters. The benefits to be derived from an initial holiday from taxes and low taxes thereafter can be magnified by an international company that is prepared and able to adjust the prices on its intra-corporation transactions to those prices that best suit its own interests.

Another element of domestic non-neutrality in the United States lies in the fact that tax credits against corporate profits

---

[1] Oil companies are a case apart and usually prefer a branch organisation with no deferral privilege to a subsidiary enterprise (with deferral). See Krause and Dam, *Federal Tax Treatment*, p. 13. The crux of the matter is depletion allowances.

[2] Ibid., pp. 13–19.

tax accorded to U.S. corporations are allowed only on domestic investments and are not allowed on foreign investments. This biases investment toward domestic locations. The proposal contained in The Foreign Trade and Investment Act of 1972, that corporate profits tax be levied at the time subsidiary profits are earned rather than at the time of repatriation, would also bias investment toward domestic locations. The effect would probably be small. It would make foreign direct investment less attractive but it would also involve a serious departure from tax neutrality within the host country. The departure would be the most serious, the greater the differential between corporate tax rates in the host and the investing country. The proposal might endanger the profitability and the long-run viability of certain subsidiaries since it would put them at a serious disadvantage in the process of expansion out of retained earnings.

The proposal of the 1972 Act would also have regional impact. It would tend to discourage investments in developing nations relative to investments in Europe and Canada. Developing nations are more likely to have low rates of corporate profits tax and are more likely to have attracted the subsidiary by means of a tax holiday. The regional bias might be instrumental in achieving some degree of protection for the workers in the vulnerable industries. However, there is little evidence to suggest that the proposal would provide enough protection to prevent the transmission of technology and capital to developing countries. Separate (non-subsidiary) enterprises would provide an adequate substitute for foreign subsidiaries. While these independent companies might result in higher costs of exports to the American importer-cum-parent – perhaps because of different tariff treatment – it is unlikely that the differences in costs would be sufficient to outweigh the labour cost differential.

To this point no mention has been made of the possibility of taxing the actual capital export rather than or as well as the return on the exported capital. To do so would, of course, represent a substantial departure from tax neutrality and would represent the same kind of discrimination as exists when a domestic investment earns a tax credit and a foreign investment does not. In addition to the purely nationalist aspects of such a tax, there is an argument that can be made for it in terms of the adjustment problem of the balance of payments. This measure already exists on portfolio capitalfolio capital through the Interest Equalization Tax and the extension of the IET concept to direct investment was suggested by Vice-Chairman J. L. Robertson of the Federal Reserve System in 1968.[1] The tax – like an excise tax – would be variable with the balance-of-payments strains and could vary according to the purpose of the investment and the development status of the host nation. An alternative to outright taxation would be to require that direct investment outflows would deposit some percentage of the funds exported at a zero rate of interest with, say, the Federal Reserve System. The percentage would vary according to the balance-of-payments situation and could vary by purpose and by host. If the percentage deposit rate were 100 per cent, the expected rate of return to the project would be halved. Repatriation of the capital from abroad could entitle the investor to withdraw his deposits. Equally, repatriation of a sum equal to the original outflow in excess of some reasonable rate of return on the funds, could also enable the investor to withdraw his deposit. Either system would involve a flexible tax on foreign investment that would serve to restrict the rate of international investment to the flow of international saving actually being generated and the restriction would rely upon the pricing mechanism for the selection process.

CONCLUSION

The benefits from successful foreign investments are apparent. With the exception of the costs deriving from possible externalities and of costs from problems of adjustment, successful foreign investment will benefit the investing nation. The costs are to be found in the risks inherent in too great a presence abroad, of non-neutrality of treatment by host governments and consequent losses, and in the distribution of the burden imposed internally by the process of international saving. There is a growing danger that nationalism will increase the frequency of expropriation of foreign subsidiaries or of their nationalisation with less than full compensation. This possibility is pronounced

[1] On 1 April, in White Sulphur Springs, West Virginia.

in developing nations and is, perhaps, more relevant to operations such as mineral extraction.[1] The major costs are likely to be the burdens imposed domestically by the international saving – particularly when domestic deflation is part of the remedy – and by the redistribution of income and power to an executive elite. Finally there is the cost of intergenerational transfer. If the rate of foreign investment were smaller, the equilibrium exchange rate would be more favourable. Thus the joys of a *rentier* income may have been paid for by one generation only to be reaped by succeeding generations.

[1] Perhaps too with greater justification. For a discussion of Nationalism in Latin America see Peter Nehemkis, 'Latin American Testing Ground for International Business', *California Management Review* (Summer 1971) pp. 87–94.

CHAPTER VIII

PROMISE AND PROBLEMS OF THE MULTINATIONAL CORPORATE ORGANISATIONAL FORM

Before World War II, several very large companies operated production and sales activities under their own corporate name in many different countries in the world. Their number was small and their operations, though large absolutely, were neither so large as to create concern with possible dominance of a domestic industry nor were their various activities so integrated and so interdependent as to cause apprehension and mistrust in national unions and governments. Since World War II, the number of multinational corporations, and the breadth and depth of their operations has increased many times and the development pattern could continue until a relatively small group of titanic firms holds the centre of global commerce. Current multinational corporations differ from the earlier vintage because their vision is so much greater and their communications are so much more advanced. New managerial techniques, the harnessing of computers and the rapid advances in transportation have made it possible for multinational corporations to achieve a degree of integration of production and production scheduling among different nations, and of financing and marketing activities that completely alters their potential impact upon the global economy.

The managerial gains have been impressive and cannot but have helped to increase world output or, at least, potential world output for the sales of multinational corporations are dependent upon the existence of adequate aggregate demand. It is the multinational corporation that promises to or has been able to achieve all of the internal economies that are to be derived from vertical and horizontal expansion across national boundaries. In addition, by crossing national boundaries with facility (if not impunity), they are able to distribute (somewhat) more equally the demand for labour among nations. This expansionist force can earn for the multinationals the enmity of workers and trade unions in advanced countries whose positions are undermined by the ability of the multinationals to find and to institute the least costly global distribution of production. Similarly, in a world full of nation states, national identity and nationalist feelings will always tend to make national governments and their electorates suspicious of supranational organisations. Nations still need to protect their own workers, are still called upon to shield their own inefficient industries and to preserve the national set of values and culture. Not least, nations have to protect their own currencies in the world markets – that is their own balance of payments and their own terms of trade.

> Conflict will increase between the world corporation, which is a modern concept evolved to meet the requirements of the modern age, and the nation state, which is still rooted in archaic concepts unsympathetic to the needs of our complex world.[1]

This potential conflict is the key social and economic aspect of the continued fast growth of the multinational corporation. The material promise of multinational corporations can be visualised with comparative ease though it is still a long way from being attained. The possible costs of the phenomenon are vague and ill-defined and are the more terrifying for that.

The multinational corporation is already in the 1970s the dominant principle in international direct investment. That process has already been seen to have its cost as well as its benefits. This chapter provides a survey of some of the more important costs that may derive from the continued growth of the multinational-corporation form of organisation.

Two points are worth making at the outset.

(1) If multinational corporations can produce goods more cheaply and sell them more cheaply, then they will flourish. Kindleberger[2] has compared the growth of multinationals in the late twentieth century to the use of the national or nationwide corporation in the late nineteenth century in the United States,

---

[1] George W. Ball, 'Cosmocorp: The Importance of Being Stateless', *Columbia Journal of World Business* (Nov–Dec 1967) p. 27.

[2] Kindleberger, *American Business Abroad*, pp. 33–5.

and cites the gains that were derived for the United States economy from the national integration of input and product markets. Big business was subjected to opposition in those days but flourishes in the United States some eighty years later.

(2) A large part of the problem – particularly of acceptance of the multinational corporate form of organisation – is the problem of adjustment to an evolutionary, new phenomenon. It is the existing institutions and customs that must adapt. In the process of adaptation they must, in a Darwinian sense, help to create an environment that will influence the development of the new species by reducing any anti-social traits that would occur in a completely *laissez-faire* atmosphere.

Despite the definition of a multinational corporation used in Chapter III, there is no clear definition of exactly what provides the identifying feature or group of features of a corporation that is likely to be the closest to the final evolutionary form of the species. Most important is the way in which the executives think and the way in which they think about the corporation's goals and activities. Executives' attitudes have been usefully categorised as ethnocentric (home-country oriented), poly-centric (host-country oriented) and geocentric (world oriented).[1]

An *ethnocentric* attitude can make itself shown by the belief in the ethnic superiority or greater efficiency of the people from the home country. There is a suspicion that complex operations are beyond the capabilities of local personnel in foreign manu-facturing subsidiaries, that home-country managerial practices have a 'divine' quality so that they can usefully be imposed upon any subsidiary in any country, and that the only appro-priate people for top executive rank in the headquarters, are home-country nationals. A *polycentric* attitude accords so much respect to the host-country culture that it allows or encourages each subsidiary to operate as a quasi-independent firm and the parent merely requires a measure of control over financial outlays and a satisfactory return on its investment. Thus, even polycentrism restricts the highest positions in the corporation to home-country nationals because of the belief that each executive of a given nationality should remain in his own

[1] The following discussion draws heavily on Howard V. Perlmutter, 'The Tortuous Evolution of the Multinational Corporation', *Columbia Journal of World Business* (Jan–Feb 1969) pp. 9–18.

country. A polycentrically-organised firm may be the result of strong national feelings in the host countries but it will tend to deprive the organisation of the benefits of the internal economies that are the source of the major efficiency gains that a multi-national corporation can achieve. A *geocentric* approach is sensitive to the constraints imposed upon its actions by the ethnocentrism of others, but for all other purposes the frame of reference is almost truly global or international. In particular, personnel appointments are made on the basis of ability not nationality. The concept of production planning, sales and personnel are all global in scope in the affiliates as well as in the headquarters. It is an ideal rather than an accomplishment.

There is a gradual progression toward geocentrism in multi-national corporations but the process is slow and uncertain. It is possible that the rate at which a fully-geocentric organisation can be achieved will increase with the advent into the executive ranks of younger people whose outlook is reported to be more internationalist and 'one-world'. However, there is also evidence of rampant nationalism in the world (also among young people) that could retard the progress of multinational corporations towards geocentrism. There is also the possibility of schism. The geocentric-minded young people of developed European and North American countries could endorse, as it were, the multinational corporation form of organisation and help to direct its development to that of a socially-beneficent species. The young people of developing countries could emphasise ethnocentrism and either hinder the achievement of geo-centrism within the multinational corporation, or endow the corporation with a bad 'image' and obstruct its spread into their own countries. In the latter case, there is the unhappy prospect of multinational corporations dominating commerce in the developed world and in some few developing nations with whole areas of the world forming a periphery to the centre.

Different attitudes tend to manifest themselves in different divisions of multinational corporations: research and develop-ment tends to be geocentric, marketing is polycentric and finance is ethnocentric – though the latter must be beginning to break down with the internationalisation of the large capital markets. Similarly, each attitude has its own separate set of cost advantages and disadvantages, when it is the dominant outlook in a corporation. Ethnocentrism provides a simpler form of organisational structure which works well in the early phases of a parent-subsidiary relationship when the flow of knowhow is predominantly or almost exclusively in one direction. It works less efficiently over the longer run because of a high rate of executive turnover in the subsidiaries, a failure to identify with the host nation and a lack of feedback of ideas and information from the subsidiary. Polycentrism's advantages are the identity with the host nation and the relative satisfaction of subsidiary executives. Its disadvantages are duplication of effort and the consequent failure to achieve internal economies – the failure will apply more to Coase-type than to Caves-type economies.[1] In theory geocentrism represents the ultimate in gains from internal and international economies and in personnel utilisation. The disadvantages are likely to stem from size, a top-heavy bureaucracy at headquarters and very burdensome travel costs.

The future growth of the multinational-corporation form of organisation may be quite sensitive to the attitude taken by the Japanese to international investment in their nation. Yet, if the multinational corporation is to become a global phenomenon, it cannot omit such a productive and important nation from its dominion. But the integration of subsidiary/affiliates located in Japan into a worldwide geocentric form of organisation may be more difficult than the problems faced by multinationals up to this time. Multinational corporations have not, as yet, been required to achieve a significant degree of integration across a wide cultural divide. Their affiliates are predominantly located in nations with an occidental culture and business climate or the affiliates are enclave industries in developing nations. It may be more difficult to incorporate a unit in a nation that has had a long history of independence and isolation coupled with a traditional suspiciousness of foreigners. The distinctly different Japanese culture may be integrated into a global policy less quickly and less painlessly than the culture of different western nations has been.[2]

[1] See Chapter III.

[2] In this sense, Perlmutter's term 'ethnocentrism' with its connotation of race is unfortunate – it may be that cultural differences will prove bigger stumbling blocks to geocentrism than ethnic nationalism.

The potential anti-social aspects of multinational corporations are the possibilities that the group of titanic concerns can: (1) so manipulate their shipments as to pay less than their 'fair share' of taxes in host nations; (2) switch production from country to country without adequate consideration for the welfare of the workforce or for the problems of adjustment; (3) collude in restraint of trade; and (4) live up to the brainwashing, taste-forming portrait of the corporate sector provided in *The New Industrial State*.[1]

The problem of tax-saving has already been discussed and has been recognised as a difficult loophole to close. However, there is scope for special methods to assure reasonable valuations on intra-corporation shipments and the possibility of applying special bases on which tax rates will apply for multinational concerns. A third possibility is for the government to recognise the special position of multinational corporations and to arrange to bill the multinational corporation affiliate for services rendered – any taxes actually paid through normal channels would be credited toward the bill. This would assure the host government that it was not subsidising the affiliate. Problems of *The New Industrial State* have yet to be solved – particularly when the consuming public does not seem to have any serious objection to having its tastes formulated for it. However, provided antitrust legislation makes sure, at least, that smaller firms can coexist with the titans, some room for innovation and nonconformism remains.

The balance of this chapter will devote itself to five aspects of the multinational corporation's possibly negative aspects. Of these five aspects, the first three and the last two are particularly interdependent. (In considering these aspects of multinational corporate behaviour, it will be useful to change the terminology used up to this point and to reserve the label of multinational corporation for a corporation that has progressed a significant way along the road to geocentrism, and to refer to ethnocentric and polycentric corporations as international corporations.)

(1) Its ability to flourish in a nationalist setting.
(2) Extraterritoriality.

---

[1] J. K. Galbraith, *The New Industrial State* (Boston: Houghton Mifflin, 1967).

(3) Control and competition.

(4) Potential damage to the host through 'switching'.

(5) Potential aggravation of balance-of-payments problems.

(1) The flourishing of nationalist feeling is inimical to the interests of subsidiaries of international corporations and to the interests of affiliates of multinational corporations. It is likely to be more apparent in developing than in rich countries. Similarly, the antipathy for the international corporation is likely to exceed that for the multinational corporation since the latter will have an air of national anonymity whereas the former will be more acutely identified as a subsidiary of *big* business from a *big* power.[1] Antipathy to a subsidiary is the more probable in a developing nation because of the expectation that the international corporation will be ethnocentric in its dealings with its subsidiary. In developed nations, the possible degree of reliance upon indigenous managers is greater so that the probability of polycentrism in such countries is high.

The common cure recommended for strained relations between host nations and inter- and multi-national corporations is the joint venture. A joint venture can take one of two main forms: either a subsidiary is owned jointly with an indigenous corporation in a sort of partnership of corporations, or equity stock of the subsidiary/affiliate is sold to nationals directly or through some intermediary. Many nations impose a requirement of partial local ownership. Mexico's Minister of Industry and Commerce has declared that Mexico's industrial future belongs to the joint venture. Peru's Government has decreed that at least 51 per cent of the shares of foreign-owned companies must be sold to Peruvian nationals at a time table to be mutually agreed upon. Colombia, Chile and Ecuador have made similar pronouncements.[2] India requires 30 per cent local ownership; some Canadians desire similar measures be legislated and the French object to complete foreign ownership or control of a business located in France (though their objections to complete French ownership of a subsidiary in Africa are less intense). These conditions do not seem unreasonable in principle. Why should nationals not be assured

[1] It may be too late for some multinational corporations to change their images even if they could achieve geocentrism overnight.

[2] Nehemkis, *Californian Management Review* (Summer 1971).

of an opportunity to share in the benefits that derive from serving their national market? The requirement can also serve to slow down the rate of entry of foreign capital to that that can be matched by local wealth or saving. It also prevents 'foreign subsidiaries' from exercising too large a degree of home-country ethnocentrism. This is particularly important in host countries in which history makes the hosts sensitive to anything pertaining to economic colonialism – as in Latin America when the United States is the investing country.

The most probable way in which a joint venture would come about is for a foreign corporation to join with an existing indigenous firm either to expand that firm or to create a new one. Any combination is possible. The investing corporation may locate a group of interested citizens or may issue stock locally through an investment bank. Whatever means is employed, the result is inferior, from the point of view of an inter- or multi-national corporation, to a wholly-owned subsidiary. The efficiency gains that accrue to a multinational corporation derive to no small degree from its ability to arrange or to rearrange its production operations with absolute freedom. Such a rearrangement could easily have adverse effects upon the profits of one subsidiary and favourable effects upon the profits of another – when normal pricing practices were followed and independently of any manoeuvres to take advantage of variation in tax rates. Once there exists an equal partner or a minority shareholder, the multinational corporation's freedom is circumscribed and its global efficiency can suffer. The classic example of the elimination of outstanding minority shares is that of Ford Motor Company of England. In this case, it could be said that the minority shareholders were paid a handsome price for their stock. Since that time, the British works has been integrated with American, Belgian and German production units and, while exports are high, they may have been still higher if Ford of England had continued to operate as a quasi-independent. Still more interesting is a later chapter in the story when serious labour troubles at Dagenham in England in the spring of 1971 caused Henry Ford II to visit London. During the visit he met the British Prime Minister. Henry Ford's reaction to the chronic labour troubles at Dagenham was to divert away from the United

Kingdom a new, export-oriented engine plant that had been destined to be located there, and to express the expectation that the important role of Ford of England as an exporter within the Ford organisation would be considerably reduced.[1] Thus, a multinational corporation is probably better able to discipline its work forces in a wholly-owned affiliate than in a joint venture. Equally, the existence of a partner or minority shareholder precludes a possibly adverse trait – the juggling of intracorporation transfer prices for tax-saving purposes. Unfortunately, the absence of an arm's-length standard does not allow the minority shareholder ever to be quite certain that transfer prices are fair to him.

On the other hand, foreign enterprises in Japan have resorted to joint ventures out of self-interest. The wide difference in culture and in business practice between Japan and the Occident has been bridged by allowing Japanese partners and management to take the dominant role in areas in which a familiarity with Japanese ways plays a large part.[2] The joint venture can allocate management according to its comparative advantage within the firm and the actual bridging of the cultural gap is accomplished in practical terms by partners within the joint venture.

The policy of many large international corporations in response to host pressures for host citizens' equity holdings in the subsidiary or affiliate is to urge the purchase of the parent's stock. This outcome has many advantages for the parent corporation – the complete control of the subsidiary and the lesser probability of a strong minority consensus being formed in the larger more cosmopolitan group of stockholders that hold sway over the parent's policies. The local investor may and probably does want to share in the local profits which he may expect to exceed the general rate of profit achieved by the parent company.[3] These extra profits will be real and not illusory only if the rate of return to capital in the subsidiary exceeds that of similar operations elsewhere. Ignoring the possibility that the parent may be engaged in many industries,

---

[1] See *U.S. News and World Report*, 5 April 1971, p. 84.

[2] Jerome Cohen (ed.), *Soft Dollar, Hard Yen: Trade on the Pacific* (published for The Japan Society, New York, 1973).

[3] Kindleberger, *American Business Abroad*, p. 30.

if Caves' hypothesis is valid that competitive forces within an industry equalises the rate of return to capital within a single industry in all countries, then the vision of quasi-rents accruing to the subsidiary will be illusory.[1]

The standard advice to foreign subsidiaries or affiliates is to 'identify with the host country's goals and aspirations'. This is valid (polycentric) advice to existing affiliates or subsidiaries caught in a fervent or even a mild wave of nationalism. There is, however, another possible reaction to stringent local demands (such as insistence on joint ventures) and that is to exclude such countries from the network of affiliates of the multinational corporation and explicitly to seek out competing opportunities for production integration in other nations more eager for the help that foreign investment can provide. This would not preclude foreign capital from entering those nations with stringent demands on foreign firms, but it would deny to those nations the benefits of 'membership' in an extremely efficient corporate enterprise or, more importantly, a dominatingly large group of enterprises. The bargaining power of a nation depends ultimately upon what it has to offer. A prosperous and growing market is attractive and a scarce natural resource will always be seductive, but a low-income market with xenophobic tendencies has no leverage at all.

(2) The question of extraterritoriality – particularly in its dimensions of antitrust and trading patterns – is an important one in the relationship between host government, investing government and international or multinational corporation. The international corporation is in the invidious position of attempting to serve two masters and can become a whipping boy in the process. It cannot accede simultaneously to conflicting demands. When the pressure is on, executives must presumably 'play it by ear' but there must be some probability that the investing-country government holds the greater degree of leverage. Still more confusing is how would investing-country pressure be exerted upon a 'grandchild' subsidiary? Suppose that a U.S.-subsidiary located in France has its own

---

[1] Caves, *Economica* (Feb 1971, pp. 17–22. Note that if the parent is engaged in many industries it will attempt to equalise the rate of return among industries in a single country as well as equalising the rate of return in the same industry in different countries.

subsidiary in a West African nation: is that subsidiary under the jurisdiction of the United States Government in any way or could it licitly export to, say, China, goods on the United States list of forbidden commodities? This question focuses on the heart of the problem: the extent of jurisdiction, the lack of definition of its powers and its enforcement.

The ability of an investing country's government to regulate the behaviour of a subsidiary located abroad is limited by self-interest, that is by the costs and benefits of so doing.[1]

> Given the lack of clear definition of rights of nation-states, the tentative answer to the question lies essentially in their *ability to interfere*. If the national government has the ability and the willingness, 'right' tends to become a legal issue and there are no courts to deny governments the exercise of rights that they wish to employ.[2]

The desire of the investing government to interfere is based upon a potential conflict of interest between the government and the international corporation. This does not necessarily mean that the government is correct in its judgment, merely that the government is prepared to use the leverage which it possesses by virtue of the geographical base of the parent.

The ability of the host government to counteract any overt or covert interference by the investing government is subject to similar general constraints.

> Obviously, host governments have the right to impose counter-restrictions. They have a unit of the multinational enterprise within their boundaries, and they can impose regulations countering the orders of parent governments on repatriation of earnings, inflow of funds, export sales and even competitive relationships. They can also raise the political costs of interference by claiming that it goes beyond some 'rule of reason', and by demonstrating to other countries, the dangers of permitting political intervention through multinational corporations.[3]

[1] A good review of this problem is given in Jack N. Behrman, 'Multinational Corporations, Transnational Interests and National Sovereignty', *Columbia Journal of World Business* (Mar–Apr 1969) pp. 15–21.

[2] Ibid., p. 16 (italics added).

[3] Ibid., p. 18.

The essence of the situation is that the international corporation becomes one variable in a multidimensional diplomatic poker game. The parent corporation becomes a tool of foreign policy just as any other means at the disposal of a government is used on foreign policy. The crucial question is 'how far is the host government prepared to go in retaliation?'

One of the constraints which may impede host governments in their search for countervailing weapons is the longstanding convention that has governed international economic relations that there are separate compartments for matters of trade, investment and the balance of payments. These separate areas are represented by their appropriate supranational bodies, General Agreement on Tariffs and Trade (GATT), the International Bank for Reconstruction and Development (IBRD), and the International Monetary Fund (IMF) respectively. There is no world body yet created to supervise private international corporations and to regulate intergovernmental procedures that affect such corporations.[1] A further constraint has been the prevalence of the principle of nondiscrimination in international economic relations – subject to explicit exemption for economic unions such as the European Economic Community.

Provided that the host government were prepared to exert countervailing power, it could, as a first step, discriminate against subsidiaries that were being unduly subjected to extraterritorial influences – by, for example, increasing the profits tax rate on those companies. A second alternative would be to levy an extra surcharge on imports by those subsidiaries or on imports from the extraterritorially-minded investing country generally. This may betoken a degree of trade warfare that is, in itself, most undesirable but if the governments of investing countries are to be discouraged, then 'muscle' is a necessary ingredient. Such actions could easily apply to instances in which the policy of the investing country has been publicly announced but there will be difficulties in legitimising such discrimination when the policy is covert. The crucial questions are – 'what are the limits of extraterritorial interference that host countries will tolerate' and perhaps more important, 'are

[1] IBRD is primarily concerned with loans to developing nations so that there is no world body to supervise investment by private companies but the idea has support. (See (3) below.)

those limits becoming tighter'. The answer to the second question is likely to be affirmative.

There is a further aspect to extraterritoriality. Does interference from the investing government have any effect upon the dynamics of discarding ethnocentrism, and does geocentrism lead to greater resistance by the multinational corporation to extraterritorial pressures by governments? Certainly, the interference of parent governments can constrain a corporation when the interests of the two clash. Whether that provides a sufficient impetus to make the corporation seek an escape from identification with one nation is not known. Pressures by the United States Government could lead to a desire to shift the headquarters to Geneva or Grenoble and to establish what is now the parent company as just another subsidiary. The decline in the relative economic strength of the United States and the growth of the larger multinational corporations may have or may soon make this a feasible policy. This possible seeking of supranational status by the titanic firms will be expedited if a willingness or desire on the part of the multinational corporations to establish links with Eastern Europe were to be frustrated by obduracy on the part of the United States Congress. Clearly, the large oil corporations could establish their headquarters in foreign nations and there may be some nation that might find hosting the headquarters organisations a beneficial and satisfying prospect.[1]

(3) Kindleberger's comparison of the economic effects of the spread of national firms across the continental United States in the nineteenth century to the present expansionary surge of international and multinational corporations is applicable to dimensions other than their contribution to economic efficiency.[2] While the national corporations may have integrated factor markets and equalised the ratio of available capital and know-how to labour, the consequence of their integration of product markets was not necessarily a perfectly competitive price structure or rate of return. Rather, it was the beginning of

---

[1] Austria, Finland, Tunisia and Yugoslavia are possible candidates as well as the more obvious choice of Switzerland. See Howard V. Perlmutter, 'Emerging East-West Ventures: The Transideological Enterprise', *Columbia Journal of World Business* (Sep–Oct 1969) pp. 39–50.

[2] Kindleberger, *American Business Abroad*, pp. 33–5.

administered prices that were able to differ from region to region according to the efficiency and aggressiveness of regional suppliers where regional suppliers existed, and of oligopolistic compromises where no regional supplier existed. The last two decades of the nineteenth century saw the development of anti-trust legislation.

In the last third of the twentieth century, the problem of industrial regulation takes on a new characteristic. Currently the extraterritoriality application of United States antitrust legislation may impede both the desires and the opportunities for collusive agreements among multinational corporations. But the forecast that the core of the world's industrial output would be produced by 300 titanic firms by the end of the century, if not sooner, suggests that the need to be aware of supranational collusion is great. Adam Smith's dictum[1] will only cease to be relevant when human nature (or the business-man's nature) has evolved to a new and higher level.

There are two levels at which this problem can be approached: the national level and the supranational level. Approaches at the national level would argue for a reconciliation of national laws to punish efforts to restrict competition – as they applied to multinational corporations at least – and to set up machinery for international co-operation among governments in enforcing these laws. The other is to create a world organisation similar to GATT, that would keep the issues of the conduct of multi-national corporations under constant surveillance.[2] There is no easy answer to this problem but another possible means would be for nations, jointly or singly, to devise a code of ethics for multinational corporations and their affiliates alone. A corpora-tion would then become liable to this special body of law by its explicit categorisation as a multinational corporation within the meaning of the statute.

[1] 'People of the same trade seldom meet together, even for merriment and diversion, but the conversation ends in a conspiracy against the public or in some contrivance to raise prices.'

[2] This proposal has a fairly broad measure of support among people thinking of this set of problems and would undoubtedly be a step in the right direction. However there is a fundamental difference between GATT and GAME (General Agreement on Multinational Enterprises). In GATT, the governments themselves set tariff rates and quotas. In GAME they would be trying to discipline firms that set, covertly, tariff rates and quotas.

The prospect that the group of multinational corporations or of their chief executives will form a new *élite* which will dominate the economic welfare of the planet earth is interesting but too far in the future (if not too unrealistic) to consider at this time. However, a variation on an old theme (from the fifties) will almost inevitably rate newspaper headlines one day – 'What is good for Multinational Motors is good for the World'.

(4) There could be legitimate concern that the overall effect of a dominant group of multinational corporations could reduce the degree of success enjoyed by national governments in achieving national economic goals.

The most spectacular aspect of this problem is the ability of the multinational corporation to close down a productive unit or drastically to reduce employment in an affiliate without considering the repercussions of the action. The more poly-centric is the organisation the less the probability of going subsidiary plants being closed down but that does not preclude the closing down of the productive aspects of a going concern shortly after it is taken over. This possibility presents problems of job security as well as possibly aggravating macro-economic difficulties. One way to reduce the social impact of such a policy is to institute a general, funded contributory system of pension rights outside any governmental programme of old-age insurance – the rights of the worker being vested after a fairly short period of employment with any corporation (say, two years). A second means of reducing the hardship is to institute a system of severance pay (what the British call the 'golden handshake') based on years of service and current salary. Such a system would tend to reduce the take-over price paid to the firm's owners but would not, on average, reduce the total cost of the take-over to the multinational corporation. Finally, some global form of countervailing power can be created through an effective international union that operates in all nations in which the multinational corporation operates. This possibility must await a more favourable attitude towards labour unions in many countries in which they are currently banned.

Haphazard variations in aggregate demand can be magnified by the policies of multinational corporations, particularly when they switch production among affiliates in different nations.

What is not clear is whether the investment patterns of multi-national business are (or will be) cyclically less or more stable than those of domestic industry. To the extent that multi-national businesses are more globally oriented, it is possible that multinational business investment could be a stabilising force.

Finally, it has been suggested that multinational corporations weaken contracyclical policy measures instituted by the authorities through their recourse to parent corporation funds. This may be true but a great part of any ability to escape monetary stringency is likely to derive from the size of the organisation and its consequently greater credit-worthiness, and from the internationalisation of capital markets.

In countries in which the national authorities rely greatly for the success of macroeconomic stabilisation policies upon co-operation between big business and government, the presence of multinational affiliates might create fears of a less effective system. However, there is no reason to expect that multi-national corporations – even if geocentric – would prove to be uncooperative. Attaining some sort of consensus on expansion plans with multinational affiliates (particularly with joint ventures) should prove no more difficult than obtaining a consensus exclusively with indigenous firms – provided always that the parties to the consensus all feel themselves to have been treated impartially.[1]

(5) A nation's international terms of trade affect its real income so that an appreciation of a nation's currency in so far as it betokens an increase in the nation's terms of trade is beneficial (it is possible for an appreciation of a currency to be due entirely to unequal changes in absolute prices levels in different countries and for the terms of trade to be constant during an appreciation). Thus, any effect on the terms of trade that multinational corporations might exert is important. On the other hand, the influence of multinational corporations on the 'equilibrium' terms of trade may be less important for a nation in the short run, than the hardships caused by any adjustments made necessary by the speed with which multi-national corporations can cause the terms of trade to change or to oscillate about some trend. To the extent that they can cause variation in the terms of trade, multinational corporations are

[1] Japan might be expected to adopt this technique.

capable of compounding the difficulties inherent in international payments adjustments for individual nations and for the world's international monetary system. Whether or not multinational corporations will aggravate problems of payments-imbalances depends upon the sensitivity of the decision-makers to the balance-of-payments repercussions of their actions. Since the system of international payments was irremediably changed in August 1971, by President Nixon's declaration that freed the U.S. dollar from gold, the new system may increase the resiliency of nations to factors affecting their international accounts and reduce the need for sensitivity by executives of multinational concerns. This general problem area may also come under the jurisdiction or supervision of the GATT-like supranational body if that organisation should ever be created.

There are three main areas in which multinational corporations can have a noticeable effect on a nation's external balance. These are (a) the greater rate of direct investment across international boundaries that growing and titanic corporations are likely to engender; (b) the ability of multinational corporations to switch production and exports from one nation to another at short notice; and (c) the ability of multinational corporations to shift large amounts of liquid funds from one currency to another at short notice.

(a) As is implicit in Appendix VI–A, sudden shifts in the volume of direct foreign investment will compound the difficulties of achieving an adequate policy for international payments. Equally, shifts in the distribution of a constant volume of direct foreign investment by a nation according to the recipient country, according to the industry and according to the type of subsidiary created, can so change the rate of induced saving as to have net effects similar to those of variations in the rate of flow.

Whether or not the growing importance of multinational corporations will increase the *variability* of the net flow is not known. It is probably true that they will increase the rate of direct foreign investment throughout the world, but it does not follow inevitably that the rate will increase unevenly or that the variability of the flow will increase. There may be some predisposition to believe that overall variability will increase if only because of the greater expected concentration of the decision-making power.

There is one way in which the multinational corporations could aggravate a nation's international adjustment problems and that is through a tendency for inflows and outflows of foreign investments to be correlated with expected changes in a country's terms of trade. The more closely-knit the forces influencing the expectations of multinational corporations as a generic body (through, for example, interlocking directorates or common sources of and means of interpreting economic data) the greater will be the tendency for direct investments to move into a concentrated group of nations and to shun another group of nations – those whose terms of trade are expected to improve and deteriorate respectively. If the 'underlying conditions' of changes in tastes and changes in production bias are working adversely for a nation and are expected to continue to do so, there will be little incentive to invest in tangible assets in that country. In addition to the depressing effect of the adverse movement of the terms of trade on profit rates, there will be a direct terms-of-trade effect on the rate of return yielded on foreign capital when measured in 'hard currency'. The rate of return to a foreign investment will presumably be measured in the currency of the investing or the base country. Thus an investment of $1 million in Europe in year t at a rate of exchange of four 'euros' to one dollar and yielding 10 per cent will return 400,000 euros or 100,000 dollars. If the euro is depreciating relative to the dollar at a rate of 3 per cent per year because of adverse changes in Europe's terms of trade, an investment of $1 million in year t will still earn 400,000 euros in year $t+4$ but that will be equivalent to only $88,000 or an 8·8 per cent yield. When the adverse trend in the terms of trade ceases or is reversed, multinational corporations will be more likely to invest in that nation again. In this way, foreign investment practices can aggravate changes in the terms of trade of an individual nation.

(b) The Ford Motor Company decision to rely less heavily on its U.K. subsidiary in the global integration of its production and to divert, from the United Kingdom, an export-oriented production unit is the most spectacular single example of the ability of an international corporation to affect a nation's terms of trade and its balance of payments. However, fully-fledged multinational corporations can be expected to make similar decisions of smaller magnitude almost routinely. One of the main benefits of multinationality is the ability to schedule production among production units according to costs rather than according to the nationality of the production unit concerned. This suggests that the multinational corporations will exert some effect each year (usually small) upon the competitiveness of individual nations.

Variations in the rate of out-transfer of profits is another area in which multinational corporations can affect the strength of a nation's currency in foreign exchange markets. It is probably most useful to consider this dimension together with the net outflow or inflow of direct investments since, logically, the rate of profit out-transfer will be positively correlated with the rate of direct-investment outflow.

(c) There is a real danger that multinational corporations' treasurers having control over substantial amounts of working capital in many different countries could be tempted to convert this capital to make a 'capital gain' from any foreseen changes in exchange rates. Speculative activities can impose great strain upon the foreign exchange markets and, while there is no evidence that this has happened or will happen, the possibility is very clear. Equally, the problems of leads and lags in payments of current transactions could be accentuated by the growth of multinational corporations in the economic world.

Conclusion. The ultimate character of the multinational corporation form of organisation is not yet known, nor is the degree to which a relatively small number of titanic corporations will dominate world industry. However, there seems to be little room for doubt that, by the end of the twentieth century, a large number of very large firms with bases and affiliates in many countries will constitute the centre of the commercial and industrial world. Their future presence and continued growth is virtually assured by their ability to compete on price with non-multinational organisations. The social implications of this change are staggering all by themselves and, to look upon the worst side, a combination of the main corporations and attendant governments could make George Orwell seem to anticipate by only sixteen years. On the other hand, there is a better probability that multinational corporations will turn out to be positive forces for good in the world. They could certainly turn out to be a positive force for peace if they develop what Perlmutter has called 'transideological' links or simply because bombing customers and accounts receivable is not a good way to do business.[1]

Their potential economic effects are many. The biggest problem is one of safeguarding against the formation of an executive superlite and a consequent lack of competition among the big corporations. The difficulties that the organisational structure, particularly if concentrated, presents for national economic policy-makers can be significant. But since corporations need adequate markets and a stable framework for their own planning, the executive bodies are likely to develop a hypersensitivity for the possibility of disruptive side-effects coming from any policy shifts instituted by themselves.

The main difficulties may come from labour relations. There must, almost inevitably, be a tendency to attempt to weaken national unions. It is therefore desirable that some form of international union be developed as a countervailing power – at least in countries in which unionisation of labour is accepted. Unfortunately, since it is union members in developed nations who may suffer most or gain least from the development of multinational corporations with their geographic freedom of production, protracted labour strife may characterise the period of adjustment.[2]

The multinational firm is still either an embryo or a novelty. Its predecessors have already become the main vehicle for international business and investment. Whatever the costs and benefits of foreign investment may be, citizens of different nations are likely to find difficulty in refusing to pay the costs or in accepting the benefits.

[1] See Perlmutter, *Columbia Journal of World Business* (Jan–Feb 1969) p. 18. Note that defence secrets become a very delicate problem when nearly all large corporations are staffed by people with geocentric attitudes and have links in all ideological blocs.

[2] This possibility applies to all large investing countries and can affect Japan as seriously as the United States.

CHAPTER IX

BUSINESS INVESTMENT ABROAD: THE JURY IS STILL OUT

That no clear cut answer can be given on the question of the overall social desirability of business investment abroad, is quite manifest from the preceding eight chapters. The reasons for the inconclusiveness are many. Two of these reasons stand out. Business investment abroad is too complex and too diverse a phenomenon for the whole range of enterprise to be lumped together into a single aggregate and to be judged as one homogeneous mass. The second reason is that the process is not mature. The character of business investment abroad is still in the process of change and evolution. As the character of international business evolves and, simultaneously, the flow of investments and the absolute importance of foreign-owned assets increase, what is being witnessed in the fifties, sixties and seventies is not the continuing costs associated with a new economic order but the much more painful costs of adaptation from one economic order to a new one.

It is the costs of adjustment and adaptation that give rise to the main forces of opposition to an unhindered spread of international investment. In the sense that no one can know what the final outcome of allowing international business to evolve in an unimpeded way, all opposition must be based on present costs rather than on some imaginary future, but the transitional costs are more direct as well as more perceptible. International investment and business abroad confront the concept of the nation state. In so doing they oppose a set of socio-politico-economic institutions that have marked man's economic progress from the Middle Ages. The nation state may prove ultimately to be a temporary institution and the historic role of international business may be to lead the world to a new order of world government. The other transitional change is the unending one of shifting terms of trade among areas, among nations, among industries and among trades and professions. As some industries advance, others recede. The internationalisation of business tends, in developed nations at least, to expedite the process of change and decline for certain people. In addition to increasing the social costs of adjustment, business abroad provides a scapegoat and a target for conservatism.

All acts of investment involve intertemporal considerations and, in the imperfect world of human beings, there is no simple yes or no answer to intertemporal problems. The question of the ultimate desirability of a world in which international business is a powerful if not dominating force would be less intractable if the new order did not betoken a centralisation of economic power. The prospect of a technocracy peopled by a managerial *élite* and drawn from big nations is not an appealing one because the world has ample evidence that it needs to be wary of the motivations and practices of big business and big countries. Historic excesses must give pause to any potential host. But it is not only the citizen of the host country that needs to fear the implications of dominance by international business. In the short run at least, foreign mercantile adventures have damaged the citizens of the investing country and the use of national funds and national resources to protect private mercantile interests has not yet disappeared from this planet.

For all the opposition and difficulties, there remain two obdurate forces that are likely to allow large international business to grow until it reaches some stage of balance with its politico-economic environment. This elusive concept of balance is not necessarily a stationary one but will be characterised by a much slower rate of evolution than is currently being experienced. The two forces are: that international investment can make a contribution to higher global living standards by improving both global resource allocation and the application of technology; and that international business can thrive under the existing form of industrial organisation and competition. It is improbable that opponents – hurt in the process of evolution – will manage to prevent these forces from working themselves out. The opponents may, however, retard the process and even alter the features of the ultimate form of the new international industrial state.

The evolution of the basic corporate form in the private-enterprise world from a predominantly national concept to a global force presents a severe set of problems. These problems cannot be considered apart from other contemporaneous forces such as the continuation of population pressures in many nations, the rising expectations of poor people and poor nations, nationalism and ecological concern at both the national and the global levels. The role of these accompanying forces on the evolution of international business is not easy to foresee. If rising expectations argue for increased receptivity of foreign capital in poor nations, feelings of nationalism argue for reduced receptivity. If national concern with pollution encourages dirty industry to move to other parts of the world, the internationalisation of business is encouraged; if global concern with the eco-sphere is paramount, the ability of business to relocate will be impeded.

The development of business investment abroad generates a conflict between what is and what might be. The investment intensifies what one writer has called 'the porosity of national boundaries'. This tends to throw international political and economic policies into conflict, at least in the short run, and, in poor nations particularly, it juxtaposes nationalism and materialism. Nor are rich investing nations immune to the increasing porosity of national boundaries because the gains and losses that derive from international investment are not spread evenly over the population.

Despite the lack of precision that must apply to any considera-tion of business investment abroad in the aggregate, some indications are available of the general directions that policy should follow.

Fundamental to any system of economic relations in a world of nation states is that each country should safeguard its own economic interests. It follows from this that host countries should discriminate among potential investors and require governmental approval of any inflows of direct-investment capital. Host countries cannot rely upon base or investing countries to limit the outflow of foreign investment in the interests of the host countries. Another facet of the problem of hosting direct investments is the degree to which blandishments (in the form of relief from taxation) should be offered to potential investors. It is quite likely that developing nations as a group are competing with each other so that the sum total of tax holidays affects the distribution of a given amount of direct investment funds rather than an increase in the total flow. Some agreement (or collusion) among developing countries might increase the total benefits derived by these countries. UNCTAD could provide the forum for consideration of a united front.

For investing nations the main policy concern is that the return on any investment should exceed its opportunity cost. If the investing nations do not receive a return (net) then it may as well have distributed an equivalent amount of foreign aid on a government-to-government basis to the benefit of its foreign policy. The distribution of unilateral transfers among nations would probably be quite different from the pattern of distribution of 'failing' projects. If the outflow of capital attains a rate at which severe difficulties of adjustment are generated domestically, the opportunity cost would be drastically increased and some control over the rate of capital exports would be needed.[1] A second 'externality' is to be found in the intangible costs of pressures exerted on foreign (political) policy by the existence of foreign subsidiaries. Recent examples of this pressure have been the side effects of the British-Rhodesia confrontation and reconciliation in Black Africa and the rest of the third world, the mutual alienation between the United States and the Allende Government in Chile, and the French involvement in Indo-China prior to 1954. It is pertinent that the Foreign Relations Committee of the U.S. Senate announced its intention of exploring the impact of International Telephone and Telegraph had on American foreign policy in Chile.[2]

Any investment in a regime which is politically unstable can generate pressures which reduce the flexibility of foreign policy when a revolution finally takes place. Corporations do not normally regard the changing of the social and political structure of the host country as a concern of a foreign corporation. However, in some clear cases, corporations no longer enjoy the freedom to disassociate themselves from the manner of the regime in which they operate subsidiaries. The classic example

[1] This represents the validation of the argument of organised labour in the United States against foreign investment.

[2] *The Washington Post* (23 March 1972) p. A 35.

of this inter-relationship between foreign and domestic operations is that of certain American corporations with subsidiaries
located in the Union of South Africa and neighbouring
Portuguese colonies.[1]

The speed with which international investment flows and
their directly-induced effects can impinge upon a nation's
balance of payments suggests that the growth of business investment abroad has repercussions on the international monetary
system. Factors affecting rates of international saving must be
more easily adjustable than they have been in the 'Bretton
Woods era' from 1945 to 1971. Moreover, if international
investments are to be allowed to increase the rate of capital
formation in the host country, then the mere creation of international liquidity is not an adequate response.

Finally, there is the prospect of supranationalism. This
possibility exists in two dimensions. Control bodies that will
regulate the behaviour of multinational corporations and of
sovereign states towards subsidiaries are necessarily supranational in concept. Proponents of such controls point to the
achievements of the GATT and the IMF (but not usually to
the International Air Transport Association).[2] The creation of
such a body should reduce the tensions among nations and any
excesses of cartelisation as well as ameliorating the final
structure of the new international industrial state. The existence
of a supranational firm with corporate headquarters outside of
any of the main sovereign states so that it effectively renounces
nationality for its base of operations, may still become reality.

---

[1] In the spring of 1972, five Protestant churches in the United States
were preparing a campaign against corporations with involvements in
southern Africa. These corporations include General Motors Corporation,
Gulf Oil Corporation, Mobil Oil Corporation, Goodyear Tire and Rubber
Company and International Business Machines Corporation. Other groups
have cited Polaroid Corporation.

[2] See, in particular, Raymond Vernon, 'Multinational Business and
National Economic Goals', *Industrial Organization*, XXV (Summer 1971)
pp. 693–705.

BIBLIOGRAPHY

BOOKS

Yair Aharoni, *The Foreign Investment Decision Process* (Cambridge, Mass.: Harvard University Press, 1966).

Hugh G. J. Aitken, *American Capital and Canadian Resources* (Cambridge, Mass.: Harvard University Press, 1961).

Jack N. Behrman, *U.S. International Business and Governments* (New York: McGraw-Hill, 1971).

Richard E. Caves and Grant L. Reuber *et al.*, *Capital Transfers and Economic Policy: Canada, 1951–1962* (Cambridge, Mass.: Harvard University Press, 1971).

John H. Dunning, *Studies in International Investment* (London: George Allen and Unwin, 1970).

Foreign Ownership and the Structure of Canadian Industry: Report of the Task Force on the Structure of Canadian Industry (Privy Council Office, Ottawa, 1968). (Watkins Report.)

G. C. Hufbauer and F. M. Adler, *Overseas Manufacturing Investment and the Balance of Payments* (Washington, D.C.: U.S. Treasury Department, 1968).

Allan W. Johnstone, *United States Direct Investment in France* (Cambridge, Mass.: The M.I.T. Press, 1965).

Charles P. Kindleberger, *American Business Abroad* (New Haven: Yale University Press, 1969).

Charles P. Kindleberger (ed.), *The International Corporation* (Cambridge, Mass.: The M.I.T. Press, 1970).

Lawrence B. Krause, *European Economic Integration and the United States* (Washington, D.C.: The Brookings Institution, 1968).

Lawrence B. Krause and Kenneth W. Dam, *Federal Tax Treatment of Foreign Income* (Washington, D.C.: The Brookings Institution, 1964).

Walter Krause and F. John Mathis (eds.), *International Economics and Business: Selected Readings* (Boston: Houghton Mifflin Company, 1968).

Kari Levitt, *Silent Surrender* (Toronto: Macmillan of Canada, 1970).

Isaiah A. Litvak and Christopher J. Maule (eds.), *Foreign Investment: The Experience of Host Countries* (New York: Praeger Special Studies, 1970).

Raymond F. Mikesell (ed.), *U.S. Private and Government Investment Abroad* (Eugene, Oregon: University of Oregon Books, 1962).

Judd Polk *et al.*, *U.S. Production Abroad and the Balance of Payments: A Survey of Corporate Investment Experience* (New York: National Industrial Conference Board, 1966).

W. B. Reddaway and Associates, *Effects of U.K. Direct Investment Overseas*, *An Interim Report* and *Final Report* (Cambridge: Cambridge University Press, 1967 and 1968).

Joan Robinson, *Economics: An Awkward Corner* (London: George Allen and Unwin, 1966).

Sidney E. Rolfe and Walter Damm (eds.), *The Multinational Corporation in the World Economy* (New York: Praeger Publishers, 1970) pp. 7–8.

Virgil Salera, *Multinational Business* (Boston: Houghton Mifflin Company, 1969).

J.-J. Servan Schreiber, *The American Challenge* (New York: Atheneum, 1968).

Transatlantic Investment and the Balance of Payments – special issue of *Law and Contemporary Problems* (Winter 1969).

Raymond Vernon, *Manager in the International Economy* (Englewood Cliffs, N.J.: Prentice-Hall, 1968).

Raymond Vernon, *Sovereignty at Bay: The Multinational Spread of U.S. Enterprise* (New York: Basic Books, 1971).

Jack Woddis, *Introduction to Neo-Colonialism* (New York: International Publishers, 1967).

ARTICLES

V. N. Bandera and J. T. White, 'U.S. Direct Investments and Domestic Markets in Europe', *Economia Internazionale* (February 1968) pp. 1–19.

Jack N. Behrman, 'Multinational Corporations, Transnational Interests and National Sovereignty', *Columbia Journal of World Business* (January–February 1969) pp. 9–18.

Philip W. Bell, 'Private Capital Movements and the U.S. Balance-of-Payments Position', in Joint Economic Committee of the U.S. Congress, *Factors Affecting the United States Balance of Payments* (Washington, D.C., 1962).

Richard E. Caves, 'International Corporations: The Industrial Economics of Foreign Investment', *Economica* (February 1971) pp. 1–27.

Marvin Frankel, 'Home versus Foreign Investment: A Case against Capital Export', *Kyklos* (1965) pp. 411–31.

Paul M. Goldberg and Charles P. Kindleberger, 'Toward a GATT for Investment: A Proposal for Supervision of the International Corporation', *Law and Policy in International Business* (Summer 1970) pp. 295–325.

'The Herb Gray Report', *The Canadian Forum* (December 1971).

H. Peter Gray and Gail E. Makinen, 'The Balance-of-Payments Contributions of Multinational Corporations', *Journal of Business* (July 1967) pp. 339–43.

Elizabeth Jager, 'Multinationalism and Labor: For Whose Benefit?,' *Columbia Journal of World Business* (January–February 1970) pp. 56–64.

Harry G. Johnson, 'The Transfer Problem and Exchange Stability', in Richard E. Caves and Harry G. Johnson, *Readings in International Economics* (Homewood, Ill.: Richard D. Irwin, 1968).

John Maynard Keynes, 'Foreign Investment and the National Advantage', *The Nation and Athenæum* (August 1924).

J. Carter Murphy, 'International Investment and the National Advantage', *Southern Economic Journal* (July 1960) pp. 11–17.

J. Alex Murray, 'Guidelines for U.S. Investment in Canada', *Columbia Journal of World Business* (May–June 1971) pp. 29–37.

Howard V. Perlmutter, 'The Tortuous Evolution of the Multinational Corporation', *Columbia Journal of World Business* (January–February 1969) pp. 9–18.

Howard V. Perlmutter, 'Emerging East–West Ventures: The Transideological Enterprise', *Columbia Journal of World Business* (September–October 1969) pp. 39–50.

J. David Richardson, 'Theoretical Considerations in the Analysis of Direct Foreign Investment', *Western Economic Journal* (March 1971) pp. 87–98.

Robert d'A. Shaw, 'Foreign Investment and Global Labor', *Columbia Journal of World Business* (July–August 1971) pp. 52–62.

Hans Singer, 'The Distribution of Gains between Investing and Borrowing Countries', *American Economic Review* (May 1950) pp. 473–85.

Raymond Vernon, 'Multinational Business and National Economic Goals', *Industrial Organization* (Summer 1971) pp. 693–705.

INDEX